Sound and Sense

An Introduction to Poetry

Second Edition

Sound and Sense

An Introduction to Poetry

by LAURENCE PERRINE

Southern Methodist University

HARCOURT, BRACE & WORLD INC.
NEW YORK · BURLINGAME

COPYRIGHTS AND ACKNOWLEDGMENTS

THE BODLEY HEAD, LTD.—for "Cha Till Maccruimein" by E. A. Mackintosh.

WILLIAM BURFORD—for "A Christmas Tree" from *Man Now* by William Burford.

JONATHAN CAPE LIMITED—for "The Villain" from *The Collected Poems of W. H. Davies;* "Naming of Parts" and "Judging Distances" from *A Map of Verona* by Henry Reed.

CHATTO & WINDUS LTD.—for "Dulce et Decorum Est," "Parable of the Old Men and the Young," and "The Send-Off" from *Poems* by Wilfred Owen.

MALCOLM COWLEY—for "The Long Voyage" from *The Dry Season*, copyright 1941 by Malcolm Cowley.

THE JOHN DAY COMPANY, INC.—for "The Griesly Wife" copyright © 1946 by The John Day Company, reprinted from *Selected Verse* by John Manifold by permission of The John Day Company, Inc., publisher.

J. M. DENT & SONS LTD.—for "Poem in October" and "Do not go gentle into that good night" from *The Collected Poems of Dylan Thomas.*

DOUBLEDAY & COMPANY, INC.—for "The Rich Man" from *Tobogganing on Parnassus* by Franklin P. Adams. Copyright 1911 by Doubleday & Company, Inc. Reprinted by permission of the publisher. For "The Grey Squirrel" from *Kensington Gardens* by Humbert Wolfe. Reprinted by permission of Doubleday & Company, Inc. For "I Knew a Woman," copyright 1954 by Theodore Roethke from *Words for the Wind,* by Theodore Roethke. Reprinted by permission of Doubleday & Company, Inc.

GERALD DUCKWORTH & CO. LTD.—for "The Changeling" and "Exspecto Resurrectionem" from *Collected Poems* by Charlotte Mew.

EDITIONS POETRY LONDON—for "Vergissmeinicht" from *Collected Poems* by Keith Douglas.

NORMA MILLAY ELLIS—for "Counting-out Rhyme" from *The Buck in the Snow* by Edna St. Vincent Millay. By permission of Norma Millay Ellis.

FABER AND FABER LTD.—for "The Love Song of J. Alfred Prufrock" from *Collected Poems, 1909–1935,* by T. S. Eliot; "O Where Are You Going?" "That night when joy began," and "The Unknown Citizen" from *The Collected Shorter Poems 1930–1944* by W. H. Auden; "The Shield of Achilles" from *The Shield of Achilles* by W. H. Auden; "The Horses" from *One Foot in Eden* by Edwin Muir; "Base Details" from *Collected Poems* by Siegfried Sassoon.

PADRAIC FALLON—for "Mary Hynes."

CHARLIE MAY FLETCHER—for "The Groundswell" from *Preludes and Symphonies* by John Gould Fletcher.

VICTOR GOLLANCZ, LTD.—for "A Bookshop Idyll" from *A Case of Samples* by Kingsley Amis.

GROVE PRESS, INC.—for "The Horses" from *One Foot in Eden* by Edwin Muir.

HARCOURT, BRACE & WORLD, INC.—for "Naming of Parts" and "Judging Distances" from *A Map of Verona and Other Poems,* copyright, 1947, by Henry Reed. Reprinted by permission of Harcourt, Brace & World, Inc. For "The Love Song of J. Alfred Prufrock" from *Collected Poems of T. S. Eliot,* copyright, 1936, by Harcourt, Brace & World, Inc. and reprinted with their permission. For "Splinter" from *Good Morning, America,* copyright, 1928, 1956, by Carl Sandburg. Reprinted by permission of Harcourt, Brace & World, Inc. For "A Bookshop Idyll" from *A Case of Samples* © 1956 by Kingsley Amis. Reprinted by permission of Harcourt, Brace & World, Inc. For "Piazza di Spagna, Early Morning" and "A Baroque Wall-Fountain in the Villa Sciarra" from *Things of This World* © 1956 by Richard Wilbur. Reprinted by permission of Harcourt, Brace & World, Inc. For "in Just-," copyright, 1923, 1951, by E. E. Cummings. Reprinted from *Poems 1923–1954* by E. E. Cummings by permission of Harcourt, Brace & World, Inc. For "if everything happens that can't be done," copyright, 1944, by E. E. Cummings. Reprinted from *Poems 1923–1954* by E. E. Cummings by permission of Harcourt, Brace & World, Inc.

HARPER & ROW, PUBLISHERS, INCORPORATED—for "Incident" from *Color* by Countée Cullen. Copyright 1925 by Harper & Row, Publishers, Incorporated. Reprinted by permission of the publishers.

HARVARD UNIVERSITY PRESS—for "Because I could not stop for Death," "My life had stood, a loaded gun," "There is no frigate like a book," "If I can stop one heart from breaking "

iv

True ease in writing comes from art, not chance,
As those move easiest who have learned to dance.
'Tis not enough no harshness gives offense,
The sound must seem an echo to the sense.

—Alexander Pope from An Essay on Criticism

Contents

PART ONE: *The Elements of Poetry*

1 WHAT IS POETRY? 3

    Alfred, Lord Tennyson The Eagle 5
    William Shakespeare Winter 6
    Wilfred Owen Dulce et Decorum Est 8
    . . .
    William Shakespeare Spring 11
    Anonymous The Twa Corbies 12
    Anonymous Two Rivers 13
    John Manifold The Griesly Wife 13
    Robert Frost Love and a Question 14
    A. E. Housman Terence, this is stupid stuff 15

2 READING THE POEM 18

    Thomas Hardy The Man He Killed 20
    A. E. Housman Is my team ploughing 22
    EXERCISE 24
    . . .
    Ben Jonson It is not growing like a tree 25
    Sir Philip Sidney It is most true that eyes are formed to serve 26
    Frank O'Connor Devil, Maggot and Son 27
    Thomas Hardy Hap 28
    Thomas Hardy The Subalterns 29
    Edwin Arlington Robinson John Gorham 30
    Edwin Arlington Robinson Another Dark Lady 31

3 DENOTATION AND CONNOTATION 32

    Emily Dickinson There is no frigate like a book 33
    William Wordsworth The World Is Too Much with Us 34
    Robert Graves The Naked and the Nude 35
    EXERCISES 37
    . . .

Edwin Arlington Robinson   Richard Cory   39
Franklin P. Adams   The Rich Man   40
Henry Reed   Naming of Parts   40
Henry Reed   Judging Distances   41
Siegfried Sassoon   Base Details   43
Samuel Hoffenstein   Love Song   44
Anonymous   The Written Word   44

4 IMAGERY   45

Robert Browning   Meeting at Night   46
Robert Browning   Parting at Morning   47
• • •

John Gould Fletcher   The Groundswell   48
A. E. Housman   On moonlit heath and lonesome bank   49
Gerard Manley Hopkins   Spring   50
Jonathan Swift   A Description of the Morning   51
John Keats   To Autumn   51
Amy Lowell   Wind and Silver   52

5 FIGURATIVE LANGUAGE 1: METAPHOR, PERSONIFICATION,
  METONYMY   53

Robert Frost   A Hillside Thaw   54
Walter Savage Landor   Death Stands Above Me   56
Ogden Nash   The Sea-Gull   57
John Dryden   Lines on a Paid Militia   58
EXERCISE   60
• • •

George Herbert   Love   61
Richard Wilbur   Piazza di Spagna, Early Morning   62
John Donne   A Valediction: Forbidding Mourning   62
Andrew Marvell   To His Coy Mistress   64
William Wordsworth   London, 1802   65
Elinor Wylie   Velvet Shoes   66
Anonymous   On a Clergyman's Horse Biting Him   67
EXERCISE   67
Walt Whitman   Cavalry Crossing a Ford   67
Herman Melville   The Night-March   67

6 FIGURATIVE LANGUAGE 2: SYMBOL, ALLEGORY   68

Robert Frost   The Road Not Taken   68
John Boyle O'Reilly   A White Rose   70
Robert Browning   My Star   70
Archibald MacLeish   You, Andrew Marvell   72
Robert Herrick   To the Virgins, to Make Much of Time   76
Charlotte Mew   Exspecto Resurrectionem   77
EXERCISE   77
• • •

Anonymous   Western Wind   78
William Blake   The Sick Rose   78
Alfred, Lord Tennyson   Ulysses   79
Alastair Reid   Curiosity   81
Amy Lowell   Patterns   82
George Herbert   Peace   85
William Butler Yeats   The Second Coming   87
EXERCISES   87
Edwin Arlington Robinson   The House on the Hill   88
Alfred, Lord Tennyson   The Deserted House   88
Walter de la Mare   The Horseman   89
Herman Melville   The Tuft of Kelp   89
Robert Herrick   The Coming of Good Luck   89
Adelaide Crapsey   On Seeing Weather-Beaten Trees   89

7 FIGURATIVE LANGUAGE 3: PARADOX, OVERSTATEMENT, UNDERSTATEMENT, IRONY   90

Emily Dickinson   My Life Closed Twice   91
Robert Burns   A Red, Red Rose   92
Robert Frost   The Rose Family   93
Anonymous   Of Alphus   95
William Blake   The Chimney Sweeper   96
Percy Bysshe Shelley   Ozymandias   97
EXERCISE   98
• • •
Richard Lovelace   To Lucasta, Going to the Wars   99
Richard Lovelace   To Althea, from Prison   99
Hilaire Belloc   Lines for a Christmas Card   101
Padraic Fallon   Mary Hynes   101
Anonymous   Fine Flowers in the Valley   104
Humbert Wolfe   The Grey Squirrel   105
William Shakespeare   No Longer Mourn for Me   105
W. H. Auden   The Unknown Citizen   106
Robert Frost   Departmental   107
Sir John Suckling   The Constant Lover   108
Robert Browning   My Last Duchess   109
Edwin Muir   The Horses   111
John Hall Wheelock   Earth   112

8 ALLUSION   113

Robert Frost   "Out, Out—"   114
William Shakespeare   From *Macbeth:* She should have died hereafter   116
• • •
e. e. cummings   in Just-   117
John Milton   On His Blindness   118

William Butler Yeats No Second Troy 118
William Butler Yeats Leda and the Swan 119
Alexander Pope Epitaph on Newton 119
A. E. Housman The Carpenter's Son 120
Wilfred Owen The Parable of the Old Men and the Young 121
Anonymous In the Garden 122
Benjamin Franklin Quatrain 122

9 MEANING AND IDEA 123

Anonymous Little Jack Horner 123
Sara Teasdale Barter 125
Robert Frost Stopping by Woods on a Snowy Evening 125
• • •
Robert Browning Song: The year's at the spring 127
Percy Bysshe Shelley Dirge: Rough wind, that moanest loud 127
William Cullen Bryant To a Waterfowl 128
Robert Frost Design 129
Thomas Vaux Of a Contented Mind 130
William Butler Yeats An Acre of Grass 130
Gerard Manley Hopkins The Caged Skylark 131
A. E. Housman The Immortal Part 132
Archibald MacLeish Ars Poetica 134

10 TONE 135

W. H. Davies The Villain 137
Emily Dickinson Apparently with no surprise 137
EXERCISES 139
• • •
William Butler Yeats The Coming of Wisdom with Time 140
Michael Drayton Since There's No Help 140
Phyllis McGinley This Side of Calvin 140
Robert Browning Epilogue to *Asolando* 141
John Heath-Stubbs Epitaph 142
Charles Best A Sonnet of the Moon 143
R. P. Lister Target 143
Walter Savage Landor Yes; I Write Verses 144
Walter Savage Landor To Age 145
Anonymous Love 146

11 MUSICAL DEVICES 147

Ogden Nash The Turtle 148
W. H. Auden That night when joy began 151
Algernon Charles Swinburne When the Hounds of Spring 152
EXERCISE 155
• • •
Gerard Manley Hopkins God's Grandeur 155

Carl Sandburg The Harbor 156
John Crowe Ransom Parting, Without a Sequel 157
Edna St. Vincent Millay Counting-Out Rhyme 158
Winthrop Mackworth Praed Song: The pints and the pistols, the
    pike-staves and pottles 158
Charlotte Mew The Changeling 159
Joshua Sylvester Autumnus 161

12 RHYTHM AND METER 162

EXERCISES 169
• • •
A. E. Housman Loveliest of Trees 170
Alfred, Lord Tennyson The Oak 171
William Whitehead The "Je Ne Sais Quoi" 172
e. e. cummings if everything happens that can't be done 173
A. E. Housman Oh Who Is That Young Sinner 174
Alfred Noyes The Barrel-Organ 176
Samuel Taylor Coleridge Metrical Feet 179

13 SOUND AND MEANING 180

Anonymous Pease porridge hot 180
William Shakespeare Song: Hark, hark! 181
Carl Sandburg Splinter 182
Robert Herrick Upon Julia's Voice 183
Robert Frost The Span of Life 186
EXERCISE 188
• • •
Alexander Pope Sound and Sense 190
Emily Dickinson I like to see it lap the miles 190
Percy Bysshe Shelley England in 1819 191
Edwin Arlington Robinson The Dark Hills 192
Gerard Manley Hopkins Heaven-Haven 193
John Milton On the Late Massacre in Piemont 193
A. E. Housman Eight O'Clock 194
James Joyce All Day I Hear 194
Herman Melville The Bench of Boors 195
William Carlos Williams The Dance 196

14 PATTERN 197

W. H. Auden O Where Are You Going? 199
Anonymous There was a young lady of Niger 200
John Keats On First Looking into Chapman's Homer 201
William Shakespeare That Time of Year 202
EXERCISES 203
• • •
Anonymous A Handful of Limericks 203

Robert Herrick   To Daffodils   204
Anonymous   I sing of a maiden   205
⌐*Dylan Thomas*   Poem in October   206
Dante Gabriel Rossetti   The Sonnet   208
William Shakespeare   From *Romeo and Juliet:* If I profane with
    my unworthiest hand   209
Anonymous   Edward   209
Anonymous   Lord Randal   211
Theodore Spencer   Escapist's Song   213
William Burford   A Christmas Tree   213

15   BAD POETRY AND GOOD   214

    EXERCISE   219
    • • •
    Say not the struggle nought availeth   220
    The Man Who Thinks He Can   220
    A Prayer in Spring   221
    Pray in May   221
    God's Will for You and Me   222
    Pied Beauty   222
    If I can stop one heart from breaking   223
    Death Is a Dialogue   223
    My son, my executioner   223
    Only a baby small   224
    The Send-Off   224
    Cha Till Maccruimein   225
    Little Boy Blue   226
    The Toys   227
    The Long Voyage   228
    Breathes There the Man   228
    Boy-Man   229
    America for Me   230

16   GOOD POETRY AND GREAT   231
    • • •
    Robert Frost   The Death of the Hired Man   233
    T. S. Eliot   The Love Song of J. Alfred Prufrock   238
    William Butler Yeats   Among School Children   243
    EXERCISES   246

PART TWO: *Poems for Further Reading*

    Conrad Aiken   Morning Song from "Senlin"   251
    Kingsley Amis   A Bookshop Idyll   252
    Anonymous   The Silver Swan   253

Anonymous   When in My Pilgrimage   254
Anonymous   Sir Patrick Spence   254
Matthew Arnold   To Marguerite   255
Matthew Arnold   Dover Beach   256
W. H. Auden   The Shield of Achilles   257
Thomas Lovell Beddoes   Song: Old Adam, the carrion crow   259
William Blake   The Tiger   259
William Blake   The Divine Image   260
George Gordon, Lord Byron   So we'll go no more a-roving   261
Thomas Campion   When Thou Must Home   261
William Cartwright   No Platonic Love   261
Arthur Hugh Clough   The Latest Decalogue   262
Samuel Taylor Coleridge   Kubla Khan   263
William Congreve   Song: Pious Selinda goes to prayers   264
Stephen Crane   The Trees in the Garden   264
Countée Cullen   Incident   265
Walter de la Mare   The Listeners   265
Emily Dickinson   My life had stood, a loaded gun   266
Emily Dickinson   Because I could not stop for Death   267
John Donne   The Good-Morrow   268
John Donne   The Sun Rising   268
John Donne   Song: Go and catch a falling star   269
John Donne   Batter My Heart, Three-Personed God   270
Keith Douglas   Vergissmeinicht   270
Ralph Waldo Emerson   Days   271
Robert Frost   The Silken Tent   271
Donald Hall   Six Poets in Search of a Lawyer   272
Thomas Hardy   Afterwards   273
George Herbert   Redemption   274
Robert Herrick   Corinna's Going a-Maying   274
John Heywood   Jack and His Father   276
Ralph Hodgson   Eve   276
A. E. Housman   Bredon Hill   278
Ben Jonson   Echo's Lament of Narcissus   279
John Keats   Ode on a Grecian Urn   279
John Keats   Ode on Melancholy   281
Walter Savage Landor   On His Seventy-Fifth Birthday   282
Philip Larkin   Church Going   282
D. H. Lawrence   City Life   283
Eugene Lee-Hamilton   Sea-Shell Murmurs   284
Andrew Marvell   The Garden   284
George Meredith   Lucifer in Starlight   286
Marianne Moore   A Carriage from Sweden   287
Thomas Nashe   Spring   288
John Frederick Nims   Love Poem   289
Alexander Pope   Epistle to a Young Lady, on Her Leaving the Town After the Coronation   290

Frederick Prokosch   Sunburned Ulysses   291

John Crowe Ransom   Piazza Piece   292

Edwin Arlington Robinson   Mr. Flood's Party   292

Theodore Roethke   I Knew a Woman   294

Dante Gabriel Rossetti   Silent Noon   295

William Shakespeare   Fear No More   295

William Shakespeare   Let me not to the marriage of true minds   296

William Shakespeare   Since Brass, nor Stone, nor Earth   296

William Shakespeare   My mistress' eyes are nothing like the sun   297

Karl Shapiro   Doctor, doctor, a little of your love   297

James Shirley   The glories of our blood and state   298

Sir Philip Sidney   Leave Me, O Love   299

Sir Philip Sidney   With How Sad Steps, O Moon   299

Theodore Spencer   The Circus; or One View of It   299

Edmund Spenser   Trust Not the Treason   300

James Stephens   A Glass of Beer   301

Wallace Stevens   A High-Toned Old Christian Woman   301

Henry Howard, Earl of Surrey   Description of Spring, Wherein Each Thing Renews Save Only the Lover   302

Jonathan Swift   A Satirical Elegy on the Death of a Late Famous General   302

Edward Taylor   Housewifery   303

Dylan Thomas   Do not go gentle into that good night   303

Edward Thomas   The Gallows   304

Henry Vaughan   Peace   305

Edmund Waller   On a Girdle   305

Joseph Blanco White   To Night   306

Walt Whitman   A noiseless patient spider   306

Walt Whitman   There Was a Child Went Forth   307

Walt Whitman   Out of the cradle endlessly rocking   308

Richard Wilbur   A Baroque Wall-Fountain in the Villa Sciarra   313

William Wordsworth   Strange Fits of Passion   315

William Wordsworth   Resolution and Independence   316

William Wordsworth   The Solitary Reaper   319

Sir Thomas Wyatt   They Flee from Me   320

William Butler Yeats   A Prayer for My Daughter   321

William Butler Yeats   Sailing to Byzantium   323

Edward Young   Two Passages from *Satire on Women*   324

INDEX OF AUTHORS, TITLES, AND FIRST LINES   326

INDEX OF TOPICS   334

Preface

The second edition of *Sound and Sense,* like the first, is written for the college student who is beginning a serious study of poetry. It seeks to give him a sufficient grasp of the nature and variety of poetry, some reasonable means for reading it with appreciative understanding, and a few primary ideas of how to evaluate it. The separate chapters gradually introduce the student to the elements of poetry, putting their emphasis always on *how* and *why.*

How can the reader use these elements to get at the meaning of the poem, to interpret it correctly and respond to it adequately?

Why does the poet use these elements? *What* values have they for the poet and the reader?

In matters of theory, undoubtedly, some issues are oversimplified, but I hope none seriously. The purpose has always been to give the beginning student something he can understand and use. The first assumptions of *Sound and Sense* are that poetry needs to be read carefully and thought about considerably, and that, when so read, poetry gives its readers continuing rewards in experience and understanding.

The second edition differs from the first essentially in the much greater number of poems included and for the opportunity it offered the author to reconsider and revise the text in those places where revision was appropriate. In addition three poets—Frost, Housman, Yeats—are represented by a sufficient number of poems to support study of them as individual artists. Part Two in this edition contains twice as many poems as in the first edition.

A book of this kind inevitably owes something to all who have thought or written about poetry. It would be impossible to express all indebtedness, but for personal advice, criticism, and assistance, I wish especially to thank my wife, Catherine Perrine; Professor Maynard Mack, Yale University; Charles S. Holmes, Pomona College; Donald Peet, Indiana University; James W. Byrd, East Texas State College; and Professor Willis Glover and Margaret Morton Blum, Southern Methodist University.

L. P.

Southern Methodist University, December, 1962

Part One

The Elements of Poetry

1

What Is Poetry?

Poetry is as universal as language, and almost as ancient. The most primitive peoples have used it, and the most civilized have cultivated it. In all ages, and in all countries, poetry has been written —and eagerly read or listened to—by all kinds and conditions of people—by soldiers, statesmen, lawyers, farmers, doctors, scientists, clergymen, philosophers, kings, and queens. In all ages it has been especially the concern of the educated, the intelligent, and the sensitive, though it has appealed also, in its simpler forms, to the uneducated and to children. Why? First, because it has given pleasure. People have read it or listened to it or recited it because they liked it, because it gave them enjoyment. But this is not the whole answer. Poetry in all ages has been regarded as important, not simply as one of several alternative forms of amusement, as one man might choose bowling, another chess, and another poetry. Rather, it has been regarded as something central to each man's existence, something having unique value to the fully realized life, something which he is better off for having and which he is spiritually impoverished without. To understand the reasons for this, we need to have at least a provisional understanding of what poetry is. Provisional, because man has always been more successful at appreciating poetry than at defining it.

Initially, poetry might be defined as a kind of language that

3

says *more* and says it *more intensely* than does ordinary language. In order to understand this fully, we need to understand what it is that poetry "says." For language is employed on different occasions to say quite different kinds of things. In other words, language has different uses.

Perhaps the commonest use of language is to communicate *information*. We say that it is nine o'clock, that there is a good movie downtown, that George Washington was the first president of the United States, that bromine and iodine are members of the halogen group of chemical elements. This we might call the *practical* use of language. It helps us with the ordinary business of living.

But it is not primarily to communicate information that novels and short stories and plays and poems are written. These exist to bring us a sense and a perception of life, to widen and sharpen our contacts with existence. Their concern is with *experience*. We all have an inner need to live more deeply and fully and with greater awareness, to know the experience of others and to know better our own experience. The poet, from his own store of felt, observed, or imagined experiences, selects, combines, and reorganizes. He creates new experiences for the reader, significant because focused and formed, in which the reader can participate and which he may use to give him a greater awareness and understanding of his world. Literature, in other words, can be used as a gear for stepping up the intensity and increasing the range of our experience, and as a glass for clarifying it. This is the *literary* use of language. For literature is not only an aid to living but a means of living.[1]

Suppose, for instance, that we are interested in eagles. If we want simply to acquire information about eagles, we may turn to an encyclopedia or a book of natural history. There we find that the family Falconidae, to which eagles belong, is characterized by imperforate nostrils, legs of medium length, a hooked bill, the hind toe inserted on a level with the three front ones, and the claws roundly curved and sharp; that land eagles are feathered to the toes and sea-fishing eagles halfway to the toes; that their length is about three feet, the extent of wing seven feet; that the nest is usually placed on some inaccessible cliff; that the eggs are spot-

---

[1] A third use of language is as an instrument of persuasion. This is the use we find in advertisements, propaganda bulletins, sermons, and political speeches. These three uses of language—the practical, the literary, and the hortatory—are not sharply divided. They may be thought of as three points of a triangle; most actual specimens of written language fall somewhere within the triangle. Most poetry conveys some information, and some poetry has a design on the reader. But language becomes *literature* when the desire to communicate experience predominates.

ted, and do not exceed three; and perhaps that the eagle's "great power of vision, the vast height to which it soars in the sky, the wild grandeur of its abode, have . . . commended it to the poets of all nations." [2]

But unless we are interested in this information only for practical purposes, we are likely to feel a little disappointed, as though we had grasped the feathers of the eagle but not its soul. True, we have learned many facts about the eagle, but we have missed somehow its lonely majesty, its power, and the "wild grandeur" of its surroundings which would make the eagle something living rather than a mere museum specimen. For the living eagle we must turn to literature.

THE EAGLE

He clasps the crag with crooked hands;
Close to the sun in lonely lands,
Ringed with the azure world, he stands.

The wrinkled sea beneath him crawls;
He watches from his mountain walls,
And like a thunderbolt he falls.

—*Alfred, Lord Tennyson* [1809–1892]

QUESTIONS

1. What is peculiarly effective about the expressions "crooked hands"; "close to the sun"; "ringed with the azure world"; "wrinkled"; "crawls"; and "like a thunderbolt"?

2. Notice the formal pattern of the poem, particularly the contrast of "he stands" in the first stanza and "he falls" in the second. Is there any other contrast between the two stanzas?

If the preceding poem has been read well, the reader will feel that he has enjoyed a significant experience and understands eagles better, though in a different way, than he did from the encyclopedia article alone. For if the article *analyzes* man's experience with eagles, the poem, in some sense, *synthesizes* such an experience. Indeed, the two approaches to experience—the scientific and the literary—may be said to complement each other. And it may be

---

[2] *Encyclopedia Americana,* IX, 473–74.

contended that the kind of understanding one gets from the second is at least as valuable as the kind he gets from the first.

Literature, then, exists to communicate significant experience—significant because concentrated and organized. Its function is not to tell us *about* experience, but to allow us imaginatively to *participate* in it. It is a means of allowing us, through the imagination, to live more fully, more deeply, more richly, and with greater awareness. It can do this in two ways: by *broadening* our experience, that is, by making us acquainted with a range of experience with which, in the ordinary course of events, we might have no contact, or by *deepening* our experience, that is, by making us feel more poignantly and more understandingly those everyday experiences which all of us have.

Two false approaches often taken to poetry can be avoided if we keep this conception of literature firmly in mind. The first is that approach which always looks for a lesson, a moral, a bit of moral instruction. The second is that which expects to find poetry always beautiful. Let us consider a song from Shakespeare:

WINTER

When icicles hang by the wall,
   And Dick the shepherd blows his nail,
And Tom bears logs into the hall,
   And milk comes frozen home in pail,
When blood is nipped and ways be foul,   5
Then nightly sings the staring owl,
         "Tu-whit, tu-who!"
A merry note,
While greasy Joan doth keel° the pot.   skim

When all aloud the wind doth blow,   10
   And coughing drowns the parson's saw,
And birds sit brooding in the snow,
   And Marian's nose looks red and raw,
When roasted crabs° hiss in the bowl,   crab apples
Then nightly sings the staring owl,   15
         "Tu-whit, tu-who!"
A merry note,
While greasy Joan doth keel the pot.

—*William Shakespeare [1564–1616]*

1. What are the meanings of *nail* (2) and *saw* (11)?
2. Is the owl's cry really a "merry" note? How are this adjective and the verb *sings* employed?
3. In what way does the owl's cry contrast with the other details of the poem?

In the poem "Winter" Shakespeare is attempting to communicate the quality of winter life around a sixteenth-century English country house. But instead of telling us flatly that winter in such surroundings is cold and in many respects unpleasant, though with some pleasant features too (the adjectives *cold, unpleasant,* and *pleasant* are not even used in the poem), he gives us a series of concrete homely details that suggest these qualities and enable us, imaginatively, to experience this winter life ourselves. The shepherd lad blows on his fingernails to warm his hands; the milk freezes in the pail between the cowshed and the kitchen; the roads are muddy; the folk listening to the parson have colds; the birds "sit brooding" in the snow; and the servant girl's nose is raw from cold. But pleasant things are in prospect. Logs are being brought in for a fire in the main hall, hot cider or ale is being prepared, and the kitchen maid is making a hot soup or stew. In contrast to all these homely, familiar details of country life comes in the mournful, haunting, and eerie note of the owl.

Obviously the poem contains no moral. Readers who always look in poetry for some lesson, message, or noble truth about life are bound to be disappointed. Moral-hunters see poetry as a kind of sugar-coated pill—a wholesome truth or lesson made palatable by being put into pretty words. What they are really after is a sermon—not a poem, but something inspirational. Yet "Winter," which has appealed to good readers now for nearly four centuries, is not inspirational and contains no moral preachment.

Neither is the poem "Winter" beautiful. Though it is appealing in its way and contains elements of beauty, there is little that is really beautiful in raw red noses, coughing in chapel, nipped blood, foul roads, and greasy kitchen maids. Yet some readers think that poetry deals exclusively with beauty—with sunsets, flowers, butterflies, love, and God—and that the one appropriate response to any poem is, after a moment of awed silence, "Isn't that beautiful!" For such readers poetry is a precious affair, the enjoyment

7

only of delicate souls, removed from the heat and sweat of ordinary life. But theirs is too narrow an approach to poetry. The function of poetry is sometimes to be ugly rather than beautiful. And poetry may deal with common colds and greasy kitchen maids as legitimately as with sunsets and flowers. Consider another example:

DULCE ET DECORUM EST

Bent double, like old beggars under sacks,
Knock-kneed, coughing like hags, we cursed through sludge,
Till on the haunting flares we turned our backs,
And towards our distant rest began to trudge.
Men marched asleep. Many had lost their boots,   5
But limped on, blood-shod. All went lame, all blind;
Drunk with fatigue; deaf even to the hoots
Of gas-shells dropping softly behind.

Gas! GAS! Quick, boys! An ecstasy of fumbling,
Fitting the clumsy helmets just in time,   10
But someone still was yelling out and stumbling
And flound'ring like a man in fire or lime.—
Dim through the misty panes and thick green light,
As under a green sea, I saw him drowning.

In all my dreams before my helpless sight   15
He plunges at me, guttering, choking, drowning.

If in some smothering dreams, you too could pace
Behind the wagon that we flung him in,
And watch the white eyes writhing in his face,
His hanging face, like a devil's sick of sin,   20
If you could hear, at every jolt, the blood
Come gargling from the froth-corrupted lungs
Bitten as the cud
Of vile, incurable sores on innocent tongues,—
My friend, you would not tell with such high zest   25
To children ardent for some desperate glory,
The old Lie: *Dulce et decorum est*
Pro patria mori.

—*Wilfred Owen [1893–1918]*

QUESTIONS

1. The Latin quotation, from the Roman poet Horace, means "It is sweet and becoming to die for one's country." (Wilfred Owen himself died fighting

for England in World War I, a week before the armistice.) What is the poem's comment on this statement?

2. List the elements of the poem which to you seem not beautiful and therefore unpoetic. Are there *any* elements of beauty in the poem?

3. How do the comparisons in lines 1, 14, 20, 23–24 contribute to the effectiveness of the poem?

Poetry takes all life as its province. Its primary concern is not with beauty, not with philosophical truth, not with persuasion, but with experience. Beauty and philosophical truth are aspects of experience, and the poet is often engaged with them. But poetry as a whole is concerned with all kinds of experience—beautiful or ugly, strange or common, noble or ignoble, actual or imaginary. One of the paradoxes of human existence is that all experience, when transmitted through the medium of art, is, for the good reader, enjoyable—even painful experience. In real life death and pain and suffering are not pleasurable, but in poetry they may be. In real life getting soaked in a rainstorm is not pleasurable, but in poetry it can be. In actual life, if we cry, usually we are unhappy; but if we cry in a movie, we are manifestly enjoying it. We don't ordinarily like to be terrified in real life, but we sometimes seek movies or books that will terrify us. We find some value in all intense living. To be intensely alive is the opposite of being dead. To be dull, to be bored, to be imperceptive is in one sense to be dead. Poetry comes to us bringing life, and therefore pleasure. Moreover, art focuses and so organizes experience as to give us a better understanding of it. And to understand life is partly to be master of it.

Between poetry and other forms of imaginative literature there is no sharp distinction. You may have been taught to believe that poetry can be recognized by the arrangement of its lines on the page or by its use of rime and meter. Such superficial tests are almost worthless. The Book of Job in the Bible and Melville's *Moby Dick* are highly poetical, but a versified theorem in physics is not.[3] The difference between poetry and other literature is one

[3] For instance, the following, found accidentally by Bliss Perry (*A Study of Poetry,* Boston, Houghton Mifflin, 1920, p. 155) in a textbook on *The Parallelogram of Forces.* Printed as verse, it has the same meter and rime scheme as Tennyson's *In Memoriam:*

> And hence no force, however great,
> Can draw a cord, however fine,
> Into a horizontal line
> Which shall be absolutely straight.

only of degree. Poetry is the most condensed and concentrated form of literature, saying most in the fewest number of words. It is language whose individual lines, either because of their own brilliance or because they focus so powerfully what has gone before, have a higher voltage than most language has. It is language which grows frequently incandescent, giving off both light and heat.

Ultimately, therefore, poetry can be recognized only by the response made to it by a good reader. But there is a catch here. We are not all good readers. If we were, there would be no purpose for this book. And if you are a poor reader, much of what has been said about poetry so far must have seemed nonsensical. "How," you may ask, "can poetry be described as moving or exciting, when I have found it dull and boring? Poetry is just a fancy way of writing something that could be said more simply." So might a color-blind man deny that there is such a thing as color.

The act of communication involved in reading poetry is like the act of communication involved in receiving a message by radio. Two factors are involved: a transmitting station and a receiving set. The completeness of the communication depends on both the power and clarity of the transmitter and the sensitivity of the receiver (and on whether it is tuned to the proper wave length). When a person reads a poem and no experience is transmitted, either the poem is not a good poem or the reader is a poor reader or not properly tuned. With new poetry, we cannot always be sure which is at fault. With older poetry, if it has acquired critical acceptance—has been enjoyed by generations of good readers—we may assume that the receiving set is at fault. Fortunately, the fault is not irremediable. Though we cannot all become expert readers, we can become good enough to find both pleasure and value in much good poetry, or we can increase the amount of pleasure which we already find in poetry and the number of kinds of poetry we find it in. To help you increase your sensitivity and range as a receiving set is the purpose of this book.

Poetry, finally, is a kind of multi-dimensional language. Ordinary language—the kind we use to communicate information—is one dimensional. It is directed at only part of the listener, his understanding. Its one dimension is intellectual. Poetry, which is language used to communicate experience, has at least four dimensions. If it is to communicate experience, it must be directed at the *whole* man, not just at his understanding. It must involve not only his intelligence but also his senses, his emotions, and his imagination. Poetry, to the intellectual dimension, adds a sensuous dimension, an emotional dimension, and an imaginative dimension.

Poetry achieves its extra dimensions—its greater pressure per word and its greater tension per poem—by drawing more fully and more consistently than does ordinary language on a number of language resources, none of which is peculiar to poetry. These various resources form the subjects of a number of the following chapters. Among them are connotation, imagery, metaphor, symbol, paradox, irony, allusion, sound repetition, rhythm, and pattern. Using these resources and the materials of life, the poet shapes and "makes" his poem. Successful poetry is never effusive language. If it is to come alive it must be as cunningly put together and as efficiently organized as a plant or a tree. It must be an organism whose every part serves a useful purpose and cooperates with every other part to preserve and express the life that is within it.

● ● ●

SPRING

> When daisies pied and violets blue
>   And lady-smocks all silver-white
> And cuckoo-buds of yellow hue
>   Do paint the meadows with delight,
> The cuckoo then, on every tree,   5
> Mocks married men; for thus sings he,
>   "Cuckoo!
> Cuckoo, cuckoo!" O, word of fear,
> Unpleasing to a married ear!
>
> When shepherds pipe on oaten straws,   10
>   And merry larks are ploughmen's clocks,
> When turtles tread, and rooks, and daws,
>   And maidens bleach their summer smocks,
> The cuckoo then, on every tree,
> Mocks married men; for thus sings he,   15
>   "Cuckoo!
> Cuckoo, cuckoo!" O, word of fear,
> Unpleasing to a married ear!

—*William Shakespeare [1564–1616]*

QUESTIONS

1. Vocabulary: *pied* (1), *lady-smocks* (2), *oaten straws* (10), *turtles* (12), *tread* (12), *daws* (12).

2. This song is a companion piece to "Winter." In what respects are the two poems similar? How do they contrast? What details show that this poem,

11

like "Winter," was written by a realist, not simply by a man carried away with the beauty of spring?

3. The word *cuckoo* is "unpleasing to a married ear" because it sounds like *cuckold*. Cuckolds were a frequent butt of humor in earlier English literature. If you do not know the meaning of the word, look it up.

4. Is the tone of this poem solemn or light and semi-humorous?

THE TWA CORBIES

As I was walking all alane,°	alone
I heard twa corbies° making a mane;°	two ravens; moan
The tane° unto the t'other say,	one
"Where sall we gang° and dine today?"	shall we go
"In behint yon auld fail dyke,°	old turf wall 5
I wot° there lies a new-slain knight;	know
And naebody kens° that he lies there,	knows
But his hawk, his hound, and lady fair.	
"His hound is to the hunting gane,	
His hawk to fetch the wild-fowl hame,	10
His lady's ta'en another mate,	
So we may mak our dinner sweet.	
"Ye'll sit on his white hause-bane,°	neck-bone
And I'll pick out his bonny blue een;°	eyes 14
Wi ae° lock o' his gowden° hair	With one; golden
We'll theek° our nest when it grows bare.	thatch
"Mony a one for him makes mane,	
But nane sall ken where he is gane;	
O'er his white banes when they are bare,	
The wind sall blaw for evermair."	20

—*Anonymous*

QUESTIONS

1. Here is an implied story of false love, murder, and disloyalty. What purpose is served by having the story told from the point of view of the "twa corbies"? How do they emphasize the atmosphere of the poem?

2. Although we do not know exactly what happened to the knight, much is suggested. What is implied by the fact that "mony a one for him makes mane" but no one knows what has become of him except his hawk, his hound, and his lady? What is implied by the fact that he is "new-slain" but his lady has already taken another mate? Does the poem lose or gain in effect by not being entirely clear.

3. The language of the old English and Scottish folk ballads, of which this is one, presents a considerable initial obstacle, but if you accept it you will probably find that it contributes a unique flavor. An English critic has written of this poem: "Modernize the spelling [of the last stanza], and you have destroyed . . . the key of the poem: the thin high music of the lament, the endlessly subtle variations on the *a* sound, the strange feeling that all things have been unified with the shrillness of the wind through the heather." [4] Does this seem to you a valid comment?

4. How would you describe the experience created by the poem?

TWO RIVERS

Says Tweed to Till—
  "What gars° ye rin sae still?"   makes
Says Till to Tweed—
"Though ye rin with speed
  And I rin slaw,
For ae man that ye droon
  I droon twa."

—*Anonymous*

THE GRIESLY WIFE

"Lie still, my newly married wife,
  Lie easy as you can.
You're young and ill accustomed yet
  To sleeping with a man."

The snow lay thick, the moon was full   5
  And shone across the floor.
The young wife went with never a word
  Barefooted to the door.

He up and followed sure and fast,
  The moon shone clear and white.   10
But before his coat was on his back
  His wife was out of sight.

He trod the trail wherever it turned
  By many a mound and scree,°   stony slope
And still the barefoot track led on,   15
  And an angry man was he.

[4] T. R. Henn, *The Apple and the Spectroscope*, London, Methuen, 1951, p. 11.

He followed fast, he followed slow,
    And still he called her name,
But only the dingoes° of the hills   wild dogs
    Yowled back at him again.   20

His hair stood up along his neck,
    His angry mind was gone,
For the track of the two bare feet gave out
    And a four-foot track went on.

Her nightgown lay upon the snow   25
    As it might upon the sheet,
But the track that led from where it lay
    Was never of human feet.

His heart turned over in his chest,
    He looked from side to side,   30
And he thought more of his gumwood fire
    Than he did of his griesly° bride.   uncanny

And first he started walking back
    And then began to run,
And his quarry wheeled at the end of her track   35
    And hunted him in turn.

Oh, long the fire may burn for him
    And open stand the door,
And long the bed may wait empty:
    He'll not be back any more.   40

—*John Manifold* [1915–   ]

QUESTION

1. This modern imitation of an old ballad is by an Australian poet, as the references to dingoes (19) and gumwood (31) indicate. What kind of animal did the griesly wife turn into? Why does not the poet tell us?

LOVE AND A QUESTION

A Stranger came to the door at eve,
    And he spoke the bridegroom fair.
He bore a green-white stick in his hand,
    And, for all burden, care.
He asked with the eyes more than the lips   5
    For a shelter for the night,
And he turned and looked at the road afar
    Without a window light.

The bridegroom came forth into the porch
  With "Let us look at the sky,   10
And question what of the night to be,
  Stranger, you and I."
The woodbine leaves littered the yard,
  The woodbine berries were blue,
Autumn, yes, winter was in the wind;   15
  "Stranger, I wish I knew."

Within, the bride in the dusk alone
  Bent over the open fire,
Her face rose-red with the glowing coal
  And the thought of the heart's desire.   20
The bridegroom looked at the weary road,
  Yet saw but her within,
And wished her heart in a case of gold
  And pinned with a silver pin.

The bridegroom thought it little to give   25
  A dole of bread, a purse,
A heartfelt prayer for the poor of God,
  Or for the rich a curse;
But whether or not a man was asked
  To mar the love of two   30
By harboring woe in the bridal house,
  The bridegroom wished he knew.

—*Robert Frost [1874–1963]*

QUESTIONS

1. The bridegroom in this poem is faced with a *dilemma* (a choice between two actions neither of which is satisfactory). How is the question he
ponders in the last stanza to be answered?
2. What is the symbolic significance of the Stranger? Does this poem
deal with a unique experience or does it have universal meaning?
3. Like "The Twa Corbies" and "The Griesly Wife" this poem is a BALLAD
(a narrative but songlike poem written in a stanzaic form repeated throughout
the poem). Compare the three poems in intent and significance.

TERENCE, THIS IS STUPID STUFF

"Terence, this is stupid stuff:
  You eat your victuals fast enough;
There can't be much amiss, 'tis clear,
  To see the rate you drink your beer.
But oh, good Lord, the verse you make,   5
  It gives a chap the belly-ache.

The cow, the old cow, she is dead;
It sleeps well the horned head:
We poor lads, 'tis our turn now
To hear such tunes as killed the cow.   10
Pretty friendship 'tis to rhyme
Your friends to death before their time
Moping melancholy mad:
Come, pipe a tune to dance to, lad."

    Why, if 'tis dancing you would be,   15
There's brisker pipes than poetry.
Say, for what were hop-yards meant,
Or why was Burton built on Trent?
Oh many a peer of England brews
Livelier liquor than the Muse,   20
And malt does more than Milton can
To justify God's ways to man.
Ale, man, ale's the stuff to drink
For fellows whom it hurts to think:
Look into the pewter pot   25
To see the world as the world's not.
And faith, 'tis pleasant till 'tis past:
The mischief is that 'twill not last.
Oh I have been to Ludlow fair
And left my necktie God knows where,   30
And carried half-way home, or near,
Pints and quarts of Ludlow beer:
Then the world seemed none so bad,
And I myself a sterling lad;
And down in lovely muck I've lain,   35
Happy till I woke again.
Then I saw the morning sky:
Heigho, the tale was all a lie;
The world, it was the old world yet,
I was I, my things were wet,   40
And nothing now remained to do
But begin the game anew.

    Therefore, since the world has still
Much good, but much less good than ill,
And while the sun and moon endure   45
Luck's a chance, but trouble's sure,
I'd face it as a wise man would,
And train for ill and not for good.
'Tis true, the stuff I bring for sale
Is not so brisk a brew as ale: 50
Out of a stem that scored the hand
I wrung it in a weary land.

But take it: if the smack is sour,
The better for the embittered hour;
It should do good to heart and head   55
When your soul is in my soul's stead;
And I will friend you, if I may,
In the dark and cloudy day.

There was a king reigned in the East:
There, when kings will sit to feast,   60
They get their fill before they think
With poisoned meat and poisoned drink.
He gathered all that springs to birth
From the many-venomed earth;
First a little, thence to more,   65
He sampled all her killing store;
And easy, smiling, seasoned sound,
Sate the king when healths went round.
They put arsenic in his meat
And stared aghast to watch him eat;   70
They poured strychnine in his cup
And shook to see him drink it up:
They shook, they stared as white's their shirt:
Them it was their poison hurt.
—I tell the tale that I heard told.   75
Mithridates, he died old.

—*A. E. Housman* [*1859–1936*]

QUESTIONS

1. *Terence* (1) is Housman's poetic name for himself. Housman's poetry is largely pessimistic or sad; and this poem, placed near the end of his volume *A Shropshire Lad,* is his defense of the kind of poetry he wrote. Who is the speaker in the first fourteen lines? Who is the speaker in the rest of the poem? What is "the stuff I bring for sale" (49)?

2. Hops (17) and malt (21) are principal ingredients of beer and ale. Burton-upon-Trent (18) is an English city famous for its breweries. Milton (21), in the invocation of his epic poem *Paradise Lost,* declares that his purpose is to "justify the ways of God to men." What, in Housman's eyes, is the efficacy of liquor in helping one live a difficult life?

3. What six lines of the poem most explicitly sum up the poet's philosophy? Most people like reading material that is cheerful and optimistic ("There's enough suffering and unhappiness in the world already"). What for Housman is the value of pessimistic and tragic literature?

4. *Mithridates* (76) was a king of Pontus and a contemporary of Julius Caesar; his "tale" is told in Pliny's *Natural History.* What is the connection of this last verse paragraph with the rest of the poem?

17

2

Reading the Poem

The primary purpose of this book is to develop your ability to understand and appreciate poetry. Here are some preliminary suggestions:

(1) Read a poem more than once. A good poem will no more yield its full meaning on a single reading than will a Beethoven symphony on a single hearing. Two readings may be necessary simply to let you get your bearings. And if the poem is a work of art, it will repay repeated and prolonged examination. One does not listen to a good piece of music once and forget it; one does not look at a good painting once and throw it away. A poem is not like a newspaper, to be hastily read and cast into the wastebasket. It is to be hung on the wall of one's mind.

(2) Keep a dictionary by you and use it. It is futile to try to understand poetry without troubling to learn the meanings of the words of which it is composed. One might as well attempt to play tennis without a ball. One of your primary purposes while in college should be to build a good vocabulary, and the study of poetry gives you an excellent opportunity. A few other reference books will also be invaluable. Particularly desirable are a good book on mythology (your instructor can recommend one) and a Bible.

(3) Read so as to hear the sounds of the words in your mind. Poetry is written to be heard: its meanings are conveyed through

sound as well as through print. Every word is therefore important. The best way to read a poem is just the opposite of the best way to read a newspaper. One reads a newspaper as rapidly as he can; one should read a poem as slowly as he can. When you cannot read a poem aloud, lip-read it: form the words with your tongue and mouth though you do not utter them. With ordinary reading material, lip reading is a bad habit; with poetry it is a good habit.

(4) Always pay careful attention to what the poem is saying. Though one should be conscious of the sounds of the poem, he should never be so exclusively conscious of them that he pays no attention to what the poem means. For some readers reading a poem is like getting on board a rhythmical roller coaster. The car starts, and off they go, up and down, paying no attention to the landscape flashing past them, arriving at the end of the poem breathless, with no idea of what it has been about.[1] This is the wrong way to read a poem. One should make the utmost effort to follow the thought continuously and to grasp the full implications and suggestions. Because a poem says so much, several readings may be necessary. But on the very first reading one should determine which noun goes with which verb.

(5) Practice occasionally reading a poem aloud. When you find one you especially like, make your roommate listen to it. Try to read it to him in such a way that he will like it too. (a) Read it affectionately, but not affectedly. The two extremes which oral readers often fall into are equally deadly. One is to read as if one were reading a tax report or a railroad timetable, unexpressively, in a monotone. The other is to elocute, with artificial flourishes and vocal histrionics. It is not necessary to put emotion into reading a poem. The emotion is already there. It only wants a fair chance to get out. It will express *itself* if the poem is read naturally and sensitively. (b) Of the two extremes, reading too fast offers greater danger than reading too slow. Read slowly enough that each word is clear and distinct and that the meaning has time to sink in. Remember that your roommate does not have the advantage, as you do, of having the text before him. Your ordinary rate of reading will probably be too fast. (c) Read the poem so that the rhythmical pattern is felt but not exaggerated. Remember that poetry is written in sentences, just as prose is, and that punctuation is a signal as to how it should be read. Give all grammatical pauses their full due. Do not distort the natural pronunciation of words or a normal accentuation of the sentence to fit into what you have decided is

---

[1] Some poems encourage this type of reading. When this is so, usually the poet has not made the best use of his rhythm to support his sense.

its metrical pattern. One of the worst ways to read a poem is to read it ta-*dum* ta-*dum* ta-*dum* with an exaggerated emphasis on every other syllable. On the other hand, it should not be read as if it were prose. An important test of your reading will be how you handle the end of a line when there is no punctuation there. A frequent mistake of the beginning reader is to treat each line as if it were a complete thought, whether grammatically complete or not, and to drop his voice at the end of it. A frequent mistake of the sophisticated reader is to take a running start upon approaching the end of a line and fly over it as if it were not there. The line is a rhythmical unit, and its end should be observed whether there is punctuation or not. If there is no punctuation, one observes it ordinarily by the slightest of pauses or by holding onto the last word in the line just a little longer than usual. One should not drop his voice. In line 12 of the following poem, one should hold onto the word *although* longer than if it occurred elsewhere in the line. But one should not lower his voice on it: it is part of the clause that follows in the next stanza.

THE MAN HE KILLED

    Had he and I but met
    By some old ancient inn,
We should have sat us down to wet
    Right many a nipperkin! °   half-pint cup

    But ranged as infantry,   5
    And staring face to face,
I shot at him as he at me,
    And killed him in his place.

    I shot him dead because—
    Because he was my foe,   10
Just so: my foe of course he was;
    That's clear enough; although

    He thought he'd 'list, perhaps
    Off-hand-like—just as I—
Was out of work—had sold his traps—   15
    No other reason why.

    Yes; quaint and curious war is!
    You shoot a fellow down
You'd treat if met where any bar is,
    Or help to half-a-crown.   20

                              —*Thomas Hardy [1840–1928]*

1. Vocabulary: *traps* (15).

2. In informational prose the repetition of a word like *because* (9–10) would be an error. What purpose does the repetition serve here? Why does the speaker repeat to himself his "clear" reason for killing a man (10–11)? The word *although* (12) gets more emphasis than it ordinarily would because it comes not only at the end of a line but at the end of a stanza. What purpose does this emphasis serve? Can the redundancy of "old ancient" (2) be poetically justified?

3. Someone has defined poetry as "the expression of elevated thought in elevated language." Comment on the adequacy of this definition in the light of Hardy's poem.

As aids to the understanding of a poem, we may ask ourselves a number of questions about it. One of the most important is: *Who is the speaker and what is the occasion?* A cardinal error of beginning readers is to assume always that the speaker is the poet himself. A far safer course is to assume always that the speaker is someone other than the poet himself. For even when the poet does speak directly and express his own thoughts and emotions, he does so ordinarily as a representative human being rather than as an individual who lives at a particular address, dislikes dill pickles, and favors blue neckties. We must always be cautious about identifying anything in a poem with the biography of the poet. Like the novelist and the playwright, he is fully justified in changing actual details of his own experience to make the experience of the poem more universal. We may well think of every poem, therefore, as being to some degree *dramatic,* that is, the utterance of a fictional character rather than of the poet himself. Many poems will be expressly dramatic.

In "The Man He Killed" the speaker is a soldier; the occasion is his having been in battle and killed a man—obviously for the first time in his life. We can tell a good deal about him. He is not a career soldier: he enlisted only because he was out of work. He is a workingman: he speaks a simple and colloquial language (*nipperkin, 'list, off-hand-like, traps*), and he has sold the tools of his trade—he may have been a tinker or plumber. He is a friendly, kindly sort who enjoys a neighborly drink of ale in a bar and will gladly lend a friend a half crown when he has it. He has known what it is to be poor. In any other circumstances he would have been horrified at taking a human life. He has been given pause as it is. He is trying to figure it out. But he is not a deep thinker, and thinks he has supplied a reason when he has only supplied a name.

"I killed the man . . . because he was my foe." The critical question, of course, is *Why was the man his "foe"?* Even the speaker is left unsatisfied by his answer, though he is not analytical enough to know what is wrong with it. Obviously this poem is expressly dramatic. We need know nothing about Thomas Hardy's life (he was never a soldier and never killed a man) to realize that the poem is dramatic. The internal evidence of the poem tells us so.

A second important question that we should ask ourselves upon reading any poem is *What is the central purpose of the poem?* [2] The purpose may be to tell a story, to reveal human character, to impart a vivid impression of a scene, to express a mood or an emotion, or to convey to us vividly some idea or attitude. Whatever the purpose is, we must determine it for ourselves and define it mentally as precisely as possible. Only then can we fully understand the function and meaning of the various details in the poem, by relating them to this central purpose. Only then can we begin to assess the value of the poem and determine whether it is a good one or a poor one. In "The Man He Killed" the central purpose is quite clear: it is to make us realize more keenly the irrationality of war. The puzzlement of the speaker may be our puzzlement. But even if we are able to give a more sophisticated answer than his as to why men kill each other, we ought still to have a greater awareness, after reading the poem, of the fundamental irrationality in war which makes men kill who have no grudge against each other and who might under different circumstances show each other considerable kindness.

IS MY TEAM PLOUGHING

"Is my team ploughing,
   That I was used to drive
And hear the harness jingle
   When I was man alive?"

Aye, the horses trample,   5
   The harness jingles now;
No change though you lie under
   The land you used to plough.

[2] Our only reliable evidence of the poem's purpose, of course, is the poem itself. External evidence, when it exists, though often helpful, may also be misleading. Some critics have objected to the use of such terms as "purpose" and "intention" altogether; we cannot know, they maintain, what was *attempted* in the poem; we can know only what was *done*. Philosophically this position is impeccable. Yet it is possible to make *inferences* about what was attempted, and such inferences furnish a convenient and helpful way of talking about poetry.

"Is football playing
　Along the river shore,
With lads to chase the leather,
　Now I stand up no more?"　　　　　10

Aye, the ball is flying,
　The lads play heart and soul;
The goal stands up, the keeper　　　15
　Stands up to keep the goal.

"Is my girl happy,
　That I thought hard to leave,
And has she tired of weeping
　As she lies down at eve?"　　　　20

Aye, she lies down lightly,
　She lies not down to weep:
Your girl is well contented.
　Be still, my lad, and sleep.

"Is my friend hearty,　　　　　　25
　Now I am thin and pine,
And has he found to sleep in
　A better bed than mine?"

Yes, lad, I lie easy,
　I lie as lads would choose;　　　30
I cheer a dead man's sweetheart,
　Never ask me whose.

　　　　　　　　—A. E. Housman [1859–1936]

QUESTIONS

　1. What is meant by *whose* in line 32?
　2. Is Housman cynical in his observation of human nature and human life?
　3. The word *sleep* in the concluding stanzas suggests three different meanings. What are they? How many meanings are suggested by the word *bed*?

Once we have answered the question, *What is the central purpose of the poem?* we can consider another question, equally important to full understanding: *By what means is that purpose achieved?* It is important to distinguish means from ends. A student on an examination once used the poem "Is my team ploughing" as evidence that A. E. Housman believed in immortality, because in it a man speaks from the grave. This is as naive as to say that Thomas Hardy in "The Man He Killed" joined the army because he was out of work. The purpose of Housman's poem is to communicate poignantly a certain truth about human life: that life goes on after our deaths pretty much as it did before—our dying does not disturb the universe. This purpose is achieved by means of a fanciful dramatic framework in which a dead man converses with his still living friend. The framework tells us nothing about whether Housman believed in immortality (as a matter of fact, he did not). It is simply an effective means by which we *can* learn how Housman felt a man's death affected the life he left behind. The question, *By what means is the purpose of the poem achieved?* is partially answered by describing the poem's dramatic framework, if any. The complete answer requires an accounting of various resources of communication which it will take us the rest of this book to discuss.

The most important preliminary advice we can give for reading poetry is to maintain always, while reading it, the utmost mental alertness. The most fatal idea one can get about poetry is that its purpose is to soothe and relax, and that the best place to read it is lying in a hammock with a cool drink beside one and low music in the background. One *can* read poetry lying in a hammock, but only if he refuses to put his mind in the same attitude as his body. Its purpose is not to soothe and relax, but to arouse and awake, to shock one into life, to make one more alive. Poetry is not a substitute for a sedative.

An analogy can be drawn between reading poetry and playing tennis. Both offer great enjoyment if the game is played hard. A good tennis player must be constantly on the tip of his toes, concentrating on his opponent's every move. He must be ready for a drive to the right or a drive to the left, a lob overhead or a drop shot barely over the net. He must be ready for top spin or underspin, a ball that bounces crazily to the left or crazily to the right. He must jump for the high ones and run for the far ones. He will enjoy the game almost exactly in proportion to the effort he puts into it. The same is true of poetry. Great enjoyment is there, but this enjoyment demands a mental effort equivalent to the physical effort one puts into tennis.

The reader of poetry has one advantage over the tennis player. The poet is not trying to win a match. He may expect the reader to stretch for his shots, but he *wants* the reader to return them.

EXERCISE

Most of the poems in this book are accompanied by study questions, but these are by no means exhaustive. Following is a list of questions which you may yourself apply to any poem, or which your instructor may wish to use, in whole or in part, to supplement the questions to any particular poem. You will not be able to answer many of them until you have read further into the book.

1. Who is the speaker? What kind of person is he?
2. To whom is he speaking? What kind of person is he?
3. What is the occasion?
4. What is the setting in time (time of day, season, century, etc.)?
5. What is the setting in place (indoors or out, city or country, nation, etc.)?
6. What is the central purpose of the poem?
7. State the central idea or theme of the poem in a sentence.
8. Discuss the tone of the poem. How is it achieved?
9. a. Outline the poem so as to show its structure and development; or
   b. Summarize the events of the poem.
10. Paraphrase the poem.
11. Discuss the diction of the poem. Point out words that are particularly well chosen and explain why.
12. Discuss the imagery of the poem. What kinds of imagery are used?
13. Point out examples of metaphor, simile, personification, and metonymy, and explain their appropriateness.
14. Point out and explain any symbols. If the poem is allegorical, explain the allegory.
15. Point out and explain examples of paradox, overstatement, understatement, and irony. What is their function?
16. Point out and explain any allusions. What is their function?
17. Point out significant examples of sound repetition and explain their function.
18. a. What is the meter of the poem?
    b. Copy the poem and mark its scansion.
19. Discuss the adaptation of sound to sense.
20. Describe the form or pattern of the poem.
21. Criticize and evaluate the poem.

• • •

IT IS NOT GROWING LIKE A TREE

It is not growing like a tree
In bulk, doth make Man better be;
Or standing long an oak, three hundred year,
To fall a log at last, dry, bald, and sere:
      A lily of a day   5
      Is fairer far in May,
Although it fall and die that night;
It was the plant and flower of Light.
In small proportions we just beauties see;
And in short measures life may perfect be.   10

—Ben Jonson [1573?–1637]

1. Your instructor may occasionally ask you, as a test of your understanding of a poem at its lowest level, or as a means of clearing up misunderstanding, to paraphrase its content. To PARAPHRASE a poem means to restate it in different language, so as to make its prose sense as plain as possible. The paraphrase may be longer or shorter than the poem, but it should contain as far as possible all the ideas in the poem in such a way as to make them clear to a puzzled reader. Figurative language should be reduced when possible to literal language; metaphors should be turned into similes. Though it is neither necessary nor possible to avoid using any word occurring in the original, you should in general use your own language.

The central idea of the above poem is approximately this: Life is to be measured by its excellence, not by its length. The poem may be paraphrased as follows:

A man does not become more excellent by simply growing in size, as a tree grows, nor by merely living for a very long time, as an oak does, only to die at length, old, bald, and wizened. A lily which lives only for one day in the spring is far more estimable than the long-lived tree, even though it dies at nightfall, for while it lives it is the essence and crown of beauty and excellence. Thus we may see perfect beauty in small things. Thus human life, too, may be most excellent though very brief.

2. A paraphrase is useful only if you understand that it is the barest, most inadequate approximation of what the poem really "says," and is no more equivalent to the poem than a corpse is equivalent to a man. Once having made a paraphrase, you should endeavor to see how far short of the poem it falls, and why. In what respects does the above poem say more, and say it more memorably, than the paraphrase?

3. Does *bald* (4) apply only to the man or also to the log? May line 8 be interpreted in a way other than the way the paraphrase interprets it? What is the meaning of *just* (9)? Could *measures* (10) mean anything in addition to "amounts"? Comment on the effectiveness of the comparisons to tree and lily.

IT IS MOST TRUE THAT EYES ARE FORMED TO SERVE

It is most true that eyes are formed to serve
    The inward light, and that the heavenly part
    Ought to be king, from whose rules who do swerve,
    Rebels to Nature, strive for their own smart.
It is most true, what we call Cupid's dart,   5
    An image is, which for ourselves we carve;
    And, fools, adore in temple of our heart,
    Till that good God make Church and Churchman starve.

True, that true Beauty Virtue is indeed,
  Whereof this Beauty can be but a shade,   10
  Which elements with mortal mixture breed:
True, that on earth we are but pilgrims made,
  And should in soul up to our country move:
True, and yet true that I must Stella love.

—*Sir Philip Sidney* [*1554–1586*]

QUESTIONS

1. This sonnet might be paraphrased as follows:

It is very true that the eyes were created to serve the soul, and that the
soul ought to rule the senses. Those who fail to observe this principle
are rebels against Nature and will injure themselves.

It is very true that what we call the arrow of Cupid is a false idol
which we have made for ourselves and which we foolishly worship in
our hearts until God punishes us by causing true religion in us to
perish.

It is true that the only divine Beauty is Virtue, and that earthly
beauty is but a shadow of that divine beauty and is itself produced
only by intermixture of that divine beauty with earthly things.

It is true that we are here on earth only temporarily and should be
preparing ourselves during this time for heaven. All these things are
true; yet I cannot help loving Stella.

In what respects is this paraphrase less satisfactory than the poem? Where does
it perhaps fail to do the poem justice in a literal sense? Can you think of other
ways of interpreting line 8? line 11?

2. Express the central idea of the poem in a sentence.

DEVIL, MAGGOT AND SON

Three things seek my death,
  Hard at my heels they run—
Hang them, sweet Christ, all three,—
  Devil, maggot and son.

So much does each of them crave   5
  The morsel that falls to his share,
He cares not a thrauneen° what   straw
  Falls to the other pair.

If the devil, that crafty one,
  Can capture my soul in sin   10
He'll leave my flesh to the worm,
  My money to my kin.

27

My sons think more of the money
    That will come to them when I die
Than a soul that they could not spend,   15
    A body that none would buy.

And how would the maggots fare
    On a soul too thin to eat
And money too tough to chew?
    The maggots must have meat.   20

Christ, speared by the blind man,
    Christ, nailed to a naked tree,
The three that are seeking my end
    Hang them, sweet Christ, all three!

—*Frank O'Connor* [1903–   ]
(*translated from the Irish*)

QUESTIONS

1. Who and what kind of person is the speaker?
2. Note (21): According to medieval Christian belief, the Roman soldier Longinus, who thrust a spear into Christ's side at the crucifixion, was blind. What element in this poem most underscores its horror?

HAP

If but some vengeful god would call to me
From up the sky, and laugh: "Thou suffering thing,
Know that thy sorrow is my ecstasy,
That thy love's loss is my hate's profiting!"

Then would I bear it, clench myself, and die,   5
Steeled by the sense of ire unmerited;
Half-eased in that a Powerfuller than I
Had willed and meted me the tears I shed.

But not so. How arrives it joy lies slain,
And why unblooms the best hope ever sown?   10
—Crass Casualty obstructs the sun and rain,
And dicing Time for gladness casts a moan. . . .
These purblind Doomsters had as readily strown
Blisses about my pilgrimage as pain.

—*Thomas Hardy* [1840–1928]

QUESTIONS

    1. Vocabulary: *hap* (title), *Casualty* (11).
    2. What is "the best hope ever sown" (10)?
    3. Why are *Casualty* (11) and *Time* (12) capitalized? What picture is evoked by line 11?
    4. Explain the psychological reaction expressed in lines 5–8.
    5. Paraphrase the poem.

THE SUBALTERNS

"Poor wanderer," said the leaden sky,
   "I fain would lighten thee,
But there are laws in force on high
   Which say it must not be."

"I would not freeze thee, shorn one," cried   5
   The North, "knew I but how
To warm my breath, to slack my stride;
   But I am ruled as thou."

"Tomorrow I attack thee, wight,"
   Said Sickness. "Yet I swear   10
I bear thy little ark no spite,
   But am bid enter there."

"Come hither, Son," I heard Death say;
   "I did not will a grave
Should end thy pilgrimage today,   15
   But I, too, am a slave!"

We smiled upon each other then,
   And life to me had less
Of that fell look it wore ere when
   They owned their passiveness.   20

—Thomas Hardy [1840–1928]

QUESTIONS

    1. Vocabulary: *subalterns* (title), *wight* (9), *fell* (19).
    2. In what respect do this poem and "Hap," though both by the same author, say directly opposite things? How do you explain the contradiction?
    3. In what respect do these two poems say the same thing?

JOHN GORHAM

"Tell me what you're doing over here, John Gorham,
Sighing hard and seeming to be sorry when you're not;
Make me laugh or let me go now, for long faces in the moonlight
Are a sign for me to say again a word that you forgot."—

"I'm over here to tell you what the moon already   5
May have said or maybe shouted ever since a year ago;
I'm over here to tell you what you are, Jane Wayland,
And to make you rather sorry, I should say, for being so."—

"Tell me what you're saying to me now, John Gorham,
Or you'll never see as much of me as ribbons any more;   10
I'll vanish in as many ways as I have toes and fingers,
And you'll not follow far for one where flocks have been before."—

"I'm sorry now you never saw the flocks, Jane Wayland,
But you're the one to make of them as many as you need.
And then about the vanishing. It's I who mean to vanish;   15
And when I'm here no longer you'll be done with me indeed."—

"That's a way to tell me what I am, John Gorham!
How am I to know myself until I make you smile?
Try to look as if the moon were making faces at you,
And a little more as if you meant to stay a little while."—   20

"You are what it is that over rose-blown gardens
Makes a pretty flutter for a season in the sun;
You are what it is that with a mouse, Jane Wayland,
Catches him and lets him go and eats him up for fun."—

"Sure I never took you for a mouse, John Gorham;   25
All you say is easy, but so far from being true
That I wish you wouldn't ever be again the one to think so;
For it isn't cats and butterflies that I would be to you."—

"All your little animals are in one picture—
One I've had before me since a year ago to-night;   30
And the picture where they live will be of you, Jane Wayland,
Till you find a way to kill them or to keep them out of sight."—

"Won't you ever see me as I am, John Gorham,
Leaving out the foolishness and all I never meant?
Somewhere in me there's a woman, if you know the way to find her.   35
Will you like me any better if I prove it and repent?"—

"I doubt if I shall ever have the time, Jane Wayland;
And I dare say all this moonlight lying round us might as well
Fall for nothing on the shards of broken urns that are forgotten,
As on two that have no longer much of anything to tell."   40

—*Edwin Arlington Robinson [1869–1935]*

QUESTIONS

1. Vocabulary: *shards* (39).
2. Define as precisely as possible the occasion in the poem.
3. What kind of person is John Gorham? Jane Wayland? Do you think the poet is more sympathetic with one than with the other?
4. We are never told exactly what was said (4) or what happened (6) "a year ago." Does the withholding of this information weaken the poem, or is the author's purpose complete without it?

ANOTHER DARK LADY

Think not, because I wonder where you fled,
That I would lift a pin to see you there;
You may, for me, be prowling anywhere,
So long as you show not your little head:
No dark and evil story of the dead   5
Would leave you less pernicious or less fair—
Not even Lilith, with her famous hair;
And Lilith was the devil, I have read.

I cannot hate you, for I loved you then.
The woods were golden then. There was a road   10
Through beeches; and I said their smooth feet showed
Like yours. Truth must have heard me from afar,
For I shall never have to learn again
That yours are cloven as no beech's are.

—*Edwin Arlington Robinson [1869–1935]*

QUESTIONS

1. This sonnet contains two literary allusions. Lilith (7–8) is a famous female demon, or vampire, of Jewish folklore; her name means "night monster." Can you identify the allusion in the title?
2. Should we guess from the evidence of this poem that its author (who also wrote "John Gorham" and who never married) was betrayed in love?

3

Denotation and Connotation

A primary distinction between the practical use of language and the literary use is that in literature, especially in poetry, a *fuller* use is made of individual words. To understand this, we need to examine the composition of a word.

The average word has three component parts: sound, denotation, and connotation. It begins as a combination of tones and noises, uttered by the lips, tongue, and throat, for which the written word is a notation. But it differs from a musical tone or a noise in that it has a meaning attached to it. The basic part of this meaning is its DENOTATION or denotations: that is, the dictionary meaning or meanings of the word. Beyond its denotations, a word may also have connotations. The CONNOTATIONS are what it suggests beyond what it expresses: its overtones of meaning. It acquires these connotations by its past history and associations, by the way and the circumstances in which it has been used. The word *home*, for instance, by denotation means only a place where one lives, but by connotation it suggests security, love, comfort, and family. The words *childlike* and *childish* both mean "characteristic of a child," but *childlike* suggests meekness, innocence, and wide-eyed wonder, while *childish* suggests pettiness, willfulness, and temper tantrums. If we name over a series of coins: *nickel, peso, lira, shilling, sen, doubloon*—the word *doubloon*, to four out of five readers, will immediately suggest pirates, though one will find nothing about pirates in looking up its meaning in the dictionary. Pirates are part of its connotation.

Connotation is very important to the poet, for it is one of the means by which he can concentrate or enrich his meaning—say more in fewer words. Consider, for instance, the following short poem:

THERE IS NO FRIGATE LIKE A BOOK

There is no frigate like a book
To take us lands away,
Nor any coursers like a page
Of prancing poetry.
This traverse may the poorest take
Without oppress of toll;
How frugal is the chariot
That bears the human soul!

—Emily Dickinson [1830–1886]

In this poem Emily Dickinson is considering the power of a book or of poetry to carry us away, to let us escape from our immediate surroundings into a world of the imagination. To do this she has compared literature to various means of transportation: a boat, a team of horses, a wheeled land vehicle. But she has been careful to choose kinds of transportation and names for them that have romantic connotations. *Frigate* suggests exploration and adventure; *coursers,* beauty, spirit, and speed; *chariot,* speed and the ability to go through the air as well as on land. (Compare "Swing Low, Sweet Chariot," and the myth of Phaëthon, who tried to drive the chariot of Apollo, and the famous painting of Aurora with her horses, once hung in almost every school.) How much of the meaning of the poem comes from this selection of vehicles and words is apparent if we try to substitute for them, say, *steamship, horses,* and *streetcar.*

QUESTIONS

1. What is lost if *miles* is substituted for *lands* (2), or *cheap* for *frugal* (7)?

2. How is *prancing* (4) peculiarly appropriate to poetry as well as to coursers? Could the poet have without loss compared a book to coursers and poetry to a frigate?

3. Is this account appropriate to all kinds of poetry or just to certain kinds?

33

That is, was the poet thinking of poems like Wilfred Owen's "Dulce et De-corum Est" (page 8) or of poems like Coleridge's "Kubla Khan" (page 263) and Walter de la Mare's "The Listeners" (page 265)?

Just as a word has a variety of connotations, so also it may have more than one denotation. If we look up the word *spring* in the dictionary, for instance, we will find that it has between twenty-five and thirty distinguishable meanings: It may mean (1) a pounce or leap, (2) a season of the year, (3) a natural source of water, (4) a coiled elastic wire, etc. This variety of denotation, complicated by additional tones of connotation, makes language confusing and difficult to use. Any person using words must be careful to define by context precisely the meanings that he wishes. But the difference between the writer using language to communicate information and the poet is this: the practical writer will always attempt to confine his words to one meaning at a time; the poet will often take advantage of the fact that the word has more than one meaning by using it to mean more than one thing at the same time. Thus when Edith Sitwell in one of her poems writes, "This is the time of the wild spring and the mating of tigers," she uses the word *spring* to denote both a season of the year and a sudden leap, and she uses *tigers* rather than *lambs* or *birds* because it has a connotation of fierceness and wildness that the other two lack. In the following sonnet the word *wreathèd* (line 14) means "twisted or convoluted," but it may also mean "hung with seaweed." Both meanings are appropriate to the image of Triton.

THE WORLD IS TOO MUCH WITH US

The world is too much with us; late and soon,
Getting and spending, we lay waste our powers:
Little we see in Nature that is ours;
We have given our hearts away, a sordid boon!
The Sea that bares her bosom to the moon;   5
The winds that will be howling at all hours,
And are up-gathered now like sleeping flowers;
For this, for everything, we are out of tune;
It moves us not.—Great God! I'd rather be
A Pagan suckled in a creed outworn;   10
So might I, standing on this pleasant lea,
Have glimpses that would make me less forlorn;
Have sight of Proteus rising from the sea;
Or hear old Triton blow his wreathèd horn.

—*William Wordsworth [1770–1850]*

1. Vocabulary: *boon* (4), *Proteus* (13), *Triton* (14).

2. Try to explain why the poet chose his wording rather than the following alternatives: *earth* for *world* (1), *buying and selling* for *getting and spending* (2), *exposes* for *bares* (5), *back* for *bosom* (5), *dozing* for *sleeping* (7), *posies* for *flowers* (7), *nourished* for *suckled* (10), *visions* for *glimpses* (12), *sound* for *blow* (14).

3. Should *Great God!* (9) be considered as a vocative (term of address) or an expletive (exclamation)? Or something of both?

4. State the theme of the poem in a sentence.

A frequent misconception of poetic language is that the poet seeks always the most beautiful or noble-sounding words. What he really seeks are the most *meaningful* words, and these vary from one context to another. Language has many levels and varieties, and the poet may choose from them all. His words may be grandiose or humble, fanciful or matter of fact, romantic or realistic, archaic or modern, technical or everyday, monosyllabic or polysyllabic. Usually his poem will be pitched pretty much in one key. The words in Emily Dickinson's "There is no frigate like a book" and those in Thomas Hardy's "The Man He Killed" (page 20) are chosen from quite different areas of language, but each poet has chosen the words most meaningful for his own poetic context. Sometimes a poet may import a word from one level or area of language into a poem composed mostly of words from a different level or area. If he does this clumsily, the result will be incongruous and sloppy. If he does it skillfully, the result will be a shock of surprise and an increment of meaning for the reader. In fact, the many varieties of language open to the poet provide his richest resource. His task is one of constant exploration and discovery. He searches always for the secret affinities of words which allow them to be brought together with soft explosions of meaning.

THE NAKED AND THE NUDE [1]

For me, the naked and the nude
(By lexicographers construed
As synonyms that should express
The same deficiency of dress
Or shelter) stand as wide apart   5
As love from lies, or truth from art.

[1] Mr. Graves has recorded "The Naked and the Nude" (LP, Library of Congress, PL 20).

Lovers without reproach will gaze
On bodies naked and ablaze;
The hippocratic eye will see
In nakedness, anatomy;   10
And naked shines the Goddess when
She mounts her lion among men.

The nude are bold, the nude are sly
To hold each treasonable eye.
While draping by a showman's trick   15
Their dishabille in rhetoric,
They grin a mock-religious grin
Of scorn at those of naked skin.

The naked, therefore, who compete
Against the nude may know defeat;   20
Yet when they both together tread
The briary pastures of the dead,
By Gorgons with long whips pursued,
How naked go the sometime nude!

—*Robert Graves* [1895–   ]

QUESTIONS

1. Vocabulary: *lexicographers* (2), *construed* (2), *hippocratic* (9), *dishabille* (16), *Gorgons* (23).

2. What kind of language is used in lines 2–5? Why? (For example, why is *deficiency* used in preference to *lack*? Purely because of meter?)

3. What is meant by *rhetoric* (16)? Why is the word *dishabille* used in this line instead of some less fancy word?

4. Explain why the poet chose his wording instead of the following alternatives: *brave* for *bold* (13), *clever* for *sly* (13), *clothing* for *draping* (15), *smile* for *grin* (17).

5. What, for the poet, is the difference in connotation between *naked* and *nude*? Try to explain reasons for the difference. If your own sense of the two words differs from that of Graves, state the difference, and give reasons to support your sense of them.

6. Explain the reversal in the last line.

The person using language to convey information is largely indifferent to the sound of his words and is hampered by their connotations and multiple denotations. He tries to confine each word to a single exact meaning. He uses, one might say, a fraction of the word and throws the rest away. The poet, on the other hand, tries to use as much of the word as he can. He is interested in sound and uses it to reinforce meaning (see Chapter 13). He is interested in connotation and uses it to enrich and convey meaning. And he may use more than one denotation.

The purest form of practical language is scientific language. The scientist needs a precise language for conveying information precisely. The fact that words have multiple denotations and various overtones of meaning is a hindrance to him in accomplishing his purpose. His ideal language would be a language with a one-to-one correspondence between word and meaning; that is, every word would have one meaning only, and for every meaning there would be only one word. Since ordinary language does not fulfill these conditions, he has invented one that does. A statement in his language looks something like this:

$$SO_2 + H_2O = H_2SO_3.$$

In such a statement the symbols are entirely unambiguous; they have been stripped of all connotation and of all denotations but one. The word *sulfurous,* if it occurred in poetry, might have all kinds of connotations: fire, smoke, brimstone, hell, damnation. But H_2SO_3 means one thing and one thing only: sulfurous acid.

The ambiguity and multiplicity of meanings that words have, then, are an obstacle to the scientist but a resource to the poet. Where the scientist wants singleness of meaning, the poet wants richness of meaning. Where the scientist needs and has invented a strictly one-dimensional language, in which every word is confined to one denotation, the poet needs a multi-dimensional language, and creates it partly by using a multi-dimensional vocabulary, in which, to the dimension of denotation, he adds the dimensions of connotation and of sound.

The poet, we may say, plays on a many-stringed instrument. And he sounds more than one note at a time.

The first problem in reading poetry, therefore, or in reading any kind of literature, is to develop a sense of language, a feeling for words. One needs to become acquainted with their shape, their color, and their flavor. There are two ways of doing this: extensive use of the dictionary and extensive reading.

EXERCISES

1. Robert Frost has said that "Poetry is what evaporates from all translations." On the basis of this chapter, can you explain why this statement is true? How much of a word can be translated?

2. Which of the following words have the most "romantic" connotations?
   a. horse ( ) steed ( ) equine quadruped ( )
   b. China ( ) Cathay ( )
   Which of the following is the most emotionally connotative?
   c. mother ( ) female parent ( ) dam ( )
   Which of the following have the more favorable connotations?
   d. average ( ) mediocre ( )
   e. secret agent ( ) spy ( )
   f. adventurer ( ) adventuress ( )

3. Fill each blank with the word richest in meaning in the given context. Explain.
   a. I still had hopes, my latest hours to crown,
      Amidst these humble bowers to lay me down;
      To husband out life's _____ at the close,   *candle, taper*
      And keep the flame from wasting by repose.
                    —*Goldsmith*
   b. She was a _____ of delight.   *ghost, phantom,*
      When first she gleamed upon my sight.   *spectre, spook*
                    —*Wordsworth*
   c. His sumptuous watch-case, though concealed it lies,
      Like a good conscience, _____ joy supplies.   *perfect, solid,*
                   —*Edward Young*   *thorough*
   d. Charmed magic _____ opening on the foam   *casements, windows*
      Of _____ seas, in faery lands forlorn.—*Keats*   *dangerous, perilous*
   e. Thou _____ unravished bride of quietness.   *still, yet*
                    —*Keats*
   f. I'll _____ the guts into the neighbor room.   *bear, carry, convey,*
                   —*Shakespeare*   *lug*
   g. The iron tongue of midnight hath _____   *said, struck, told*
      twelve.   —*Shakespeare*
   h. In poetry each word reverberates like the note of
      a well-tuned _____ and always leaves be-   *banjo, guitar, lyre*
      hind it a multitude of vibrations.   —*Joubert*
   i. I think that with this _____ new alliance   *holy, sacred*
         I may ensure the public, and defy
      All other magazines of art or science.   —*Byron*
   j. Care on thy maiden brow shall put
      A wreath of wrinkles, and thy foot
      Be shod with pain: not silken dress
      But toil shall _____ thy loveliness.   *clothe, tire, weary*
              —*C. Day Lewis*

4. Ezra Pound has defined great literature as being "simply language charged with meaning to the utmost possible degree." Would this be a good definition of poetry? The word *charged* is roughly equivalent to *filled*. Why is

charged a better word in Pound's definition? What do its associations with
storage batteries, guns, and dynamite suggest about poetry?

• • •

RICHARD CORY

Whenever Richard Cory went down town,
We people on the pavement looked at him:
He was a gentleman from sole to crown,
Clean favored, and imperially slim.

And he was always quietly arrayed,   5
And he was always human when he talked;
But still he fluttered pulses when he said,
"Good-morning," and he glittered when he walked.

And he was rich—yes, richer than a king—
And admirably schooled in every grace: 10
In fine, we thought that he was everything
To make us wish that we were in his place.

So on we worked, and waited for the light,
And went without the meat, and cursed the bread;
And Richard Cory, one calm summer night,   15
Went home and put a bullet through his head.

                              —*Edwin Arlington Robinson [1869–1935]*

QUESTIONS

1. In how many senses is Richard Cory a gentleman?
2. The word *crown,* meaning the top of the head, is familiar to you from
"Jack and Jill"; but why does Robinson use the unusual phrase "from sole to
crown" instead of the common "from head to foot" or "from top to toe"?
3. List the words in the poem which express or suggest the idea of aris-
tocracy or royalty.
4. Try to explain why the poet chose his wording rather than the following alternatives: *sidewalk* for *pavement* (2), *good-looking* for *clean favored*
(4), *thin* for *slim* (4), *dressed* for *arrayed* (5), *courteous* for *human* (6),
wonderfully for *admirably* (10), *trained* for *schooled* (10), *manners* for *every
grace* (10), *in short* for *in fine* (11). What other examples of effective diction
do you find in the poem?
5. Why is *Richard Cory* a good name for the character in this poem?
6. This poem is a good example of how ironic contrast (see Chapter 7)
generates meaning. The poem makes no direct statement about life; it simply
relates an incident. What larger meanings about life does it suggest?

7. A leading American critic has said of this poem: "In 'Richard Cory' . . . we have a superficially neat portrait of the elegant man of mystery; the poem builds up deliberately to a very cheap surprise ending; but all surprise endings are cheap in poetry, if not, indeed, elsewhere, for poetry is written to be read not once but many times." [2] Do you agree with this evaluation of the poem? Discuss.

THE RICH MAN

The rich man has his motor-car,
    His country and his town estate.
He smokes a fifty-cent cigar
    And jeers at Fate.

He frivols through the livelong day,   5
    He knows not Poverty her pinch.
His lot seems light, his heart seems gay,
    He has a cinch.

Yet though my lamp burns low and dim,
    Though I must slave for livelihood—   10
Think you that I would change with him?
    You bet I would!

—*Franklin P. Adams [1881–1960]*

QUESTIONS

1. What meanings has *lot* (7)?
2. Bearing in mind the criticism cited of Robinson's "Richard Cory," state whether you think that poem or this has more poetic value. Which poem is merely clever? Which is something more?

NAMING OF PARTS [3]

To-day we have naming of parts. Yesterday,
We had daily cleaning. And to-morrow morning,
We shall have what to do after firing. But to-day,
To-day we have naming of parts. Japonica
Glistens like coral in all of the neighboring gardens,   5
    And to-day we have naming of parts.

This is the lower sling swivel. And this
Is the upper sling swivel, whose use you will see,

[2] Yvor Winters, *Edwin Arlington Robinson*, Norfolk, Conn., New Directions, 1946, p. 52.
[3] Mr. Reed has recorded "Naming of Parts" (LP, Library of Congress, PL 20).

When you are given your slings. And this is the piling swivel,
Which in your case you have not got. The branches   ⸗ 10
Hold in the gardens their silent, eloquent gestures,
      Which in our case we have not got.

This is the safety-catch, which is always released
With an easy flick of the thumb. And please do not let me
See anyone using his finger. You can do it quite easy   15
If you have any strength in your thumb. The blossoms
Are fragile and motionless, never letting anyone see
      Any of them using their finger.

And this you can see is the bolt. The purpose of this
Is to open the breech, as you see. We can slide it   20
Rapidly backwards and forwards: we call this
Easing the spring. And rapidly backwards and forwards
The early bees are assaulting and fumbling the flowers:
      They call it easing the Spring.

They call it easing the Spring: it is perfectly easy   25
If you have any strength in your thumb: like the bolt,
And the breech, and the cocking-piece, and the point of balance,
Which in our case we have not got; and the almond-blossom
Silent in all of the gardens and the bees going backwards and forwards,
      For to-day we have naming of parts.   30

                                         —*Henry Reed* [1914–]

QUESTIONS

    1. What basic contrasts are represented by the trainees and the gardens?
    2. What is it that the trainees "have not got"?
    3. How many senses have the phrases "easing the Spring" (stanza 4) and
"point of balance" (27)?
    4. What differences of language and rhythm do you find between those
lines concerning "naming of parts" and those describing the gardens?
    5. Does the repetition of certain phrases throughout the poem have any
special function, or is it only a kind of refrain?

JUDGING DISTANCES [4]

    Not only how far away, but the way that you say it
    Is very important. Perhaps you may never get
    The knack of judging a distance, but at least you know
    How to report on a landscape: the central sector,
    The right of arc and that, which we had last Tuesday,   5
          And at least you know

[4] Mr. Reed has recorded "Judging Distances" (LP, Library of Congress, PL 20).

That maps are of time, not place, so far as the army
Happens to be concerned—the reason being,
Is one which need not delay us. Again, you know
There are three kinds of tree, three only, the fir and   10
    the poplar,
And those which have bushy tops to; and lastly
    That things only seem to be things.

A barn is not called a barn, to put it more plainly,
Or a field in the distance, where sheep may be safely grazing.
You must never be over-sure. You must say, when reporting: 15
At five o'clock in the central sector is a dozen
Of what appear to be animals; whatever you do,
    Don't call the bleeders *sheep*.

I am sure that's quite clear; and suppose, for the sake of
    example,
The one at the end, asleep, endeavors to tell us   20
What he sees over there to the west, and how far away,
After first having come to attention. There to the west,
On the fields of summer the sun and the shadows bestow
    Vestments of purple and gold.

The still white dwellings are like a mirage in the heat,   25
And under the swaying elms a man and a woman
Lie gently together. Which is, perhaps, only to say
That there is a row of houses to the left of arc,
And that under some poplars a pair of what appear to be humans
    Appear to be loving.   30

Well that, for an answer, is what we might rightly call
Moderately satisfactory only, the reason being,
Is that two things have been omitted, and those are important.
The human beings, now: in what direction are they,
And how far away, would you say? And do not forget   35
    There may be dead ground in between.

There may be dead ground in between; and I may not have got
The knack of judging a distance; I will only venture
A guess that perhaps between me and the apparent lovers,
(Who, incidentally, appear by now to have finished,)   40
At seven o'clock from the houses, is roughly a distance
    Of about one year and a half.

                          —*Henry Reed* [1914–]

1. In what respect are maps "of time, not place" in the army?
2. Though they may be construed as belonging to the same speaker, there are two speaking voices in this poem. Identify each, and put quotation marks around the lines spoken by the second voice.
3. Two kinds of language are used in this poem—army "officialese," and the language of human experience. What are the characteristics of each? What is the purpose of each? Which is more precise?
4. The word *bleeders* (18)—i.e., "bloody creatures"—is British profanity. To which of the two kinds of language does it belong? Or is it perhaps a third kind of language?
5. As in "Naming of Parts" (these two poems are part of a series of three with the general title "Lessons of War") the two kinds of language used might possibly be called "unpoetic" and "poetic." Is the "unpoetic" language *really* unpoetic? In other words, is its use inappropriate in these two poems? Explain.
6. The phrase "dead ground" (36) takes on symbolic meaning in the last stanza. What is its literal meaning? What is its symbolic meaning? What does the second speaker mean by saying that the distance between himself and the lovers is "about one year and a half"? In what respect is the contrast between the recruits and the lovers similar to that between the recruits and the gardens in "Naming of Parts"? What meanings are generated by the former contrast?

BASE DETAILS

If I were fierce, and bald, and short of breath,
    I'd live with scarlet Majors at the Base,
And speed glum heroes up the line to death.
    You'd see me with my puffy petulant face,
Guzzling and gulping in the best hotel,   5
    Reading the Roll of Honor. "Poor young chap,"
I'd say—"I used to know his father well;
    Yes, we've lost heavily in this last scrap."
And when the war is done and youth stone dead,
I'd toddle safely home and die—in bed.   10

—*Siegfried Sassoon* [1886–]

1. Vocabulary: *petulant* (4).
2. In what two ways may the title be interpreted? (Both words have two pertinent meanings.) What applications has *scarlet* (2)? What is the force of *fierce* (1)? Try to explain why the poet chose his wording rather than the

following alternatives: *fleshy* for *puffy* (4), *eating and drinking* for *guzzling and gulping* (5), *battle* for *scrap* (8), *totter* for *toddle* (10).

3. Who evidently is the speaker? (The poet, a British captain in World War I, was decorated for bravery on the battlefield.) Does he mean what he says? What is the purpose of the poem?

LOVE SONG

Your little hands,
Your little feet,
Your little mouth—
Oh, God, how sweet!

Your little nose,   5
Your little ears,
Your eyes, that shed
Such little tears!

Your little voice,
So soft and kind;   10
Your little soul,
Your little mind!

—*Samuel Hoffenstein [1890–1947]*

QUESTION

1. The connotations of a word, like its denotations, are controlled by context, and are thus subject to change. What are the connotations of *little* in lines 1–10? in lines 11–12?

THE WRITTEN WORD

A

The spoken or written word
Should be as clean as a bone,
As clear as is the light,
As firm as is a stone.
Two words will never serve
As well as one alone.

B

The written word
Should be clean as bone,
Clear as light,
Firm as stone.
Two words are not
As good as one.

QUESTION

1. Which of the above versions of a poem, by an anonymous writer, is the better? Why?

4

Imagery

Experience comes to us largely through the senses. My experience of a spring day, for instance, may consist partly of certain emotions I feel and partly of certain thoughts I think, but most of it will be a cluster of sense impressions. It will consist of *seeing* blue sky and white clouds, budding leaves and daffodils; of *hearing* robins and bluebirds singing in the early morning; of *smelling* damp earth and blossoming hyacinths; and of *feeling* a fresh wind against my cheek. The poet seeking to express his experience of a spring day must therefore provide a selection of the sense impressions he has. Like Shakespeare (page 11), he must give the reader "daisies pied" and "lady-smocks all silver-white" and "merry larks" and the song of the cuckoo and maidens bleaching their summer smocks. Without doing so he will probably fail in evoking the emotions which accompanied his sensations. His language, therefore, must be more *sensuous* than ordinary language. It must be more full of imagery.

IMAGERY may be defined as the representation through language of sense experience. Poetry appeals directly to our senses, of course, through its music and rhythm, which we actually hear when it is read aloud. But indirectly it appeals to our senses through imagery, the representation to the imagination of sense experience. The word *image* perhaps most often suggests a mental picture, something seen in the mind's eye—and *visual* imagery is the most frequently occurring kind of imagery in poetry. But an image may also represent a sound; a smell; a taste; a tactile experience, such as hardness, wetness, or cold; an internal sensation, such as hunger, thirst, or nausea; or movement or tension in the muscles or joints. If we wished to be scientific, we could extend this list further, for psychologists no longer confine themselves to five or even six senses; but for purposes of discussing poetry the above classification should ordinarily be sufficient.

MEETING AT NIGHT

The gray sea and the long black land;
And the yellow half-moon large and low;
And the startled little waves that leap
In fiery ringlets from their sleep,
As I gain the cove with pushing prow,   5
And quench its speed i' the slushy sand.

Then a mile of warm sea-scented beach;
Three fields to cross till a farm appears;
A tap at the pane, the quick sharp scratch
And blue spurt of a lighted match,   10
And a voice less loud, through its joys and fears,
Than the two hearts beating each to each!

—*Robert Browning* [1812–1889]

"Meeting at Night" is a poem about love. It makes, one might say, a number of statements about love: being in love is a sweet and exciting experience; when one is in love everything seems beautiful to him, and the most trivial things become significant; when one is in love his sweetheart seems the most important object in the world. But the poet actually *tells* us none of these things directly. He doesn't even use the word *love* in his poem. His business is to communicate experience, not information. He does this largely in two ways. First, he presents us with a specific situation, in which a lover goes to meet his sweetheart. Second, he describes the lover's journey so vividly in terms of sense impressions that the reader not only sees and hears what the lover saw and heard but also shares his anticipation and excitement.

Every line in the poem contains some image, some appeal to the senses: the gray sea, the long black land, the yellow half-moon, the startled little waves with their fiery ringlets, the blue spurt of the lighted match—all appeal to our sense of sight and convey not only shape, but also color and motion. The warm sea-scented beach appeals to the senses, of both smell and touch. The pushing prow of the boat on the sand, the tap at the pane, the quick sharp scratch of the match, the low speech of the lovers, and the sound of their two hearts beating—all appeal to the sense of hearing.

PARTING AT MORNING

> Round the cape of a sudden came the sea,
> And the sun looked over the mountain's rim:
> And straight was a path of gold for him,
> And the need of a world of men for me.

> —*Robert Browning [1812–1889]*

QUESTIONS

1. This poem is a sequel to "Meeting at Night." *Him* (3) refers to the sun. Does the last line mean that the lover needs the world of men or that the world of men needs the lover? Or both?

2. Does the sea *actually* come suddenly around the cape or *appear* to? Why does Browning mention the *effect* before its *cause* (the sun looking over the mountain's rim)?

3. Do these two poems, taken together, suggest any larger truths above love? Browning, in answer to a question, said that the second part is the man's confession of "how fleeting is the belief (implied in the first part) that such raptures are self-sufficient and enduring—as for the time they appear."

The sharpness and vividness of any image will ordinarily depend on how specific it is and on the poet's use of effective detail. The word *hummingbird,* for instance, conveys a more definite image than does *bird;* and *ruby-throated hummingbird* is sharper and more specific still. It is not necessary, however, for a vivid representation, that something be completely described. One or two especially sharp and representative details will ordinarily serve the alert reader, allowing his imagination to fill in the rest. Tennyson, in "The Eagle" (page 5), gives only one detail about the eagle itself—that he clasps the crag with "crooked hands"—but this detail is an effective and memorable one. Robinson tells us that Richard Cory (page 39) was clean favored, slim, and quietly arrayed; but the detail that really brings Cory before us is that he "glittered when he walked." Browning, in "Meeting at Night," calls up a whole scene with "A tap at the pane, the quick sharp scratch/

And blue spurt of a lighted match."

Since imagery is a peculiarly effective way of evoking vivid experience, and since it may be used by the poet in such a way as to convey emotion and suggest ideas as well as to cause a mental reproduction of sensations, it is an invaluable resource of the poet. In general, he will seek concrete or image-bearing words in preference to abstract or non-image-bearing words. We cannot evaluate a poem, however, by the amount or quality of its imagery alone. Sense impression is only one of the elements of experience. A poet may attain his ends by other means. We must never judge any single element of a poem except in reference to the total intention of that poem.

• • •

THE GROUNDSWELL

Marcia Funebre

With heavy doleful clamor, hour on hour, and day on day
The muddy groundswell lifts and breaks and falls and slides away.

The cold and naked wind runs shivering over the sands,
Salt are its eyes, open its mouth, its brow wet, blue its hands.

It finds naught but a starving gull whose wings trail at its side,   5
And the dull battered wreckage, grey jetsam of the tide.

The lifeless chilly slaty sky with no blue hope is lit,
A rusty waddling steamer plants a smudge of smoke on it.

Stupidly stand the factory chimneys staring over all,
The grey grows ever denser, and soon the night will fall: 10

The wind runs sobbing over the beach and touches with its hands
Straw, chaff, old bottles, broken crates, the litter of the sands.

Sometimes the bloated carcase of a dog or fish is found,
Sometimes the rumpled feathers of a sea-gull shot or drowned.

Last year it was an unknown man who came up from the sea,   15
There is his grave hard by the dunes under a stunted tree.

With heavy doleful clamor, hour on hour, and day on day
The muddy groundswell lifts and breaks and falls and slides away.

—John Gould Fletcher [1886–1950]

1. Vocabulary: *groundswell* (title), *jetsam* (6).
2. *Marcia Funebre* is a musical term. In what ways is this poem analogous to a funeral march? What functions are served by the repetition of the first couplet as the last?
3. How does the imagery support the mood of the poem?
4. Imagery may be carried by nouns, adjectives, verbs, and adverbs. How important is each in this poem? Study especially the effectiveness of the verbs and participles (verbal adjectives).
5. How do the connotations of *blue* in lines 4 and 7 differ? Why?

ON MOONLIT HEATH AND LONESOME BANK

On moonlit heath and lonesome bank
    The sheep beside me graze;
And yon the gallows used to clank
    Fast by the four cross ways.

A careless shepherd once would keep   5
    The flocks by moonlight there,
And high amongst the glimmering sheep
    The dead man stood on air.

They hang us now in Shrewsbury jail:
    The whistles blow forlorn,   10
And trains all night groan on the rail
    To men that die at morn.

There sleeps in Shrewsbury jail to-night,
    Or wakes, as may betide,
A better lad, if things went right,   15
    Than most that sleep outside.

And naked to the hangman's noose
    The morning clocks will ring
A neck God made for other use
    Than strangling in a string.   20

And sharp the link of life will snap,
    And dead on air will stand
Heels that held up as straight a chap
    As treads upon the land.

So here I'll watch the night and wait   25
    To see the morning shine,
When he will hear the stroke of eight
    And not the stroke of nine;

And wish my friend as sound a sleep
    As lads' I did not know,   30
That shepherded the moonlit sheep
    A hundred years ago.

                                        —A. E. Housman [1859–1936]

QUESTIONS

1. Housman explains in a note to lines 5–6 that "Hanging in chains was called keeping sheep by moonlight." Where is this idea repeated?

2. What is the speaker's attitude toward his friend? toward other young men who have died by hanging? What is the purpose of the reference to the young men hanged "a hundred years ago"?

3. Discuss the kinds of imagery present in the poem and their role in the development of the dramatic situation.

4. Discuss the use of language in stanza 5.

SPRING

Nothing is so beautiful as spring—
    When weeds, in wheels, shoot long and lovely and lush;
    Thrush's eggs look little low heavens, and thrush
Through the echoing timber does so rinse and wring
The ear, it strikes like lightning to hear him sing;   5
    The glassy peartree leaves and blooms, they brush
    The descending blue; that blue is all in a rush
With richness; the racing lambs too have fair their fling.

What is all this juice and all this joy?
    A strain of the earth's sweet being in the beginning   10
In Eden garden.—Have, get, before it cloy,
    Before it cloud, Christ, lord, and sour with sinning,
Innocent mind and Mayday in girl and boy,
    Most, O maid's child, thy choice and worthy the winning.

                                —Gerard Manley Hopkins [1844–1889]

QUESTIONS

1. The first line makes an abstract statement. How is this statement brought to carry conviction?

2. The sky is described as being "all in a rush/With richness" (7–8). In what other respects is the poem "rich"?

3. The author was a Catholic priest as well as a poet. To what two things does he compare the spring in lines 9–14? In what ways are the comparisons appropriate?

A DESCRIPTION OF THE MORNING

Now hardly here and there a hackney-coach
Appearing, showed the ruddy morn's approach.
Now Betty from her master's bed had flown,
And softly stole to discompose her own.
The slip-shod 'prentice from his master's door   5
Had pared the dirt, and sprinkled round the floor.
Now Moll had whirled her mop with dextrous airs,
Prepared to scrub the entry and the stairs.
The youth with broomy stumps began to trace
The kennel's edge, where wheels had worn the place.   10
The small-coal man was heard with cadence deep,
Till drowned in shriller notes of chimney-sweep.
Duns at his lordship's gate began to meet;
And Brickdust Moll had screamed through half the street.
The turnkey now his flock returning sees,   15
Duly let out a-nights to steal for fees.
The watchful bailiffs take their silent stands;
And schoolboys lag with satchels in their hands.

—*Jonathan Swift [1667–1745]*

QUESTIONS

1. Vocabulary: *hardly* (1), *hackney–coach* (1), *kennel* (10), *duns* (13), *turnkey* (15), *bailiffs* (17).

2. The images in this poem differ sharply from those in the previous poem. Do they differ also from the expectations set up by the title? What is the poem's purpose? ·

3. The poem gives a good brief picture of London street life in the eighteenth century. List the various types of people mentioned and explain what each is doing. (The "youth with broomy stumps" in line 9 is apparently searching for salvage.)

TO AUTUMN

Season of mists and mellow fruitfulness,
    Close bosom-friend of the maturing sun:
Conspiring with him how to load and bless
    With fruit the vines that round the thatch-eaves run;
To bend with apples the mossed cottage-trees,   5
    And fill all fruit with ripeness to the core;
        To swell the gourd, and plump the hazel shells
With a sweet kernel; to set budding more,
    And still more, later flowers for the bees,
    Until they think warm days will never cease,   10
        For Summer has o'er-brimmed their clammy cells.

Who hath not seen thee oft amid thy store?
　Sometimes whoever seeks abroad may find
Thee sitting careless on a granary floor,
　　Thy hair soft-lifted by the winnowing wind;　　　15
Or on a half-reaped furrow sound asleep,
　　Drowsed with the fume of poppies, while thy hook
　　Spares the next swath and all its twinèd flowers:
And sometimes like a gleaner thou dost keep
　　Steady thy laden head across a brook;　　　20
Or by a cider-press, with patient look,
　　Thou watchest the last oozings hours by hours.

Where are the songs of Spring? Ay, where are they?
　Think not of them, thou hast thy music too,—
While barred clouds bloom the soft-dying day,　　　25
　　And touch the stubble-plains with rosy hue;
Then in a wailful choir the small gnats mourn
　　Among the river sallows, borne aloft
　　　Or sinking as the light wind lives or dies;
And full-grown lambs loud bleat from hilly bourn;　　　30
Hedge-crickets sing; and now with treble soft
The red-breast whistles from a garden-croft;
　　And gathering swallows twitter in the skies.

　　　　　　　　　　　　—John Keats [1795–1821]

QUESTIONS

1. Vocabulary: *hook* (17), *sallows* (28), *bourn* (30), *croft* (32).

2. How many kinds of imagery do you find in the poem? Give examples of each.

3. Are the images arranged haphazardly or are they carefully organized? In answering this question, consider: (a) With what aspect of autumn is each stanza particularly concerned? (b) What kind of imagery is dominant in each stanza? (c) What time of the season is presented in each stanza? (d) Is there any progression in time of day?

4. As what is Autumn personified in stanza 2? Is there any suggestion of personification in the other two stanzas?

5. Although the poem is primarily descriptive, what attitude toward transcience and passing beauty is implicit in it?

WIND AND SILVER

Greatly shining,
The Autumn moon floats in the thin sky;
And the fish-ponds shake their backs and flash their dragon scales
As she passes over them.

　　　　　　　　　　　　—Amy Lowell [1874–1925]

5

Figurative Language 1

Metaphor · Personification · Metonymy

Poetry provides the one permissible way of saying
one thing and meaning another.—ROBERT FROST

Let us assume that your roommate has just come in out of a rainstorm and you say to him, "Well, you're a pretty sight! Got slightly
wet, didn't you?" And he replies, "Wet? I'm drowned! It's raining
cats and dogs outside, and my raincoat's just like a sieve!"

It is likely that you and your roommate understand each other
well enough, and yet if you examine this conversation literally,
that is to say unimaginatively, you will find that you have been
speaking nonsense. Actually you have been speaking figuratively.
You have been saying less than what you mean, or more than what
you mean, or the opposite of what you mean, or something else
than what you mean. You did not mean that your roommate was
a pretty sight but that he was a wretched sight. You did not mean
that he got slightly wet but that he got very wet. Your roommate
did not mean that he got drowned but that he got drenched. It
was not raining cats and dogs; it was raining water. And your
roommate's raincoat is so unlike a sieve that not even a baby
would confuse them.

If you are familiar with Molière's play *Le Bourgeois Gentil-
homme,* you will remember how delighted M. Jourdain was to dis-

53

cover that he had been speaking prose all his life. You may be equally surprised to discover that you have been speaking a kind of sub-poetry all your life. The difference between your figures of speech and the poet's is that yours are worn and trite, his fresh and original.

On first examination, it might seem absurd to say one thing and mean another. But we all do it, and with good reason. We do it because we can say what we want to say more vividly and force-fully by figures than we can by saying it directly. And we can say *more* by figurative statement than we can by literal statement. Figures of speech are another way of adding extra dimensions to language. We shall examine their usefulness more particularly at the end of this chapter.

Broadly defined, a FIGURE OF SPEECH is any way of saying something other than the ordinary way, and some rhetoricians have classified as many as 250 separate figures. For our purposes, how-ever, a figure of speech is more narrowly definable as a way of saying one thing and meaning another, and we need be concerned with no more than a dozen.

METAPHOR and SIMILE are both comparisons between things essentially unlike. The only distinction is that in simile the com-parison is *expressed,* by the use of some word such as *like, as, than, similar to,* or *resembles.* In metaphor the comparison is *implied;* that is, the figurative term is *substituted for* or *identified with* the literal term. When Shakespeare writes in "Spring" (page 11) that "merry larks are ploughmen's clocks," he is using a metaphor, for he identifies larks with clocks. When Tennyson writes that the eagle "clasps the crag with crooked hands" (page 5), he is using a metaphor, for he substitutes crooked hands for claws. Later, when he says that the eagle falls "like a thunderbolt," he uses a simile.

A HILLSIDE THAW

> To think to know the country and not know
> The hillside on the day the sun lets go
> Ten million silver lizards out of snow!
> As often as I've seen it done before
> I can't pretend to tell the way it's done.   5
> It looks as if some magic of the sun
> Lifted the rug that bred them on the floor
> And the light breaking on them made them run.
> But if I thought to stop the wet stampede,
> And caught one silver lizard by the tail,   10
> And put my foot on one without avail,

And threw myself wet-elbowed and wet-kneed
In front of twenty others' wriggling speed,—
In the confusion of them all aglitter,
And birds that joined in the excited fun   15
By doubling and redoubling song and twitter,
I have no doubt I'd end by holding none.

It takes the moon for this. The sun's a wizard
By all I tell; but so's the moon a witch.
From the high west she makes a gentle cast   20
And suddenly, without a jerk or twitch,
She has her spell on every single lizard.
I fancied when I looked at six o'clock
The swarm still ran and scuttled just as fast.
The moon was waiting for her chill effect.   25
I looked at nine: the swarm was turned to rock
In every lifelike posture of the swarm,
Transfixed on mountain slopes almost erect.
Across each other and side by side they lay.
The spell that so could hold them as they were   30
Was wrought through trees without a breath of storm
To make a leaf, if there had been one, stir.
It was the moon's: she held them until day,
One lizard at the end of every ray.
The thought of my attempting such a stay!   35

—*Robert Frost [1874–1963]*

QUESTIONS

1. The literal equivalents of the silver lizards and the lizards turned to rock are never named in the poem. What are they?

2. A poet may use a variety of metaphors or similes in developing a subject, or may, as Frost does here, develop a single metaphor at length (this poem is an excellent example of an EXTENDED or SUSTAINED METAPHOR). What are the advantages of each type of development?

3. Though primarily descriptive of nature, this poem also reveals a good deal about the nature of the speaker and of the poet. What is his relationship to nature? Is he serious in ascribing to the moon the transformation effected in the second half of the poem? If not, what quality of mind is here displayed, and how is it seen elsewhere in the poem?

PERSONIFICATION consists in giving the attributes of a human being to an animal, an object, or an idea. It is really a subtype of metaphor, an implied comparison in which the figurative term of the comparison is always a human being. When Wordsworth writes of the "Sea that bares her bosom to the moon" (page 34), he is personifying an object.[1] When Keats describes Autumn as a harvester "sitting careless on a granary floor" or "on a half-reaped furrow sound asleep" (page 52), he is personifying an idea. Personifications differ in the degree to which they ask the reader actually to visualize the literal term in human form. In Keats's comparison we are asked to make a complete identification of Autumn with a human being. In Wordsworth's, the identification is much less complete. In "The Twa Corbies" (page 12), we are asked to think of the two ravens as speaking, thinking, and feeling like human beings, but not as having human form. In Browning's reference to "the startled little waves" (page 46) a personification is barely suggested; we should make a mistake if we tried to visualize the waves in human form or even, really, to think of them as having human emotions. Closely related to personification is APOSTROPHE, which consists in addressing someone absent or something nonhuman as if it were alive and present and could reply to what is being said. The speaker in Robinson's "Another Dark Lady" (page 31) apostrophizes his departed sweetheart; William Blake apostrophizes the tiger throughout his famous poem (page 259); Keats apostrophizes as well as personifies Autumn (page 51). Personification and apostrophe are both ways of giving "life" and immediacy to one's language, but since neither, especially apostrophe, requires great imaginative power on the part of the poet, they may degenerate into mere mannerisms and are to be found as often in bad and mediocre poetry as in good. We need to distinguish between their effective use and their merely conventional use.

DEATH STANDS ABOVE ME

> Death stands above me, whispering low
> I know not what into my ear;
> Of his strange language all I know
> Is, there is not a word of fear.

> —*Walter Savage Landor [1775–1864]*

---

[1] The various figures of speech blend into each other, and it is sometimes difficult to classify a specific example as definitely metaphor or symbol, symbolism or allegory, understatement or irony, irony or paradox. I have thus been arbitrary in classifying "crooked hands" as a metaphor and "bares her bosom" as personification. The important consideration is not that we classify figures definitively but that we construe them correctly.

1. To what degree is Death personified, and what is the effect of this personification? What is implied by the poet's not knowing what is said in Death's "strange language"?

2. Define as precisely as possible the poet's attitude toward the possibility of some kind of future life.

THE SEA-GULL

Hark to the whimper of the sea-gull;
He weeps because he's not an ea-gull.
Suppose you were, you silly sea-gull,
Could you explain it to your she-gull?

—*Ogden Nash* [1902–   ]

QUESTION

1. What is lost in effectiveness, and why, if the last two lines are rewritten thus:

But if it were, how could the sea-gull
Explain the matter to its she-gull?

Synecdoche (the use of the part for the whole) and ME-TONYMY (the use of a closely related idea for the idea itself) are so much alike that it is hardly worth while to distinguish between them, and the latter term is increasingly coming to be used for both. In both some significant detail or aspect of an experience is substituted for the experience itself. Thus when Shakespeare says that the cuckoo's song is unpleasing to a "married ear," he means to a married *man*, and when he says that the yellow cuckoo-buds "paint the meadow with delight," he means with bright color (page 11). Similarly, in Robert Graves's "The Naked and the Nude" (page 36) the "hippocratic eye" is really a doctor; in Housman's "Is my team ploughing" (page 23) "the leather" is a football; and in Hardy's "The Subalterns" (page 29) "a grave" is death. But in each case the metonymy implies its literal equivalent and something *more*, or at least something more vivid and precise. For the abstraction death, Hardy substitutes something that can be seen and fallen into; by referring to bright color as "delight" Shakespeare evokes not only the visual effect but the emotional response that it arouses. Many metonymies, like many metaphors, have become so much a part of the language that they no longer strike us as figurative: such is the case with *redskin* for Indian, *paleface* for white man, and *salt* and *tar* for sailor. Such figures are referred to as dead metaphors or dead figures. A fresh use of metonymy, however, can be both pleasing to the imagination and economical by directing the imagination to the significant aspect of the experience.

LINES ON A PAID MILITIA

The country rings around with loud alarms,
And raw in fields the rude militia swarms;
Mouths without hands; maintained at vast expense,
In peace a charge, in war a weak defense:
Stout once a month they march, a blustering band,   5
And ever, but in times of need, at hand.
This was the morn when, issuing on the guard,
Drawn up in rank and file they stood prepared
Of seeming arms to make a short essay,
Then hasten to be drunk, the business of the day.   10

—*John Dryden [1631–1700]*
(*from* Cymon and Iphigenia)

QUESTIONS

1. Vocabulary: *essay* (9).
2. Comment on the meanings or force of *charge* (4), *business* (10).
3. The art of this passage depends on effective juxtapositions. Point out and comment on the most effective.
4. Explain the meaning of *mouths without hands* (3). Although this book proposes that the single term *metonymy* be used for the figures once distinguished as metonymy and synecdoche, it may be instructive to make the distinction here. Which is *mouths?* which is *hands?* Why?

We said at the beginning of this chapter that figurative language often provides a more effective means of saying what we mean than does direct statement. What are some of the reasons for that effectiveness?

First, figurative language affords us imaginative pleasure. Imagination, in one sense, might be described as that faculty or ability of the mind that proceeds by sudden leaps from one point to another, which goes up a stair by leaping in one jump from the bottom to the top rather than by climbing up one step at a time.[2]

[2] It is also the faculty of mind which is able to "picture" or "image" absent objects as if they were present. It was with imagination in this sense that we were concerned in the chapter on imagery.

The mind takes delight in these sudden leaps, in seeing likenesses between unlike things. We have all taken pleasure in staring into a fire and seeing castles and cities and armies in it, or in looking into the clouds and shaping them into animals or faces, or in seeing a man in the moon. We name our plants and flowers after fancied resemblances: jack-in-the-pulpit, babies'-breath, Queen Anne's lace. Figures of speech are therefore satisfying in themselves, providing us a source of pleasure in the exercise of the imagination.

Second, figures of speech are a way of bringing additional imagery into verse, of making the abstract concrete, of making poetry more sensuous. When Landor personifies death (page 56) he makes audible and visible what had previously been only a concept; when Robert Frost's bridegroom thinks of his bride (page 15) and wishes "her heart in a case of gold and pinned with a silver pin," he objectifies an inner feeling in precise visual terms; when Robert Browning compares the crisping waves to "fiery ringlets" (page 46) he starts with one image and transforms it into three. Figurative language is a way of multiplying the sense appeal of poetry.

Third, figures of speech are a way of adding emotional intensity to otherwise merely informative statements and of conveying attitudes along with information. If we say, "So-and-so is a rat," or "My feet are killing me," our meaning is as much emotional as informative. When the speaker in "Another Dark Lady" (page 31) compares his sweetheart's feet to those of beech trees, he is expressing an emotional attitude toward her, and even more so when he later draws a contrast (comparing them to the devil's). When Wilfred Owen compares a soldier caught in a gas attack to a man drowning under a green sea (page 8), he conveys to us a feeling of despair as well as a visual image.

Fourth, figures of speech are a means of concentration, a way of saying much in brief compass. Like words, they may be multidimensional. Consider, for instance, the merits of comparing life to a candle, as Shakespeare does in a passage from *Macbeth* (page 116). Life is like a candle in that it begins and ends in darkness; in that while it burns, it gives off light and energy, is active and colorful; in that it gradually consumes itself, gets shorter and shorter; in that it can be snuffed out at any moment; in that it is brief at best, burns only for a short duration. Possibly your imagination can suggest other similarities. But at any rate, Macbeth's compact metaphorical description of life as a "brief candle" suggests certain truths about life that would require dozens of words to state in literal language. At the same time it makes the abstract concrete, provides imaginative pleasure, and adds a degree of emotional intensity.

Obviously one of the necessary abilities for reading poetry is the ability to interpret figurative language. Every use of figurative language involves a risk of misinterpretation, though the risk is well worth taking. For the person who can translate the figure, the dividends are immense. Fortunately all people have imagination to some degree, and imagination can be cultivated. By practice one's ability to interpret figures of speech can be increased.

EXERCISE

Identify each of the following quotations as literal or figurative. If figurative, explain what is being compared to what, and explain the appropriateness of the comparison. EXAMPLE: "Talent is a cistern; genius is a fountain." ANSWER: A metaphor. Talent = cistern; genius = fountain. Talent exists in finite supply; it can be used up. Genius is inexhaustible, ever renewing.

1. O tenderly the haughty day
   Fills his blue urn with fire.—*Emerson*

2. It is with words as with sunbeams—the more they are condensed, the deeper they burn.—*Robert Southey*

3. Joy and Temperance and Repose
   Slam the door on the doctor's nose.—*Anonymous*

4. The pen is mightier than the sword.—*Edward Bulwer-Lytton*

5. The strongest oaths are straw
   To the fire i' the blood.—*Shakespeare*

6. The Cambridge ladies . . . live in furnished souls.—*E. E. Cummings*

7. The green lizard and the golden snake,
   Like unimprisoned flames, out of their trance awake.—*Shelley*

8. Dorothy's eyes, with their long brown lashes, looked very much like her mother's.—*Laetitia Johnson*

9. Is this the face that launched a thousand ships?—*Marlowe*

10. What should such fellows as I do crawling between earth and heaven?—
    Shakespeare

11. Love's feeling is more soft and sensible
    Than are the tender horns of cockled snails.—*Shakespeare*

12. The tawny-hided desert crouches watching her.—*Francis Thompson*

13. . . . Let us sit upon the ground
    And tell sad stories of the death of kings.—*Shakespeare*

14. See, from his head, his hands, his side [*his:* Christ's, on the cross]
Sorrow and love flow mingled down.—*Isaac Watts*

15. Now half [of the departing guests] to the setting moon are gone,
And half to the rising day.—*Tennyson*

16. I do not know whether my present poems are better than the earlier ones.
But this is certain: they are much sadder and sweeter, like pain dipped in
honey.—*Heinrich Heine*

17. The clouds shepherded by the slow, unwilling wind.—*Shelley*

18. Let us eat and drink, for tomorrow we shall die.—*Isaiah 22:13*

19. Let us eat and drink, for tomorrow we may die.
                            —*Common misquotation of the above*

• • •

LOVE

Love bade me welcome; yet my soul drew back,
    Guilty of dust and sin.
But quick-eyed Love, observing me grow slack
    From my first entrance in,
Drew nearer to me, sweetly questioning   5
    If I lacked anything.

"A guest," I answered, "worthy to be here."
    Love said, "You shall be he."
"I, the unkind, ungrateful? Ah, my dear,
    I cannot look on Thee."   10
Love took my hand, and smiling, did reply,
    "Who made the eyes but I?"

"Truth, Lord, but I have marred them: let my shame
    Go where it doth deserve."
"And know you not," says Love, "who bore the blame?"   15
    "My dear, then I will serve."
"You must sit down," says Love, "and taste my meat."
    So I did sit and eat.

                            —*George Herbert [1593–1633]*

QUESTIONS

1. This little drama has two characters. Characterize the guest. Characterize the host. What is the relationship between them?

2. Should "Love" be considered a personification or a metonymy? Explain.

3. To what kind of feast is the guest being invited? Is the "meat" (17) any
meat or something special?

PIAZZA DI SPAGNA, EARLY MORNING

I can't forget
How she stood at the top of that long marble stair
Amazed, and then with a sleepy pirouette
Went dancing slowly down to the fountain-quieted square;

Nothing upon her face   5
But some impersonal loneliness,—not then a girl,
But as it were a reverie of the place,
A called-for falling glide and whirl;

As when a leaf, petal, or thin chip
Is drawn to the falls of a pool and, circling a moment above it,   10
Rides on over the lip—
Perfectly beautiful, perfectly ignorant of it.

—Richard Wilbur [1921–]

QUESTIONS

1. Explore the similarities between the two things compared.
2. Comment upon "fountain-quieted" (4).
3. Explain the metaphor in line 7.

A VALEDICTION: FORBIDDING MOURNING

As virtuous men pass mildly away,
    And whisper to their souls to go,
While some of their sad friends do say,
    The breath goes now, and some say, no:

So let us melt, and make no noise,   5
    No tear-floods, nor sigh-tempests move,
'Twere profanation of our joys
    To tell the laity our love.

Moving of th' earth brings harms and fears,
    Men reckon what it did and meant,   10
But trepidation of the spheres,
    Though greater far, is innocent.

Dull sublunary lovers' love
    (Whose soul is sense) cannot admit
Absence, because it doth remove   15
    Those things which elemented it.

But we by a love so much refined,
  That ourselves know not what it is,
Inter-assurèd of the mind,
  Care less, eyes, lips, and hands to miss.   20

Our two souls therefore, which are one,
  Though I must go, endure not yet
A breach, but an expansion,
  Like gold to airy thinness beat.

If they be two, they are two so   25
  As stiff twin compasses are two,
Thy soul the fixed foot, makes no show
  To move, but doth, if th' other do.

And though it in the center sit,
  Yet when the other far doth roam,   30
It leans, and hearkens after it,
  And grows erect, as that comes home.

Such wilt thou be to me, who must
  Like th' other foot, obliquely run;
Thy firmness makes my circle just,   35
  And makes me end, where I begun.

                                            —*John Donne* [*1572–1631*]

QUESTIONS

1. Vocabulary: *valediction* (title), *profanation* (7), *laity* (8), *trepidation* (11), *innocent* (12), *sublunary* (13), *elemented* (16). Line 11 is a reference to the spheres of the Ptolemaic cosmology, whose movement caused no such disturbance as does a movement of the earth, i.e., an earthquake.

2. Is the speaker in the poem about to die? Or about to leave on a journey?

3. The poem is organized around a contrast of two kinds of lovers: the "laity" (8) and, as their opposite, the "priesthood." What two major contrasts are drawn between these two kinds of lovers?

4. Find and explain three similes and one metaphor used to describe the parting of true lovers. The figure in the last three stanzas is one of the most famous in English literature. Demonstrate its appropriateness by obtaining a drawing compass or by using two pencils to imitate the two legs.

5. What kind of language is used in the poem? Is the language consonant with the figures of speech?

TO HIS COY MISTRESS

Had we but world enough, and time,
This coyness, lady, were no crime.
We would sit down and think which way
To walk, and pass our long love's day;
Thou by the Indian Ganges' side   5
Shouldst rubies find; I by the tide
Of Humber would complain. I would
Love you ten years before the Flood;
And you should, if you please, refuse
Till the conversion of the Jews.   10
My vegetable love should grow
Vaster than empires, and more slow.
An hundred years should go to praise
Thine eyes, and on thy forehead gaze;
Two hundred to adore each breast,   15
But thirty thousand to the rest;
An age at least to every part,
And the last age should show your heart.
For, lady, you deserve this state,
Nor would I love at lower rate.   20
    But at my back I always hear
Time's wingèd chariot hurrying near;
And yonder all before us lie
Deserts of vast eternity.
Thy beauty shall no more be found,   25
Nor in thy marble vault shall sound
My echoing song; then worms shall try
That long preserved virginity,
And your quaint honor turn to dust,
And into ashes all my lust.   30
The grave's a fine and private place,
But none, I think, do there embrace.
    Now therefore, while the youthful hue
Sits on thy skin like morning dew,
And while thy willing soul transpires   35
At every pore with instant fires,
Now let us sport us while we may;
And now, like amorous birds of prey,
Rather at once our time devour,
Than languish in his slow-chapped power.   40
Let us roll all our strength, and all
Our sweetness, up into one ball;
And tear our pleasures with rough strife
Thorough° the iron gates of life.   through

Thus, though we cannot make our sun   45
Stand still, yet we will make him run.

—*Andrew Marvell [1621–1678]*

QUESTIONS

1. Vocabulary: *mistress* (title), *Humber* (7), *transpires* (35), *chapped* (40).

2. Outline the speaker's argument in three sentences, beginning with *If*, *But*, and *Therefore*. Is the speaker urging his mistress to marry him?

3. Explain the appropriateness of "vegetable love" (11). What simile in the third section contrasts with it, and how? What image in the third section contrasts with the distance between the Ganges and the Humber in section one?

4. Explain the figures in lines 22, 24, and 40 and their implications.

5. Explain the last two lines. For what is *sun* a metonymy?

6. Is this poem principally about love or about time? If the latter, what might making love represent? What philosophy is the poet advancing here?

LONDON, 1802

Milton! thou shouldst be living at this hour:
England hath need of thee: she is a fen
Of stagnant waters: altar, sword, and pen,
Fireside, the heroic wealth of hall and bower,
Have forfeited their ancient English dower   5
Of inward happiness. We are selfish men;
Oh! raise us up, return to us again;
And give us manners, virtue, freedom, power.
Thy soul was like a star, and dwelt apart:
Thou hadst a voice whose sound was like the sea: 10
Pure as the naked heavens, majestic, free,
So didst thou travel on life's common way,
In cheerful godliness; and yet thy heart
The lowliest duties on herself did lay.

—*William Wordsworth [1770–1850]*

QUESTIONS

1. Wordsworth, in 1802, was discouraged by "the vanity and parade" he found in England as contrasted with the "desolation" caused by the French Revolution in France. He also believed England indolent in not championing the Spanish in their struggle for freedom from "the usurped power of the French." Milton (1608–1674), the great English poet, served the Commonwealth as an undersecretary of state. This poem was written for a past political and social situation; are its emotion and ideas therefore dead? Why?

2. Find examples of metaphor, simile, personification, apostrophe, and metonymy. What aspects of English life are referred to in lines 3–4?

VELVET SHOES

Let us walk in the white snow
In a soundless space;
With footsteps quiet and slow,
At a tranquil pace,
Under veils of white lace.   5

I shall go shod in silk
And you in wool,
White as white cow's milk,
More beautiful
Than the breast of a gull.   10

We shall walk through the still town
In a windless peace;
We shall step upon white down,
Upon silver fleece,
Upon softer than these.   15

We shall walk in velvet shoes:
Wherever we go
Silence will fall like dews
On white silence below.
We shall walk in the snow.   20

—Elinor Wylie [1885–1928]

QUESTIONS

1. A published analysis of this poem states that it has "two main pairs of conflicting motives: (1) the delicacy and fragility of the clothing contrasted with the sharp coldness of winter (if the author had said, 'Let us put on appropriate galoshes,' there could, of course, have been no poem); (2) the conflict between the pleasure of the imaginary excursion and the hard fact that no such trip will take place or is possible." [3] Is this an adequate reading of the poem? To answer this question, you will have to determine whether such phrases as "veils of white lace" (5), "shod in silk" (6), "wool" (7), "white down" (13), "silver fleece" (14), and "velvet shoes" (16) should be interpreted literally or figuratively.

2. Find an example of metonymy in the last stanza and explain its effectiveness.

3. Strictly, a white cow's milk (8) is no whiter than that of a brown cow. But can this line be justified *poetically*? Why?

[3] *College English,* IX (March, 1948), 319–20.

ON A CLERGYMAN'S HORSE BITING HIM

The steed bit his master;
How came this to pass?
He heard the good pastor
Cry, "All flesh is grass."

—Anonymous

EXERCISE

The two following poems were both written by American poets who lived during the Civil War. Whitman published the first in a volume of Civil War poems called *Drum-Taps* (1865). Melville also published a book of war poems, *Battle-Pieces* (1866); however, this poem did not appear in it. Compare and contrast these two poems as to their purpose and meaning. What is the main difference between them?

CAVALRY CROSSING A FORD

A line in long array where they wind betwixt green islands,
They take a serpentine course, their arms flash in the sun—hark to the musical clank,
Behold the silvery river, in it the splashing horses loitering stop to drink,
Behold the brown-faced men, each group, each person a picture, the negligent rest on the saddles,
Some emerge on the opposite bank, others are just entering the ford—while,
Scarlet and blue and snowy white,
The guidon flags flutter gayly in the wind.

—Walt Whitman [1819–1892]

THE NIGHT-MARCH

With banners furled, and clarions mute,
　　An army passes in the night;
And beaming spears and helms salute
　　The dark with bright.

In silence deep the legions stream,　　　　　　　　　　5
　　With open ranks, in order true;
Over boundless plains they stream and gleam—
　　No chief in view!

Afar, in twinkling distance lost,
　　(So legends tell) he lonely wends　　　　　　　　10
And back through all that shining host
　　His mandate sends.

—Herman Melville [1819–1891]

6

Figurative Language 2

Symbol · Allegory

THE ROAD NOT TAKEN [1]

Two roads diverged in a yellow wood,
And sorry I could not travel both
And be one traveler, long I stood
And looked down one as far as I could
To where it bent in the undergrowth;   5

Then took the other, as just as fair,
And having perhaps the better claim,
Because it was grassy and wanted wear;
Though as for that the passing there
Had worn them really about the same,   10

And both that morning equally lay
In leaves no step had trodden black.
Oh, I kept the first for another day!
Yet knowing how way leads on to way,
I doubted if I should ever come back.   15

[1] Mr. Frost recorded "The Road Not Taken" (LP, National Council of Teachers of English, RL 20–1; or LP, Library of Congress, PL 20; or LP, Caedmon, TC 1060.)

I shall be telling this with a sigh
Somewhere ages and ages hence:
Two roads diverged in a wood, and I—
I took the one less traveled by,
And that has made all the difference.   20

—Robert Frost [1874–1963]

QUESTIONS

1. Does the speaker feel that he made the wrong choice in taking the road "less traveled by"? If not, why does he sigh? What does he regret?

2. Why does the choice between two roads that seem very much alike make such a big difference many years later?

A SYMBOL may be roughly defined as something that means *more* than what it is. "The Road Not Taken," for instance, concerns a choice made between two roads by a person out walking in the woods. He would like to explore both roads. He tells himself that he will explore one and then come back and explore the other, but he knows that he shall probably be unable to do so. By the last stanza, however, we realize that the poet is talking about something more than the choice of paths in a wood, for such a choice would be relatively unimportant, while this choice is one which will make a great difference in the speaker's life and which he will remember with a sigh "ages and ages hence." We must interpret his choice of a road as a symbol for any choice in life between alternatives which appear almost equally attractive but which will result through the years in a large difference in the kind of experience one knows.

Image, metaphor, and symbol shade into each other and are sometimes difficult to distinguish. In general, however, an image means only what it is; a metaphor means something other than what it is; and a symbol means what it is and something more too.[2] If I say that a shaggy brown dog was rubbing its back against a white picket fence, I am talking about nothing but a dog and am therefore presenting an image; if I say, "Some dirty dog stole my wallet at the party," I am not talking about a dog at all, and am therefore using a metaphor; but if I say, "You can't teach an old dog new tricks," I am talking not only about dogs but about living

[2] This account does not hold for nonliterary symbols such as the letters of the alphabet or algebraic signs, e.g., the symbol ∞ for infinity or $=$ for equals. Here, the symbol is meaningless except when it stands for something else, and the connection between the sign and what it stands for is purely arbitrary.

creatures of any species, and am therefore speaking symbolically.

Symbols vary in the degree of identification and definition that their authors give them. Frost, in his poem, forces us to interpret the choice of roads symbolically by the degree of importance he gives it in the last stanza. Sometimes poets will be much more specific in identifying their symbols. Sometimes they will not identify them at all. Consider, for instance, the following two poems:

A WHITE ROSE

The red rose whispers of passion,
    And the white rose breathes of love;
Oh, the red rose is a falcon,
    And the white rose is a dove.

But I send you a cream-white rosebud,
    With a flush on its petal tips;
For the love that is purest and sweetest
    Has a kiss of desire on the lips.

            —*John Boyle O'Reilly [1844–1890]*

QUESTIONS

1. Could the poet have made the white rose a symbol of passion and the red rose a symbol of love? Why not?

2. In the second stanza, why does the speaker send a rosebud rather than a rose?

MY STAR

All that I know
    Of a certain star
Is, it can throw
    (Like the angled spar)
Now a dart of red,   5
    Now a dart of blue;
Till my friends have said
    They would fain see, too,
My star that dartles the red and the blue!
Then it stops like a bird; like a flower, hangs furled: 10
    They must solace themselves with the Saturn above it.
What matter to me if their star is a world?
    Mine has opened its soul to me; therefore I love it.

            —*Robert Browning [1812–1889]*

In his first two lines O'Reilly indicates so clearly that his red rose is a symbol of physical desire and his white rose of spiritual attachment that when we get to the metaphor in the third line we unconsciously substitute passion for the red rose in our minds, knowing without thinking that what O'Reilly is really likening is falcons and passion, not falcons and roses. Similarly in the second stanza, the symbolism of the white rosebud with pink tips is specifically indicated in the last two lines, although, as a matter of fact, it would have been clear from the first stanza. In Browning's poem, on the other hand, there is nothing specific to tell us that Browning is talking about anything other than just a star, and it is only the star's importance to him that makes us suspect that he is talking about something more.

The symbol is the richest and at the same time the most difficult of the poetical figures. Both its richness and its difficulty result from its imprecision. Although the poet may pin down the meaning of his symbol to something fairly definite and precise, as O'Reilly does in "A White Rose," more often the symbol is so general in its meaning that it is able to suggest a great variety of more specific meanings. It is like an opal that flashes out different colors when slowly turned in the light. The choice in "The Road Not Taken," for instance, concerns some choice in life, but what choice? Was it a choice of profession? (Frost took the road "less traveled by" in deciding to become a poet.) A choice of hobby? A choice of wife? It might be any or all or none of these. We cannot determine what particular choice the poet had in mind, if any, and it is not important that we do so. The general meaning of the poem is clear enough. It is an expression of regret that the possibilities of life-experience are so sharply limited. One must live with one wife, have one native country, follow one profession. The speaker in the poem would have liked to explore both roads, but could explore only one. The person with a craving for life, however satisfied with his own choice, will always long for the realms of experience that had to be passed by. Because the symbol is a rich one, the poem suggests other meanings too. It affirms a belief in the possibility of choice, and says something of the nature of choice—how each choice limits the range of possible future choices, so that we make our lives as we go, both freely choosing and being determined by past choices. Though not primarily a philosophical poem, it obliquely comments on the issue of free will versus determinism and indicates the poet's own position. It is able to do all these things, concretely and compactly, by its use of an effective symbol.

"My Star," if we interpret it symbolically, likewise suggests a variety of meanings. It has been most often interpreted as a tribute to Browning's wife, Elizabeth Barrett Browning. As one critic writes, "She shone upon his life like a star of various colors; but the moment the world attempted to pry into the secret of her genius, she shut off the light altogether."[3] The poem has also been taken to refer to Browning's own peculiar genius—"his gift for seeing in events and things a significance hidden from other men."[4] A third suggestion is that Browning was thinking of his own peculiar poetic style. He loved harsh, jagged sounds and rhythms and grotesque images; most people of his time found beauty only in the smoother-flowing, melodic rhythms and more conventionally poetic images of his contemporary Tennyson's style, which could be symbolized by Saturn in the poem. The point is not that any one of these interpretations is right, nor is any one of them necessarily wrong. We cannot say what the poet had specifically in mind. Literally the poem is an expression of affection for a particular star in the sky that has a unique beauty and fascination for the poet but in which no one else can see the qualities that the poet sees. If we interpret the poem symbolically, the star is a symbol for anything in life that has unique meanings and value for an individual, which other people cannot see. Beyond this, the meaning is "open." And because the meaning is "open," the reader is justified in bringing his own experience to its interpretation. Browning's cherished star might remind him, for instance, of an old rag doll which he particularly loved as a child, though its button eyes were off and its stuffing coming out and it had none of the crisp bright beauty of waxen dolls with real hair admired by other children.

Between the extremes represented by "The White Rose" and "My Star" a poem may exercise all degrees of control over the range and meaning of its symbolism. Consider another example:

YOU, ANDREW MARVELL[5]

> And here face down beneath the sun
> And here upon earth's noonward height
> To feel the always coming on
> The always rising of the night:

[3] William Lyon Phelps, *Robert Browning: How to Know Him*, Indianapolis, Bobbs-Merrill, 1932, p. 165.

[4] Quoted from William Clyde DeVane, *A Browning Handbook*, New York, Crofts, 1935, p. 202.

[5] Mr. MacLeish has recorded "You, Andrew Marvell" (78 rpm, Harvard Vocarium, P-1220).

To feel creep up the curving east
The earthly chill of dusk and slow
Upon those under lands the vast
And ever-climbing shadow grow

And strange at Ecbatan the trees
Take leaf by leaf the evening strange   10
The flooding dark about their knees
The mountains over Persia change

And now at Kermanshah the gate
Dark empty and the withered grass
And through the twilight now the late   15
Few travelers in the westward pass

And Baghdad darken and the bridge
Across the silent river gone
And through Arabia the edge
Of evening widen and steal on   20

And deepen on Palmyra's street
The wheel rut in the ruined stone
And Lebanon fade out and Crete
High through the clouds and overblown

And over Sicily the air   25
Still flashing with the landward gulls
And loom and slowly disappear
The sails above the shadowy hulls

And Spain go under and the shore
Of Africa the gilded sand   30
And evening vanish and no more
The low pale light across that land

Nor now the long light on the sea:
And here face downward in the sun
To feel how swift how secretly   35
The shadow of the night comes on . . .

—*Archibald MacLeish [1892–   ]*

QUESTIONS

1. We ordinarily speak of *nightfall;* why does MacLeish speak of the *rising* of the night? What implicit metaphorical comparison is suggested by phrases like "rising of the night," "the flooding dark," "the bridge across the

silent river gone," "deepen on Palmyra's street," "Spain go under," etc.?

2. Does the comparative lack of punctuation serve any function in the poem?

3. Ecbatan was founded in 700 B.C. and is associated in history with Cyrus the Great, founder of the Persian Empire, and with Alexander the Great. It and Kermanshah were ancient cities of Persia. Where are Baghdad, Palmyra, Lebanon, Crete?

On the literal level, "You, Andrew Marvell" is about the coming on of night. The poet, lying at noon full-length in the sun somewhere in the United States,[6] pictures in his mind the earth's shadow, halfway around the world, moving silently westward over Persia, Syria, Crete, Sicily, Spain, Africa, and finally the Atlantic—approaching swiftly, in fact, the place where he himself lies. But the title of the poem tells us that, though particularly concerned with the passage of a day, it is more generally concerned with the swift passage of time; for the title is an allusion to a famous poem on this subject by Andrew Marvell ("To His Coy Mistress," page 64) and especially to two lines of that poem:

> But at my back I always hear
> Time's wingèd chariot hurrying near.

Once we are aware of this larger concern of the poem, two symbolical levels of interpretation open out to us. Marvell's poem is primarily concerned with the swift passing of man's life; and the word *night*, we know if we have had any experience with other literature, is a natural and traditional metaphor or symbol for death. The poet, then, is thinking not only about the passing of a day but about the passing of his life. He is at present "upon earth's noonward height"—in the full flush of manhood—but he is acutely conscious of the declining years ahead and of "how swift how secretly" his death comes on.

If we are to account fully for all the data of the poem, however, a third level of interpretation is necessary. What has dictated the poet's choice of geographical references? The places named, of course, progress from east to west; but they have a further linking characteristic. Ecbatan, Kermanshah, Baghdad, and Palmyra are all ancient or ruined cities, the relics of past empires and crumbled civilizations. Lebanon, Crete, Sicily, Spain, and North Africa are

---

[6] MacLeish has himself identified the fixed location of the poem as being Illinois on the shore of Lake Michigan.

places where civilization once flourished more vigorously than it does at present. On a third level, then, the poet is concerned, not with the passage of a day nor with the passage of a lifetime, but with the passage of historical epochs. The poet's own country—the United States—now shines "upon earth's noonward height" as a favored nation in the sun of history, but its civilization, too, will pass.

Meanings ray out from a symbol, like the corona around the sun, or like connotations around a richly suggestive word. But the very fact that a symbol may be so rich in its meanings makes it necessary that we use the greatest tact in its interpretation. Though Browning's "My Star" might, if memory and reason be stretched, make us think of a rag doll, still we should not go around telling people that in this poem Browning uses the star to symbolize a rag doll, for this interpretation is private, idiosyncratic, and narrow. The poem allows it, but does not itself suggest it. Moreover, we should never assume that because the meaning of a symbol is more or less open, we may make it mean anything we choose. We would be wrong, for instance, in interpreting the choice in "The Road Not Taken" as some choice between good and evil, for the poem tells us that the two roads are much alike and that both lie "in leaves no step had trodden black." Whatever the choice is, it is a choice between two goods. Whatever our interpretation of a symbolical poem, it must be tied firmly to the facts of the poem. We must not let loose of the string and let our imaginations go ballooning up among the clouds. Because the symbol is capable of adding so many dimensions to a poem, it is a peculiarly effective resource of the poet, but it is also peculiarly susceptible of misinterpretation by the untrained or incautious reader.

Accurate interpretation of the symbol requires delicacy, tact, and good sense. The reader must keep his balance while walking a tightrope between too little and too much—between underinterpretation and overinterpretation. If he falls off, however, it is much more desirable that he fall off on the side of too little. The reader who reads "The Road Not Taken" as being only about a choice between two roads in a wood has at least gotten part of the experience that the poem communicates, but the reader who reads into it anything he chooses might as well discard the poem and simply daydream.

Above all, we should avoid the disease of seeing symbols everywhere, like a man with hallucinations, whether there are symbols there or not. It is better to miss a symbol now and then than to walk constantly among shadows and mirages.

TO THE VIRGINS, TO MAKE MUCH OF TIME

Gather ye rosebuds while ye may,
Old Time is still a-flying;
And this same flower that smiles today
Tomorrow will be dying.

The glorious lamp of heaven, the Sun,   5
The higher he's a-getting,
The sooner will his race be run,
And nearer he's to setting.

That age is best which is the first,
When youth and blood are warmer;   10
But being spent, the worse and worst
Times still succeed the former.

Then be not coy, but use your time;
And while ye may, go marry;
For having lost but once your prime,   15
You may forever tarry.

—*Robert Herrick [1591–1674]*

QUESTIONS

1. The first two stanzas might be interpreted literally if the third and fourth stanzas did not force us to interpret them symbolically. What do the rosebuds symbolize (stanza 1)? What does the course of a day symbolize (stanza 2)? Does the poet fix the meaning of the rosebud symbol in the last stanza, or merely name *one* of its specific meanings?

2. How does the title help us interpret the meaning of the symbol? Why did Herrick use *virgins* instead of *maidens?*

3. Why is such haste necessary in gathering the rosebuds? True, the blossoms die quickly, but they are replaced by others. Who *really* is dying?

4. What are the "worse and worst" times (11)? Why?

5. Why did the poet use his wording rather than the following alternative: *blooms* for *smiles* (3), *course* for *race* (7), *used* for *spent* (11), *spend* for *use* (13)?

ALLEGORY is a narrative or description which has a second meaning beneath the surface one. Although the surface story or description may have its own interest, the author's major interest is in the ulterior meaning. When Pharaoh in the Bible, for instance, has a dream in which seven fat kine are devoured by seven lean kine, the story does not really become significant until Joseph interprets its allegorical meaning: that Egypt is to enjoy seven years ot fruitfulness and prosperity followed by seven years of famine. Allegory has sometimes been defined as an extended metaphor or as a series of related symbols. But it is usually distinguishable from either of these. It is unlike the extended metaphor in that the literal equivalent of the figurative term is seldom given. It is unlike symbolism in that its meaning is more single: there is usually a one-to-one correspondence between its details and a set of ulterior meanings. Meanings do not ray out from it, as from the symbol.

Allegory is less popular in modern literature than it was in medieval writing, and is much less often found in short poems than in long works, such as *The Faerie Queene, Everyman,* and *Pilgrim's Progress.* It has sometimes, especially with political allegory, been used to conceal meaning rather than to reveal it (or rather, to conceal it from some people while revealing it to others). Though less rich than the symbol, it is an effective way of making the abstract concrete, and has occasionally been effectively used even in fairly short poems.

EXSPECTO RESURRECTIONEM

Oh! King Who hast the key
　　Of that dark room
The last which prisons us but held not Thee,
　　Thou know'st its gloom.
　Dost Thou a little love this one　　　　　　　　　5
　　Shut in tonight,
Young and so piteously alone,
　　Cold—out of sight?
Thou know'st how hard and bare
The pillow of that new-made narrow bed.　　　　10
　　Then leave not there
　　So dear a head!

　　　　　　　　　　　　—*Charlotte Mew [1869–1928]*

QUESTIONS

1. The title means "I hope for resurrection." What are the *King* (1), the *key* (1), the *dark room* (2), the *narrow bed* (10)?
2. What figure of speech is *head* (12)?

EXERCISE

Determine whether *sleep,* in the following poems, is literal, metaphorical, symbolical, or other. In each case explain and justify your answer: (a) "On moonlit heath and lonesome bank," line 13 (page 49); (b) same poem, line 29; (c) "Stopping by Woods on a Snowy Evening" (page 125); (d) "The Chimney Sweeper" (page 96); (e) "Is my team ploughing" (page 22); (f) "The Second Coming" (page 87); (g) "Ulysses," line 5 (page 79); (h) "The Toys" (page 227); (i) "The Love Song of J. Alfred Prufrock," line 22 (page 238); (j) "Judging Distances," line 20 (page 41).

• • •

WESTERN WIND

O Western wind, when wilt thou blow
That the small rain down can rain?
Christ, that my love were in my arms,
And I in my bed again!

—Anonymous [16th century]

QUESTION

1. What is the connection between the first two lines and the last two?

THE SICK ROSE

O Rose, thou art sick!
The invisible worm
That flies in the night,
In the howling storm,

Has found out thy bed
Of crimson joy,
And his dark secret love
Does thy life destroy.

—William Blake [1757–1827]

QUESTIONS

1. As in Browning's "My Star" the meaning of the symbolism here is left open. The poem might be interpreted as being only about a rose which has been attacked on a stormy night by a cankerworm. But the connotations of certain words and details are so powerful as to suggest that something more is meant: *sick* (applied to a flower), *invisible, night, howling storm, joy, dark secret love.* May we say that the worm symbolizes any corrupting agent which destroys something beautiful by feeding upon it or making love to it?
2. Some specific interpretations of the poem are that it refers to the de-

struction of love by selfishness, possessiveness, or jealousy; of innocence by experience; of humanity by Satan; of imagination by reason. Do these suggestions seem plausible? Do you think of others?

3. Besides being a symbol, the rose is to some degree personified. What words in the poem contribute to this personification?

ULYSSES

It little profits that an idle king,
By this still hearth, among these barren crags,
Matched with an agèd wife, I mete and dole
Unequal laws unto a savage race,
That hoard, and sleep, and feed, and know not me.   5
I cannot rest from travel; I will drink
Life to the lees. All times I have enjoyed
Greatly, have suffered greatly, both with those
That loved me, and alone; on shore, and when
Through scudding drifts the rainy Hyades   10
Vext the dim sea. I am become a name;
For always roaming with a hungry heart
Much have I seen and known,—cities of men
And manners, climates, councils, governments,
Myself not least, but honored of them all;   15
And drunk delight of battle with my peers,
Far on the ringing plains of windy Troy.
I am a part of all that I have met;
Yet all experience is an arch wherethrough
Gleams that untraveled world, whose margin fades   20
For ever and for ever when I move.
How dull it is to pause, to make an end,
To rust unburnished, not to shine in use!
As though to breathe were life! Life piled on life
Were all too little, and of one to me   25
Little remains; but every hour is saved
From that eternal silence, something more,
A bringer of new things; and vile it were
For some three suns to store and hoard myself,
And this grey spirit yearning in desire   30
To follow knowledge like a sinking star,
Beyond the utmost bound of human thought.

This is my son, mine own Telemachus,
To whom I leave the scepter and the isle—
Well-loved of me, discerning to fulfil   35
This labor, by slow prudence to make mild
A rugged people, and through soft degrees
Subdue them to the useful and the good.

Most blameless is he, centered in the sphere
Of common duties, decent not to fail   40
In offices of tenderness, and pay
Meet adoration to my household gods,
When I am gone. He works his work, I mine.

There lies the port; the vessel puffs her sail:
There gloom the dark, broad seas. My mariners,   45
Souls that have toiled, and wrought, and thought with me—
That ever with a frolic welcome took
The thunder and the sunshine, and opposed
Free hearts, free foreheads—you and I are old;
Old age hath yet his honor and his toil.   50
Death closes all; but something ere the end,
Some work of noble note, may yet be done,
Not unbecoming men that strove with Gods.
The lights begin to twinkle from the rocks;
The long day wanes; the slow moon climbs; the deep   55
Moans round with many voices. Come, my friends,
'Tis not too late to seek a newer world.
Push off, and sitting well in order smite
The sounding furrows; for my purpose holds
To sail beyond the sunset, and the baths   60
Of all the western stars, until I die.
It may be that the gulfs will wash us down;
It may be we shall touch the Happy Isles,
And see the great Achilles, whom we knew.
Though much is taken, much abides; and though   65
We are not now that strength which in old days
Moved earth and heaven, that which we are, we are:
One equal temper of heroic hearts,
Made weak by time and fate, but strong in will
To strive, to seek, to find, and not to yield.   70

—*Alfred, Lord Tennyson* [*1809–1892*]

QUESTIONS

1. Vocabulary: *Hyades* (10), *meet* (42).
2. Ulysses, king of Ithaca, is a legendary Greek hero, a major figure in Homer's *Iliad*, the hero of Homer's *Odyssey*, and a minor figure in Dante's *Divine Comedy*. After ten years at the siege of Troy, Ulysses set sail for home, but having incurred the wrath of the god of the sea, he was subjected to storms and vicissitudes and was forced to wander for another ten years, having many adventures and seeing most of the Mediterranean world before again reaching Ithaca, his wife, and his son. But once back home, according to Dante, he still wished to travel and "to follow virtue and knowledge." In Tennyson's poem Ulysses is represented as about to set sail on a final voyage, from which

he will not return. Where is Ulysses standing during his speech? Whom is he addressing? Locate Ithaca on a map. Where exactly, in geographical terms, does Ulysses intend to sail (59–64)? (The Happy Isles were the Elysian fields, or Greek paradise; Achilles was another Greek prince, the hero of the *Iliad*, who was killed at the siege of Troy.)

3. Characterize Ulysses. What kind of person is he, as Tennyson represents him?

4. What does Ulysses symbolize? What way of life is being recommended?

5. Find as many evidences as you can that Ulysses' desire for travel represents something more than mere wanderlust and wish for adventure.

6. Give two reasons why Tennyson might have Ulysses travel *westward*.

7. Interpret lines 18–21, 26–29. What is symbolized by "the thunder and the sunshine" (48)? What do the two metonymies in line 49 stand for? What metaphor is implied in line 23?

8. Read Frederick Prokosch's "Sunburned Ulysses," p. 291. Written more than a century apart, both the Tennyson and Prokosch poems are portraits of Ulysses's character and spirit. In both poems the ancient hero has symbolic value. In what specific verbal figures is that value delineated? Is that value the same in both poems?

CURIOSITY

  may have killed the cat; more likely
  the cat was just unlucky, or else curious
  to see what death was like, having no cause
  to go on licking paws, or fathering
  litter on litter of kittens, predictably.   5

   Nevertheless, to be curious
  is dangerous enough. To distrust
  what is always said, what seems,
  to ask odd questions, interfere in dreams,   ·
  leave home, smell rats, have hunches   10
  does not endear him to those doggy circles
  where well-smelt baskets, suitable wives, good lunches
  are the order of things, and where prevails
  much wagging of incurious heads and tails.

   Face it. Curiosity   15
  will not cause him to die—
  only lack of it will.
  Never to want to see
  the other side of the hill,
  or that improbable country   20
  where living is an idyll
  (although a probable hell)
  would kill us all.

Only the curious
have, if they live, a tale   25
worth telling at all.

   Dogs say he loves too much, is irresponsible,
is changeable, marries too many wives,
deserts his children, chills all dinner tables
with tales of his nine lives.   30
Well, he is lucky. Let him be
nine-lived and contradictory,
curious enough to change, prepared to pay
the cat price, which is to die
and die again and again,   35
each time with no less pain.
A cat minority of one
is all that can be counted on
to tell the truth. And what he has to tell
on each return from hell   40
is this: that dying is what the living do,
that dying is what the loving do,
and that dead dogs are those who do not know
that hell is where, to live, they have to go.

                                        —*Alastair Reid* [*1926–*   ]

QUESTIONS

   1. On the surface this poem is a dissertation on cats. What deeper comments does it make? Of what are cats and dogs, in this poem, symbols?
   2. In what different senses are the words *death, die,* and *dying* here used?
   3. Compare and contrast this poem in meaning and manner with "Ulysses."

PATTERNS

I walk down the garden paths,
And all the daffodils
Are blowing, and the bright blue squills.
I walk down the patterned garden paths
In my stiff, brocaded gown.   5
With my powdered hair and jeweled fan,
I too am a rare
Pattern. As I wander down
The garden paths.

My dress is richly figured,   10
And the train
Makes a pink and silver stain
On the gravel, and the thrift
Of the borders.

Just a plate of current fashion,   15
Tripping by in high-heeled, ribboned shoes.
Not a softness anywhere about me,
Only whalebone and brocade.
And I sink on a seat in the shade
Of a lime tree. For my passion   20
Wars against the stiff brocade.
The daffodils and squills
Flutter in the breeze
As they please.
And I weep;   25
For the lime tree is in blossom
And one small flower has dropped upon my bosom.

And the plashing of waterdrops
In the marble fountain
Comes down the garden paths.   30
The dripping never stops.
Underneath my stiffened gown
Is the softness of a woman bathing in a marble basin,
A basin in the midst of hedges grown
So thick, she cannot see her lover hiding,   35
But she guesses he is near,
And the sliding of the water
Seems the stroking of a dear
Hand upon her.
What is Summer in a fine brocaded gown!   40
I should like to see it lying in a heap upon the ground.
All the pink and silver crumpled up on the ground.

I would be the pink and silver as I ran along the paths,
And he would stumble after,
Bewildered by my laughter.   45
I should see the sun flashing from his sword-hilt and the buckles
      on his shoes.
I would choose
To lead him in a maze along the patterned paths,
A bright and laughing maze for my heavy-booted lover
Till he caught me in the shade,   50
And the buttons of his waistcoat bruised my body as he clasped me,
Aching, melting, unafraid.
With the shadows of the leaves and the sundrops,
And the plopping of the waterdrops,
All about us in the open afternoon—   55
I am very like to swoon
With the weight of this brocade,
For the sun sifts through the shade.

Underneath the fallen blossom
In my bosom   60
Is a letter I have hid.
It was brought to me this morning by a rider from the Duke.
"Madam, we regret to inform you that Lord Hartwell
Died in action Thursday se'nnight."
As I read it in the white, morning sunlight,   65
The letters squirmed like snakes.
"Any answer, Madam," said my footman.
"No," I told him.
"See that the messenger takes some refreshment.
No, no answer."   70
And I walked into the garden,
Up and down the patterned paths,
In my stiff, correct brocade.
The blue and yellow flowers stood up proudly in the sun,
Each one.   75
I stood upright too,
Held rigid to the pattern
By the stiffness of my gown;
Up and down I walked,
Up and down.   80

In a month he would have been my husband.
In a month, here, underneath this lime,
We would have broke the pattern;
He for me, and I for him,
He as Colonel, I as Lady,   85
On this shady seat.
He had a whim
That sunlight carried blessing.
And I answered, "It shall be as you have said."
Now he is dead.   90

In Summer and in Winter I shall walk
Up and down
The patterned garden paths
In my stiff, brocaded gown.
The squills and daffodils   95
Will give place to pillared roses, and to asters, and to snow.
I shall go
Up and down
In my gown.
Gorgeously arrayed,   100
Boned and stayed.
And the softness of my body will be guarded from embrace
By each button, hook, and lace.

For the man who should loose me is dead,
Fighting with the Duke in Flanders,   105
In a pattern called a war.
Christ! What are patterns for?

—*Amy Lowell [1874–1925]*

QUESTIONS

1. Vocabulary: *squills* (3), *whalebone* (18), *brocade* (18), *lime* (20),
se'nnight (64), *stayed* (101). What possible meanings have the following
words: *blowing* (3), *thrift* (13), *maze* (48), *stayed* (101)?
2. Two of England's greatest generals, the Duke of Marlborough and the
Duke of Wellington, both won famous victories in Flanders—Marlborough
in 1708 and Wellington in 1815. What evidence is there in the poem that the
earlier rather than the later campaign is being referred to in line 105? What
social characteristics of the eighteenth century (sometimes called the Age of
Reason) are reflected in the poem?
3. In one of its aspects, this poem is a psychological study of a bereaved
woman. The underlying story, however, is not told chronologically. What are
the chief thoughts that pass through the woman's head? Can you justify, psychologically, the order in which they are presented?
4. In another aspect, the poem is a protest against "patterns," and the
patterns, or some of them, are obviously symbolical. What are the various
patterns in the poem? The first two are obvious; but what social pattern is
manifested in lines 65–70? What pattern did Lord Hartwell and the lady intend to break on the shady seat (81–89)? The inclusion of war as a pattern
(106) may come, at first, as a shock, for war might seem the opposite of a
pattern. But what do all of these patterns have in common? What do they
symbolize? And what elements in the poem are contrasted to the patterns?
5. What kinds of imagery predominate in the poem? Point out some particularly effective tactile images.

PEACE

Sweet Peace, where dost thou dwell? I humbly crave,
    Let me once know.
  I sought thee in a secret cave,
    And asked, if Peace were there.
A hollow wind did seem to answer, No,   5
    Go seek elsewhere.

  I did; and going did a rainbow note.
    Surely, thought I,
  This is the lace of Peace's coat:
    I will search out the matter.   10
But while I looked the clouds immediately
    Did break and scatter.

Then went I to a garden and did spy
      A gallant flower,
  The crown imperial. Sure, said I,   15
    Peace at the root must dwell.
But when I digged, I saw a worm devour
      What showed so well.

At length I met a rev'rend good old man,
      Whom when for Peace   20
  I did demand, he thus began:
    There was a Prince of old
At Salem° dwelt, who lived with good increase   Jerusalem
      Of flock and fold.

He sweetly lived; yet sweetness did not save   25
      His life from foes.
  But after death out of his grave
    There sprang twelve stalks of wheat;
Which many wond'ring at, got some of those
      To plant and set.   30

It prospered strangely, and did soon disperse
      Through all the earth:
  For they that taste it do rehearse,
    That virtue lies therein,
A secret virtue, bringing peace and mirth   35
      By flight of sin.

Take of this grain, which in my garden grows,
      And grows for you;
  Make bread of it: and that repose
    And peace which ev'rywhere   40
With so much earnestness you do pursue,
      Is only there.

—*George Herbert [1593–1633]*

QUESTIONS

1. Who was the Prince (22)? What were the twelve stalks of wheat (28)? What is the grain (37)?

2. Should the secret cave (stanza 1), the rainbow (stanza 2), and the garden (stanza 3) be taken merely in the sense of "I searched everywhere," or assigned more precise meanings?

3. Is this poem mainly symbolical or allegorical?

THE SECOND COMING

Turning and turning in the widening gyre
The falcon cannot hear the falconer;
Things fall apart; the center cannot hold;
Mere anarchy is loosed upon the world,
The blood-dimmed tide is loosed, and everywhere   5
The ceremony of innocence is drowned;
The best lack all conviction, while the worst
Are full of passionate intensity.

Surely some revelation is at hand;
Surely the Second Coming is at hand.   10
The Second Coming! Hardly are those words out
When a vast image out of *Spiritus Mundi*
Troubles my sight: somewhere in sands of the desert
A shape with lion body and the head of a man,
A gaze blank and pitiless as the sun,   15
Is moving its slow thighs, while all about it
Reel shadows of the indignant desert birds.
The darkness drops again; but now I know
That twenty centuries of stony sleep
Were vexed to nightmare by a rocking cradle,   20
And what rough beast, its hour come round at last,
Slouches towards Bethlehem to be born?

—William Butler Yeats [1865–1939]

QUESTIONS

1. Vocabulary: *gyre* (1).

2. In Christian legend the prophesied "Second Coming" may refer either
to Christ or to Antichrist. *Spiritus Mundi* (12), literally world spirit, means the
racial memory or collective unconscious mind of mankind. Yeats believed in a
cyclical theory of history in which one historical era would be replaced by an
opposite kind of era every two thousand years. Here, the anarchy in the world
following World War I (the poem was written in 1919) heralds the end of
the Christian era. What is symbolized by the falcon and the falconer (1–2)?
What is the "shape with lion body and the head of a man" (14), and what
does it symbolize? What are the "rocking cradle" (20) and the "rough beast"
(21)? Discuss the effectiveness of these symbols.

EXERCISES

1. What are the essential differences between the following poems?

THE HOUSE ON THE HILL

They are all gone away,
    The House is shut and still,
There is nothing more to say.

Through broken walls and gray
    The winds blow bleak and shrill: 5
They are all gone away.

Nor is there one to-day
    To speak them good or ill:
There is nothing more to say.

Why is it then we stray   10
    Around the sunken sill?
They are all gone away,

And our poor fancy-play
    For them is wasted skill:
There is nothing more to say.   15

There is ruin and decay
    In the House on the Hill:
They are all gone away,
There is nothing more to say.

—Edwin Arlington Robinson [1869–1935]

THE DESERTED HOUSE

Life and Thought have gone away
    Side by side,
        Leaving door and windows wide:
Careless tenants they!

    All within is dark as night: 5
    In the windows is no light;
    And no murmur at the door,
    So frequent on its hinge before.

Close the door, the shutters close,
    Or through the windows we shall see   10
    The nakedness and vacancy
Of the dark deserted house.

Come away: no more of mirth
    Is here or merry-making sound.
The house was builded of the earth,   15
    And shall fall again to ground.

Come away: for Life and Thought
      Here no longer dwell;
         But in a city glorious—
A great and distant city—have bought   20
A mansion incorruptible.
Would they could have stayed with us!

—Alfred, Lord Tennyson [1809–1892]

2. Discuss the purpose and meaning of the following poems. Is any one of them symbolical? More than one? Are all?

THE HORSEMAN

I heard a horseman
Ride over the hill;
The moon shone clear,
The night was still;
His helm was silver,
And pale was he;
And the horse he rode
Was of ivory.

—Walter de la Mare [1873–1956]

THE TUFT OF KELP

All dripping in tangles green,
Cast up by a lonely sea,
If purer for that, O Weed,
Bitterer, too, are ye?

—Herman Melville [1819–1891]

THE COMING OF GOOD LUCK

So Good Luck came, and on my roof did light,
Like noiseless snow; or as the dew of night:
Not all at once, but gently, as the trees
Are, by the sunbeams, tickled by degrees.

—Robert Herrick [1591–1674]

ON SEEING WEATHER-BEATEN TREES

Is it as plainly in our living shown,
By slant and twist, which way the wind hath blown?

—Adelaide Crapsey [1878–1914]

89

7

Figurative Language 3

Aesop tells the tale of a traveler who sought refuge with a Satyr on a bitter winter night. On entering the Satyr's lodging, he blew on his fingers, and was asked by the Satyr what he did it for. "To warm them up," he explained. Later, on being served with a piping hot bowl of porridge, he blew also on it, and again was asked what he did it for. "To cool it off," he explained. The Satyr thereupon thrust him out of doors, for he would have nothing to do with a man who could blow hot and cold with the same breath.

A PARADOX is an apparent contradiction which is nevertheless somehow true. It may be either a situation or a statement. Aesop's tale of the traveler illustrates a paradoxical situation. As a figure of speech, paradox is a statement. When Alexander Pope wrote that a literary critic of his time would "damn with faint praise," he was using a verbal paradox, for how can a man damn by praising?

When we understand all the conditions and circumstances involved in a paradox, we find that what at first seemed impossible is actually entirely plausible and not strange at all. The paradox of the cold hands and hot porridge is not strange to a man who knows that a stream of air directed upon an object of different temperature will tend to bring that object closer to its own temperature. And Pope's paradox is not strange when we realize that *damn* is being used figuratively, and that Pope means only that a too reserved praise may damage an author with the public almost as much as adverse criticism. In a paradoxical statement the contradiction usually stems from one of the words being used figuratively or in more than one sense.

The value of paradox is its shock value. Its seeming impossibility startles the reader into attention, and thus, by the fact of its apparent absurdity, it underscores the truth of what is being said.

MY LIFE CLOSED TWICE

My life closed twice before its close;
It yet remains to see
If Immortality unveil
A third event to me,

So huge, so hopeless to conceive,
As these that twice befell.
Parting is all we know of heaven,
And all we need of hell.

—Emily Dickinson [1830–1886]

QUESTIONS

1. Should lines 2–6 be interpreted as meaning: (a) I do not know yet whether there is a life after death—a continued existence in heaven and hell; or (b) I do not know yet whether my entry into heaven or hell—whichever place I go—will be as "huge" an event as two events that have already happened to me during my life? Or both?

2. The poem is organized around two, possibly three, paradoxes: (a) that the speaker's life closed twice before its close; (b) (if we accept the second alternative above) that death and entry into immortality may possibly be "lesser" events than two not extraordinary occurrences that happened during the speaker's lifetime; (c) that parting from a loved one is *both* heaven and hell. Resolve (*i.e.*, explain) each of these paradoxes.

Overstatement, understatement, and verbal irony form a continuous series, for they consist, respectively, of saying more, saying less, and saying the opposite of what one really means.

OVERSTATEMENT, or *hyperbole*, is simply exaggeration, but exaggeration in the service of truth. It is not the same as a fish story. If you say, "I'm starved!" or "You could have knocked me over with a feather!" or "I'll die if I don't pass this course!" you do not expect to be believed; you are merely adding emphasis to what you really mean. (And if you say, "There were literally millions of people at the dance!" you are merely piling one overstatement on top of another, for you really mean that "There were figuratively millions of people at the dance," or, literally, "The dance hall was very crowded.") Like all figures of speech, overstatement may be used with a variety of effects. It may be humorous or grave, fanciful or restrained, convincing or unconvincing. When Tennyson says of his eagle (page 5) that it is *Close* to the sun in lonely lands," he says what appears to be literally true, though we know from our study of astronomy that it is not. When Wordsworth reports of his daffodils in "I wandered lonely as a cloud" that they "stretched *in never-ending line*" along the margin of a bay, he too reports faithfully a visual appearance. When Frost says, at the conclusion of "The Road Not Taken" (page 69),

> I shall be saying this with a sigh
> Somewhere *ages and ages hence,*

we are scarcely aware of the overstatement, so quietly is the assertion made. Unskillfully used, however, overstatement may seem strained and ridiculous, leading us to react as Gertrude does to the player-queen's speeches in *Hamlet:* "The lady doth protest too much."

It is paradoxical that one can emphasize a truth either by overstating it or by understating it. UNDERSTATEMENT, or saying less than one means, may exist in what one says or merely in how one says it. If, for instance, upon sitting down to a loaded dinner plate, you say, "This looks like a good bite," you are actually stating less than the truth; but if you say, with Artemus Ward, that a man who holds his hand for half an hour in a lighted fire will experience "a sensation of excessive and disagreeable warmth," you are stating what is literally true but with a good deal less force than the situation might seem to warrant.

A RED, RED ROSE

> O, my luve is like a red, red rose,
>   That's newly sprung in June.
> O my luve is like the melodie
>   That's sweetly played in tune.
>
> As fair art thou, my bonnie lass,   5
>   So deep in luve am I,
> And I will luve thee still, my dear,
>   Till a'° the seas gang° dry.   all; go

Till a' the seas gang dry, my dear,
And the rocks melt wi' the sun!　　　　　　10
And I will luve thee still, my dear,
While the sands o' life shall run.

And fare thee weel, my only luve,
And fare thee weel awhile!
And I will come again, my luve,　　　　　　15
Though it were ten thousand mile!

　　　　　　　　　　—*Robert Burns* [1759–1796]

THE ROSE FAMILY

The rose is a rose,
And was always a rose.
But the theory now goes
That the apple's a rose,
And the pear is, and so's　　　　　　5
The plum, I suppose.
The dear only knows
What will next prove a rose.
You, of course, are a rose—
But were always a rose.　　　　　　10

　　　　　　　　　　—*Robert Frost* [1874–1963]

QUESTION

1. Burns and Frost use the same metaphor in paying tribute to their loved ones; otherwise their methods are opposed. Burns begins with a couple of conventionally poetic similes and proceeds to a series of overstatements. Frost begins with literal and scientific fact (the apple, pear, plum, and rose all belong to the same botanical family, the Rosaceae), and then slips in his metaphor so casually and quietly that the assertion has the effect of understatement. What is the function of *of course* and *but* in the last two lines?

Like paradox, *irony* has meanings which extend beyond its use merely as a figure of speech.

VERBAL IRONY, saying the opposite of what one means, is often confused with sarcasm and with satire, and for that reason it may be well to look at the meanings of all three terms. SARCASM and SATIRE both imply ridicule, one on the colloquial level, the other on the literary level. Sarcasm is simply bitter or cutting speech, intended to wound the feelings (it comes from a Greek word meaning to tear flesh). Satire is a more formal term, applied usually to written literature rather than to speech, and ordinarily implying a higher motive: it is ridicule (either bitter or gentle) of human folly or vice, with the purpose of bringing about reform, or at least of keeping other people from falling into similar folly or vice. Irony, on the other hand, is a literary device or figure which may be used in the service of sarcasm or ridicule or may not. It is popularly confused with sarcasm and satire because it is so often used as their tool: but irony may be used without either sarcastic or satirical intent, and sarcasm and satire may exist (though they do not usually) without irony. If, for instance, one of the members of your class raises his hand on the discussion of this point and says, "I don't understand," and your instructor replies, with a tone of heavy disgust in his voice, "Well, I wouldn't expect *you* to," he is being sarcastic but not ironical; he means exactly what he says. But if, after you have done particularly well on an examination, your instructor brings your test papers into the classroom saying, "Here's some *bad* news for you: you all got A's and B's!" he is being ironical but not sarcastic. Sarcasm, we may say, is cruel, as a bully is cruel: it intends to give hurt. Satire is both cruel and kind, as a surgeon is cruel and kind: it gives hurt in the interest of the patient or of society. Irony is neither cruel nor kind: it is simply a device, like a surgeon's scalpel, for performing any operation more skillfully.

Like all figures of speech, verbal irony runs the danger of being misunderstood. With irony the risks are perhaps greater than with other figures, for if metaphor is misunderstood, the result may be simply bewilderment; but if irony is misunderstood, the reader goes away with exactly the opposite idea from what the user meant to convey. The results of misunderstanding if, for instance, you ironically called someone a villain, might be calamitous. For this reason the user of irony must be very skillful in its use, conveying by an altered tone or by a wink of the eye or pen, that he is speaking ironically; and the reader of literature must be always alert to recognize the subtle signs that irony is intended.

No matter how broad or obvious the irony, there will always be, in any large audience, a number who will misunderstand. The humorist Artemus Ward used to protect himself against these people by writing at the bottom of his newspaper column, "This is writ ironical." But irony is most delightful and most effective, for the good reader, when it is subtlest. It sets up a special understanding between writer and reader that may add either grace or force. If irony is too obvious, it sometimes seems merely crude. But if effectively used, it, like all figurative language, is capable of adding extra dimensions to meaning.

OF ALPHUS

> No egg on Friday Alph will eat,
>   But drunken he will be
> On Friday still. Oh, what a pure
>   Religious man is he!

—*Anonymous [16th century]*

QUESTION

1. Obviously the poet thinks Alphus anything but "a pure religious man." But what would be lost if he had written instead:

> Oh, what an impure
> Irreligious man is he!

The term *irony* always implies some sort of discrepancy or incongruity. In verbal irony the discrepancy is between what is said and what is meant. In other forms the discrepancy may be between appearance and reality, or between expectation and fulfillment. These other forms of irony are, on the whole, more important resources for the poet than is verbal irony. Two types, especially, are important for the beginning student to know.

In DRAMATIC IRONY[1] the discrepancy is not between what the speaker says and what he means but between what the speaker says and what the author means. The speaker's words may be perfectly straightforward, but the author, by putting these words in a particular speaker's mouth, may be indicating to the reader ideas or attitudes quite opposed to those the speaker is voicing. This form of irony is more complex than is verbal irony, and demands a more complex response from the reader. It may be used not only to convey attitudes but also to illuminate character, for the author who uses it is indirectly commenting not only upon the

---

[1] The term *dramatic irony*, which stems from Greek tragedy, often connotes something more specific and perhaps a little different from what I am developing here. It is used for a speech or action in a story which has much greater significance to the audience than to the character who speaks or performs it, because of possession by the audience of knowledge which the character does not have, as when the enemies of Ulysses, in the *Odyssey*, wish good luck and success to a man who the reader knows is Ulysses himself in disguise, or as when Oedipus, in the play by Sophocles, bends every effort to discover the murderer of Laius so that he may avenge the death, not knowing, as the audience does, that Laius is the man whom he himself once slew. I have appropriated the term for a perhaps slightly different situation, because no other suitable term exists. Both uses have the common characteristic that the author conveys to the reader something different, or at least something more, than the character himself intends.

value of the ideas uttered but also upon the nature of the person who utters them. Such comment may be harsh, gently mocking, or sympathetic.

THE CHIMNEY SWEEPER

When my mother died I was very young,
And my father sold me while yet my tongue
Could scarcely cry " 'weep! 'weep! 'weep! 'weep!"
So your chimneys I sweep, and in soot I sleep.

There's little Tom Dacre, who cried when his head,   5
That curled like a lamb's back, was shaved; so I said,
"Hush, Tom! never mind it, for, when your head's bare,
You know that the soot cannot spoil your white hair."

And so he was quiet, and that very night,
As Tom was asleeping, he had such a sight!   10
That thousands of sweepers, Dick, Joe, Ned, and Jack,
Were all of them locked up in coffins of black.

And by came an Angel who had a bright key,
And he opened the coffins and set them all free;
Then down a green plain leaping, laughing, they run,   15
And wash in a river, and shine in the sun.

Then naked and white, all their bags left behind,
They rise upon clouds and sport in the wind;
And the Angel told Tom, if he'd be a good boy,
He'd have God for his father, and never want joy.   20

And so Tom awoke, and we rose in the dark,
And got with our bags and our brushes to work.
Though the morning was cold, Tom was happy and warm;
So if all do their duty they need not fear harm.

—*William Blake [1757–1827]*

QUESTIONS

1. In the eighteenth century small boys, sometimes no more than four or five years old, were employed to climb up the narrow chimney flues and clean them, collecting the soot in bags. Such boys, sometimes sold to the master sweepers by their parents, were miserably treated by their masters and often suffered disease and physical deformity. Characterize the boy who speaks in this poem. How do his and the poet's attitudes toward his lot in life differ? How, especially, are the meanings of the poet and the speaker different in lines 3, 7–8, and 24?

2. The dream in lines 11–20, besides being just a happy dream, is capable of symbolic interpretations. Point out possible significances of the sweepers' being "locked up in coffins of black" and the Angel's releasing them with a bright key to play upon green plains.

A third type of irony is IRONY OF SITUATION. This occurs when there is a discrepancy between the actual circumstances and those that would seem appropriate, or between what one anticipates and what actually comes to pass. If a man and his second wife, on the first night of their honeymoon, are accidentally seated at the theater next to the man's first wife, we should call the situation ironical. When, in O. Henry's famous short story "The Gift of the Magi" a poor young husband pawns his most prized possession, a gold watch, in order to buy his wife a set of combs for her hair for Christmas, and his wife sells her most prized possession, her long brown hair, in order to buy a fob for her husband's watch, we call the situation ironical. When King Midas, in the famous fable, is granted his fondest wish, that anything he touches turn to gold, and then finds that he cannot eat because even his food turns to gold, we call the situation ironical. When Coleridge's Ancient Mariner finds himself in the middle of the ocean with "Water, water, everywhere" but not a "drop to drink," we call the situation ironical. In each case the circumstances are not what would seem appropriate or what we would expect.

Dramatic irony and irony of situation are powerful devices for the poet, for, like symbol, they enable him to suggest meanings without stating them—to communicate a great deal more than he says. We have seen one effective use of irony of situation in "Richard Cory" (page 39). Another is in "Ozymandias," which follows.

Irony and paradox may be trivial or powerful devices, depending on their use. At their worst they may degenerate into mere mannerism and mental habit. At their best they may greatly extend the dimensions of meaning in a work of literature. Because irony and paradox are devices that demand an exercise of critical intelligence, they are particularly valuable as safeguards against sentimentality.

OZYMANDIAS

> I met a traveler from an antique land
> Who said: Two vast and trunkless legs of stone
> Stand in the desert. Near them, on the sand,
> Half sunk, a shattered visage lies, whose frown,
> And wrinkled lip, and sneer of cold command,   5

Tell that its sculptor well those passions read
Which yet survive (stamped on these lifeless things),
The hand that mocked them and the heart that fed;
And on the pedestal these words appear:
"My name is Ozymandias, king of kings;   10
Look on my works, ye Mighty, and despair!"
Nothing beside remains. Round the decay
Of that colossal wreck, boundless and bare
The lone and level sands stretch far away.

—*Percy Bysshe Shelley [1792–1822]*

QUESTIONS

1. *Survive* (7) is a transitive verb with *hand* and *heart* as direct objects.
Whose hand? Whose heart? What figure of speech is exemplified in *hand* and
heart?
2. Characterize Ozymandias.
3. Ozymandias was an ancient Egyptian tyrant. This poem was first published in 1817. Of what is Ozymandias a *symbol?* What contemporary reference might the poem have had in Shelley's time?
4. What is the theme of the poem and how is it "stated"?

EXERCISE

Identify each of the following quotations as literal or figurative. If figurative,
identify the figure as paradox, overstatement, understatement, or irony, and
explain the use to which it is put (emotional emphasis, humor, satire, etc.).

1. Poetry is a language that tells us, through a more or less emotional reaction, something that cannot be said.—*Edwin Arlington Robinson*

2. Have not the Indians been kindly and justly treated? Have not the tem-
poral things, the vain baubles and filthy lucre of this world, which were
too apt to engage their worldly and selfish thoughts, been benevolently
taken from them? And have they not instead thereof, been taught to set
their affections on things above?—*Washington Irving*

3. A man who could make so vile a pun would not scruple to pick a pocket.
—*John Dennis*

4. Last week I saw a woman flayed, and you will hardly believe how much
it altered her person for the worse.—*Swift*

5. . . . Where ignorance is bliss,
'Tis folly to be wise.—*Thomas Gray*

6. All night I made my bed to swim; with my tears I dissolved my couch.
—*Psalms 6:6*

7. Believe him, he has known the world too long,
And seen the death of much immortal song.—*Pope*

8. Give me my Romeo: and, when he shall die,
   Take him and cut him out in little stars,
   And he will make the face of heaven so fine
   That all the world will be in love with night,
   And pay no worship to the garish sun.—*Juliet, in Shakespeare*

9. Immortality will come to such as are fit for it; and he who would be a great soul in the future must be a great soul now.—*Emerson*

10. Whoe'er their crimes for interest only quit,
    Sin on in virtue, and good deeds *commit.*—*Edward Young*

● ● ●

TO LUCASTA, GOING TO THE WARS

Tell me not, Sweet, I am unkind,
    That from the nunnery
Of thy chaste breast and quiet mind
    To war and arms I fly.

True, a new mistress now I chase,   5
    The first foe in the field;
And with a stronger faith embrace
    A sword, a horse, a shield.

Yet this inconstancy is such
    As you too shall adore;   10
I could not love thee, Dear, so much,
    Loved I not Honor more.

            —*Richard Lovelace [1618–1658]*

QUESTIONS

    1. State the basic paradox of the poem in a sentence. How is the paradox to be resolved?
    2. Do you find any words in the poem used in more than one meaning?

TO ALTHEA, FROM PRISON

When love with unconfinèd wings
    Hovers within my gates,
And my divine Althea brings
    To whisper at the grates;
When I lie tangled in her hair   5
    And fettered to her eye,
The birds that wanton in the air
    Know no such liberty.

When flowing cups run swiftly round
　　With no allaying Thames,
Our careless heads with roses bound,
　　Our hearts with loyal flames;
When thirsty grief in wine we steep,
　　When healths and draughts go free,
Fishes that tipple in the deep
　　Know no such liberty.

When, like committed linnets, I
　　With shriller throat shall sing
The sweetness, mercy, majesty,
　　And glories of my King;
When I shall voice aloud how good
　　He is, how great should be,
Enlargèd winds that curl the flood
　　Know no such liberty.

Stone walls do not a prison make,
　　Nor iron bars a cage;
Minds innocent and quiet take
　　That for an hermitage;
If I have freedom in my love
　　And in my soul am free,
Angels alone, that soar above,
　　Enjoy such liberty.

10

15

20

25

30

—*Richard Lovelace [1618–1658]*

QUESTIONS

1. Vocabulary: *wanton* (7), *allaying* (10), *committed* (17), *enlargèd* (23).

2. Richard Lovelace was a Cavalier poet, a loyal follower of Charles I who because of his royalist sympathies was imprisoned by Parliament in the Gatehouse at Westminster in 1642, a few months before the outbreak of the English Civil War. What is the central paradox of the poem? To whom are healths being drunk in stanza 2 and songs or poems being "sung" in stanza 3?

3. Each of the first three stanzas names a different pleasure which the poet may enjoy even though in prison. What are they? Each stanza also develops and intensifies the central paradox by suggesting some further kind of "confinement" (besides physical) which is not inconsistent with "liberty." What? Each of the four stanzas ends, in its last two lines, with a comparison. Show how each of these is especially appropriate to its stanza.

4. Explain the image in lines 1–2. What is the subject of *brings* (3)? *Thames* (10) is a metonymy; what does it mean?

LINES FOR A CHRISTMAS CARD

> May all my enemies go to hell,
> Noel, Noel, Noel, Noel.

—*Hilaire Belloc [1870–1953]*

MARY HYNES

(After the Irish of Raftery)

That Sunday, on my oath, the rain was a heavy overcoat
On a poor poet, and when the rain began
In fleeces of water to buckleap like a goat
I was only a walking penance reaching Kiltartan;
And there, so suddenly that my cold spine   5
Broke out on the arch of my back in a rainbow,
This woman surged out of the day with so much sunlight
I was nailed there like a scarecrow,

But I found my tongue and the breath to balance it
And I said: "If I bow to you with this hump of rain   10
I'll fall on my collarbone, but look, I'll chance it,
And after falling, bow again."
She laughed, ah, she was gracious, and softly said to me,
"For all your lovely talking I go marketing with an ass,
I'm no hill-queen, alas, or Ireland, that grass widow,   15·
So hurry on, sweet Raftery, or you'll keep me late for Mass!"

The parish priest has blamed me for missing second Mass
And the bell talking on the rope of the steeple,
But the tonsure of the poet is the bright crash
Of love that blinds the irons on his belfry;   20
Were I making an Aisling I'd tell the tale of her hair,
But now I've grown careful of my listeners
So I pass over one long day and the rainy air
Where we sheltered in whispers.

When we left the dark evening at last outside her door,   25
She lighted a lamp though a gaming company
Could have sighted each trump by the light of her unshawled poll,
And indeed she welcomed me
With a big quart bottle and I mooned there over glasses
Till she took that bird, the phoenix, from the spit;   30
And "Raftery," says she, "a feast is no bad dowry,
Sit down now and taste it!"

If I praised Ballylea before it was only for the mountains
Where I broke horses and ran wild,
And not for its seven crooked smoky houses   35
Where seven crones are tied
All day to the listening top of a half door,
And nothing to be heard or seen
But the drowsy dropping of water
And a gander on the green.   40

But, Boys! I was blind as a kitten till last Sunday.
This town is earth's very navel!
Seven palaces are thatched there of a Monday,
And O the seven queens whose pale
Proud faces with their seven glimmering sisters,   45
The Pleiads, light the evening where they stroll,
And one can find the well by their wet footprints,
And make one's soul;

For Mary Hynes, rising, gathers up there
Her ripening body from all the love stories;   50
And, rinsing herself at morning, shakes her hair
And stirs the old gay books in libraries;
And what shall I do with sweet Boccaccio?
And shall I send Ovid back to school again
With a new headline for his copybook,   55
And a new pain?

Like a nun she will play you a sweet tune on a spinet,
And from such grasshopper music leap
Like Herod's hussy who fancied a saint's head
For grace after meat;   60
Yet she'll peg out a line of clothes on a windy morning
And by noonday put them ironed in the chest,
And you'll swear by her white fingers she does nothing
But take her fill of rest.

And I'll wager now that my song is ended,   65
Loughrea, that old dead city where the weavers
Have pined at the mouldering looms since Helen broke the thread,
Will be piled again with silver fleeces:
O the new coats and big horses! The raving and the ribbons!
And Ballylea in hubbub and uproar!   70
And may Raftery be dead if he's not there to ruffle it
On his own mare, Shank's mare, that never needs a spur!

But ah, Sweet Light, though your face coins
My heart's very metals, isn't it folly without a pardon
For Raftery to sing so that men, east and west, come 75
Spying on your vegetable garden?
We could be so quiet in your chimney corner—
Yet how could a poet hold you any more than the sun,
Burning in the big bright hazy heart of harvest,
Could be tied in a henrun? 80

Bless your poet then and let him go!
He'll never stack a haggard with his breath:
His thatch of words will not keep rain or snow
Out of the house, or keep back death.
But Raftery, rising, curses as he sees you 85
Stir the fire and wash delph,
That he was bred a poet whose selfish trade it is
To keep no beauty to himself.

—*Padraic Fallon [1906–]*

QUESTIONS

1. Vocabulary: *tonsure* (19), *poll* (27), *phoenix* (30), *Pleiads* (46). *Crash* (19) has several meanings: a heavy linen fabric; a brilliant reddish-yellow color; a loud noise: which ones are relevant here? What two relevant meanings has *tell the tale* (20–21), and why must Raftery be "careful" of his listeners (22)? *Aisling* (21) is a vision of a maiden, usually Ireland personified. *Shank's mare* (72) is shanks' mare, i.e., one's own legs. *Haggard* (82) is an enclosure of stacked grain. *Delph* (86) is china.

2. Raftery (1784?–1835) was a famous itinerant Irish bardic poet, and Mary Hynes was the peasant girl whom he made famous in his verse. The present poem, while not a translation of any Raftery poem, does depend on a sense of Raftery as a folk figure, as well as on a mixture of Irish and classical mythology. What kind of person is Raftery? Whom is he addressing? Where? When?

3. Examine and comment on the figures of speech used by Raftery. What kind of bird, literally, does Mary Hynes cook for Raftery? What is the essential quality of his language and of his praise of Mary Hynes?

4. *Kiltartan* (4) and *Loughrea* (66) are in County Galway, Ireland; *Ballylea* (33) is a mythical town. *Boccaccio* (53) was a fourteenth-century storyteller and poet whose *Decameron* revolves about the enticing figure of Fiametta. *Ovid* (54) was a first-century B.C. Roman poet, famous for his *Art of Love. Herod's hussy* (59) is Salome, the famous dancing wench of the Bible (Matthew 14:1–11). *Helen* (67) is Helen of Troy. What does Raftery's use of literary, Biblical, and classical allusions tell us about him?

5. For what qualities does Raftery praise Mary Hynes? Enumerate her accomplishments. What is the main difference between her and Raftery? Does she acquire any symbolic values in the course of the poem?

6. Why, in Raftery's thinking, will Loughrea revive, and Ballylea again become a busy center of commerce (65–70)? What will be the ultimate result of Raftery's praise?

7. Explain the paradox with which the poem ends. State the theme of the poem, in a paragraph if necessary.

FINE FLOWERS IN THE VALLEY

She sat down below a thorn,
  Fine flowers in the valley,
And there she has her sweet babe born,
  And the green leaves they grow rarely.

"Smile na sae sweet, my bonny babe,   5
  Fine flowers in the valley,
And° ye smile sae sweet, ye'll smile me dead,"   if
  And the green leaves they grow rarely.

She's ta'en out her little pen-knife,
  Fine flowers in the valley,   10
And twinnd° the sweet babe o' its life,   robbed
  And the green leaves they grow rarely.

She's howket° a grave by the light o' the moon,   dug
  Fine flowers in the valley,
And there she's buried her sweet babe in,   15
  And the green leaves they grow rarely.

As she was going to the church,
  Fine flowers in the valley,
She saw a sweet babe in the porch,°   transcept
  And the green leaves they grow rarely.   20

"O sweet babe, and thou were mine,
  Fine flowers in the valley,
I wad cleed° thee in the silk so fine,"   clad
  And the green leaves they grow rarely.

"O mother dear, when I was thine,   25
  Fine flowers in the valley,
You did na prove to me sae kind,"
  And the green leaves they grow rarely.

—*Anonymous*

1. An old ballad, this poem has its origins in the Middle Ages. How much can be inferred about the "she" of the poem—her social position, character, etc.?

2. Is the supernatural element in the poem introduced chiefly for its own sake, or for comment on the human material?

3. What, if anything, does the refrain add to the poem? (Try reading the poem without it.)

4. What figurative device is used in the last stanza? Why is it more effective than a literal statement?

THE GREY SQUIRREL

Like a small grey
coffee-pot
sits the squirrel.
He is not

all he should be,   5
kills by dozens
trees, and eats
his red-brown cousins.

The keeper, on the
other hand   10
,who shot him, is
a Christian, and

loves his enemies,
which shows
the squirrel was not   15
one of those.

—Humbert Wolfe [1885–1940]

QUESTIONS

1. In this poem irony is employed in the service of satire. Which lines of the poem are ironical? What is being satirized?

2. Explain the simile in the first three lines. Find an example of understatement in the first half of the poem.

NO LONGER MOURN FOR ME

No longer mourn for me when I am dead
Than you shall hear the surly sullen bell
Give warning to the world that I am fled
From this vile world, with vilest worms to dwell.

Nay, if you read this line, remember not   5
The hand that writ it, for I love you so,
That I in your sweet thoughts would be forgot,
If thinking on me then should make you woe.
O, if, I say, you look upon this verse
When I perhaps compounded am with clay,   10
Do not so much as my poor name rehearse,
But let your love even with my life decay,
    Lest the wise world should look into your moan
    And mock you with me after I am gone.

                              —William Shakespeare [1564–1616]

QUESTIONS

    1. What paradoxical idea informs the first twelve lines of the poem, and
how is it resolved?
    2. What word in the concluding couplet is ironical?

THE UNKNOWN CITIZEN [2]

(To JS/07/M/378 This Marble Monument Is Erected by the State)

He was found by the Bureau of Statistics to be
One against whom there was no official complaint,
And all the reports on his conduct agree
That, in the modern sense of an old-fashioned word, he was a saint,
For in everything he did he served the Greater Community.   5
Except for the War till the day he retired
He worked in a factory and never got fired,
But satisfied his employers, Fudge Motors Inc.
Yet he wasn't a scab or odd in his views,
For his Union reports that he paid his dues,   10
(Our report on his Union shows it was sound)
And our Social Psychology workers found
That he was popular with his mates and liked a drink.
The Press are convinced that he bought a paper every day
And that his reactions to advertisements were normal in every way. 15
Policies taken out in his name prove that he was fully insured,
And his Health-card shows he was once in hospital but left it cured.
Both Producers Research and High-Grade Living declare
He was fully sensible to the advantages of the Installment Plan
And had everything necessary to the Modern Man,   20
A phonograph, a radio, a car and a frigidaire.
Our researchers into Public Opinion are content
That he held the proper opinions for the time of year;
When there was peace, he was for peace; when there was war, he went.

[2] Mr. Auden has recorded "The Unknown Citizen" (LP, Library of Congress, PL 21).

He was married and added five children to the population,   25
Which our Eugenist says was the right number for a parent of his
          generation,
And our teachers report that he never interfered with their education.
Was he free? Was he happy? The question is absurd:
Had anything been wrong, we should certainly have heard.

                                        —*W. H. Auden* [1907–   ]

QUESTIONS

   1. Vocabulary: *scab* (9), *Eugenist* (26).
   2. Explain the allusion and the irony in the title. Why was the citizen
"unknown"?
   3. This obituary of an unknown state "hero" was apparently prepared by
a functionary of the state. Give an account of the citizen's life and character
from Auden's own point of view.
   4. What trends in modern life and social organization does the poem
satirize?

DEPARTMENTAL[3]

            An ant on the tablecloth
            Ran into a dormant moth
            Of many times his size.
            He showed not the least surprise.
            His business wasn't with such.   5
            He gave it scarcely a touch,
            And was off on his duty run.
            Yet if he encountered one
            Of the hive's enquiry squad
            Whose work is to find out God   10
            And the nature of time and space,
            He would put him onto the case.
            Ants are a curious race;
            One crossing with hurried tread
            The body of one of their dead   15
            Isn't given a moment's arrest—
            Seems not even impressed.
            But he no doubt reports to any
            With whom he crosses antennae,
            And they no doubt report   20
            To the higher up at court.
            Then word goes forth in Formic:
            "Death's come to Jerry McCormic,

---

[3] Mr. Frost recorded "Departmental" (LP, Caedmon, TC 1060).

Our selfless forager Jerry.
Will the special Janizary   25
Whose office it is to bury
The dead of the commissary
Go bring him home to his people.
Lay him in state on a sepal.
Wrap him for shroud in a petal.   30
Embalm him with ichor of nettle.
This is the word of your Queen."
And presently on the scene
Appears a solemn mortician;
And taking formal position   35
With feelers calmly atwiddle,
Seizes the dead by the middle,
And heaving him high in air,
Carries him out of there.
No one stands round to stare.   40
It is nobody else's affair.

It couldn't be called ungentle.
But how thoroughly departmental.

—*Robert Frost [1874–1963]*

QUESTIONS

1. Vocabulary: *dormant* (2), *Formic* (22), *Janizary* (25), *commissary* (27), *sepal* (29), *ichor* (31).

2. The poem is ostensibly about ants. Is it ultimately about ants? Give reasons to support your view that it is or isn't.

3. What is the author's attitude toward the "departmental" organization of ant society? How is it indicated? Could this poem be described as "gently ironic"? If so, in what sense?

4. Compare and contrast this poem with "The Unknown Citizen" in content and manner.

THE CONSTANT LOVER

Out upon it! I have loved
    Three whole days together;
And am like to love three more,
    If it prove fair weather.

Time shall moult away his wings   5
    Ere he shall discover
In the whole wide world again
    Such a constant lover.

But the spite on 't is, no praise
Is due at all to me; 10
Love with me had made no stays
Had it any been but she.

Had it any been but she,
And that very face,
There had been at least ere this 15
A dozen dozen in her place.

—Sir John Suckling [1609–1642]

QUESTIONS

1. What figures of speech are used in stanzas 2 and 4?
2. Traditionally, lovers vow to be faithful forever to their sweethearts. Burns, in "A Red, Red Rose" (page 92), declares he will love his sweetheart "till a' the seas gang dry." Suckling's lover, on the other hand, *complains* that he has been faithful for three whole days and may be so for three more. The discrepancy between our expectation (aroused by the title) and this fulfillment constitutes a form of irony. Is this irony employed ultimately for the purpose of making a cynical observation about love or of paying an exaggerated compliment to the lady in question? In what respect does the speaker pay his sweetheart a greater compliment than does the lover who vows to be faithful forever?
3. Does the lover's complaint in the first stanza support his assertion in the third that no praise is due at all to him for this constancy?

MY LAST DUCHESS

Ferrara

That's my last Duchess painted on the wall,
Looking as if she were alive. I call
That piece a wonder, now; Fra Pandolf's hands
Worked busily a day, and there she stands.
Will 't please you sit and look at her? I said 5
"Fra Pandolf" by design, for never read
Strangers like you that pictured countenance,
The depth and passion of its earnest glance,
But to myself they turned (since none puts by
The curtain I have drawn for you, but I) 10
And seemed as they would ask me, if they durst,
How such a glance came there; so, not the first
Are you to turn and ask thus. Sir, 'twas not
Her husband's presence only, called that spot
Of joy into the Duchess' cheek; perhaps 15
Fra Pandolf chanced to say, "Her mantle laps

Over my lady's wrist too much," or, "Paint
Must never hope to reproduce the faint
Half-flush that dies along her throat." Such stuff
Was courtesy, she thought, and cause enough   20
For calling up that spot of joy. She had
A heart—how shall I say?—too soon made glad,
Too easily impressed; she liked whate'er
She looked on, and her looks went everywhere.
Sir, 'twas all one! My favor at her breast,   25
The dropping of the daylight in the West,
The bough of cherries some officious fool
Broke in the orchard for her, the white mule
She rode with round the terrace—all and each
Would draw from her alike the approving speech,   30
Or blush, at least. She thanked men—good! but thanked
Somehow—I know not how—as if she ranked
My gift of a nine-hundred-years-old name
With anybody's gift. Who'd stoop to blame
This sort of trifling? Even had you skill   35
In speech—which I have not—to make your will
Quite clear to such an one, and say, "Just this
Or that in you disgusts me; here you miss,
Or there exceed the mark"—and if she let
Herself be lessoned so, nor plainly set   40
Her wits to yours, forsooth, and made excuse—
E'en then would be some stooping; and I choose
Never to stoop. Oh, sir, she smiled, no doubt,
Whene'er I passed her; but who passed without
Much the same smile? This grew; I gave commands;   45
Then all smiles stopped together. There she stands
As if alive. Will 't please you rise? We'll meet
The company below, then. I repeat,
The Count your master's known munificence
Is ample warrant that no just pretense   50
Of mine for dowry will be disallowed;
Though his fair daughter's self, as I avowed
At starting, is my object. Nay, we'll go
Together down, sir. Notice Neptune, though,
Taming a sea-horse, thought a rarity,   55
Which Claus of Innsbruck cast in bronze for me!

—*Robert Browning* [1812–1889]

QUESTIONS

1. Vocabulary: *officious* (27), *munificence* (49).
2. Ferrara is in Italy. The time is during the Renaissance, probably the sixteenth century. To whom is the Duke speaking? What is the occasion? Are the

Duke's remarks about his last Duchess a digression, or do they have some relation to the business at hand?

3. Characterize the Duke as fully as you can. How does your characterization differ from the Duke's opinion of himself? What kind of irony is this?

4. Why was the Duke dissatisfied with his last Duchess? Was it sexual jealousy? What opinion do you get of the Duchess's personality, and how does it differ from the Duke's opinion?

5. What characteristics of the Italian Renaissance appear in the poem (marriage customs, social classes, art)? What is the Duke's attitude toward art? Is it insincere?

6. What happened to the Duchess? Should we have been told?

THE HORSES

Barely a twelvemonth after
The seven days war that put the world to sleep,
Late in the evening the strange horses came.
By then we had made our covenant with silence,
But in the first few days it was so still   5
We listened to our breathing and were afraid.
On the second day
The radios failed; we turned the knobs; no answer.
On the third day a warship passed us, heading north,
Dead bodies piled on the deck. On the sixth day   10
A plane plunged over us into the sea. Thereafter
Nothing. The radios dumb;
And still they stand in corners of our kitchens,
And stand, perhaps, turned on, in a million rooms
All over the world. But now if they should speak,   15
If on a sudden they should speak again,
If on the stroke of noon a voice should speak,
We would not listen, we would not let it bring
That old bad world that swallowed its children quick
At one great gulp. We would not have it again.   20
Sometimes we think of the nations lying asleep,
Curled blindly in impenetrable sorrow,
And then the thought confounds us with its strangeness.

The tractors lie about our fields; at evening
They look like dank sea-monsters couched and waiting.   25
We leave them where they are and let them rust:
"They'll moulder away and be like other loam."
We make our oxen drag our rusty ploughs,
Long laid aside. We have gone back
Far past our fathers' land.   30

And then, that evening
Late in the summer the strange horses came.
We heard a distant tapping on the road,
A deepening drumming; it stopped, went on again
And at the corner changed to hollow thunder.   35
We saw the heads
Like a wild wave charging and were afraid.
We had sold our horses in our fathers' time
To buy new tractors. Now they were strange to us
As fabulous steeds set on an ancient shield   40
Or illustrations in a book of knights.
We did not dare go near them. Yet they waited,
Stubborn and shy, as if they had been sent
By an old command to find our whereabouts
And that long-lost archaic companionship.   45
In the first moment we had never a thought
That they were creatures to be owned and used.
Among them were some half-a-dozen colts
Dropped in some wilderness of the broken world,
Yet new as if they had come from their own Eden.   50
Since then they have pulled our ploughs and borne our loads,
But that free servitude still can pierce our hearts.
Our life is changed; their coming our beginning.

—*Edwin Muir* [1887–1959]

QUESTIONS

1. Vocabulary: *archaic* (45), *dropped* (49). What meanings has *quick* (19)?

2. There is a special name (*oxymoron*) for an extremely compact para-dox—one in which two successive words seemingly contradict each other, yet convey a truth. Find an example toward the end of the poem, and explain it.

3. What basic irony pervades the poem? What kind of irony is it? What ironic details contribute to it? What comment does it make on civilization?

4. Compare and contrast this poem with "The Unknown Citizen" in its meaning and in the quality of its irony.

EARTH

"A planet doesn't explode of itself," said drily
The Martian astronomer, gazing off into the air—
"That they were able to do it is proof that highly
Intelligent beings must have been living there."

—*John Hall Wheelock* [1886–   ]

8

Allusion

The famous English diplomat and letter writer Lord Chesterfield was once invited to a great dinner given by the Spanish ambassador. At the conclusion of the meal the host rose and proposed a toast to his master, the king of Spain, whom he compared to the sun. The French ambassador followed with a health to the king of France, whom he likened to the moon. It was then Lord Chesterfield's turn. "Your excellencies have taken from me," he said, "all the greatest luminaries of heaven, and the stars are too small for me to make a comparison of my royal master; I therefore beg leave to give your excellencies—Joshua!" [1]

For a reader familiar with the Bible, that is, for one who recognizes the Biblical allusion, Lord Chesterfield's story will come as a stunning revelation of his wit. For an ALLUSION—a reference to something in history or previous literature—is, like a richly connotative word or a symbol, a means of suggesting far more than it says. The one word *Joshua*, in the context of Chesterfield's toast, calls up in the reader's mind the whole Biblical story of how the Israelite captain stopped the sun and the moon in order that the Israelites might finish a battle and conquer their enemies before nightfall (Joshua 10:12–14). The force of the toast lies in its ex-

[1] Samuel Shellabarger, *Lord Chesterfield and His World,* Boston, Little, Brown, 1951, p. 132.

treme economy; it says so much in so little, and it exercises the mind of the reader to make the connection for himself.

The effect of Chesterfield's allusion is chiefly humorous or witty, but allusions may also have a powerful emotional effect. The essayist William Hazlitt writes of addressing a fashionable audience about the lexicographer Dr. Johnson. Speaking of Johnson's great heart and of his charity to the unfortunate, Hazlitt recounted how, finding a drunken prostitute lying in Fleet Street late at night, Johnson carried her on his broad back to the address she managed to give him. The audience, unable to face the picture of the famous dictionary-maker doing such a thing, broke out in titters and expostulations. Whereupon Hazlitt simply said: "I remind you, ladies and gentlemen, of the parable of the Good Samaritan." The audience was promptly silenced.[2]

Allusions are a means of reinforcing the emotion or the ideas of one's own work with the emotion or ideas of another work or occasion. Because they are capable of saying so much in so little, they are extremely useful to the poet.

"OUT, OUT—"

> The buzz-saw snarled and rattled in the yard
> And made dust and dropped stove-length sticks of wood,
> Sweet-scented stuff when the breeze drew across it.
> And from there those that lifted eyes could count
> Five mountain ranges one behind the other   5
> Under the sunset far into Vermont.
> And the saw snarled and rattled, snarled and rattled,
> As it ran light, or had to bear a load.
> And nothing happened: day was all but done.
> Call it a day, I wish they might have said   10
> To please the boy by giving him the half hour
> That a boy counts so much when saved from work.
> His sister stood beside them in her apron
> To tell them "Supper." At the word, the saw,
> As if to prove saws knew what supper meant,   15
> Leaped out at the boy's hand, or seemed to leap—
> He must have given the hand. However it was,
> Neither refused the meeting. But the hand!
> The boy's first outcry was a rueful laugh,
> As he swung toward them holding up the hand   20
> Half in appeal, but half as if to keep
> The life from spilling. Then the boy saw all—

---

[2] Jacques Barzun, *Teacher in America*, Boston, Little, Brown, 1945, p. 160.

Since he was old enough to know, big boy
Doing a man's work, though a child at heart—
He saw all spoiled. "Don't let them cut my hand off—   25
The doctor, when he comes. Don't let him, sister!"
So. But the hand was gone already.
The doctor put him in the dark of ether.
He lay and puffed his lips out with his breath.
And then—the watcher at his pulse took fright.   30
No one believed. They listened at his heart.
Little—less—nothing!—and that ended it.
No more to build on there. And they, since they
Were not the one dead, turned to their affairs.

—*Robert Frost [1874–1963]*

QUESTIONS

1. How does this poem differ from a newspaper account that might have dealt with the same incident?

2. To whom does *they* (33) refer? the boy's family? the doctor and hospital attendants? casual onlookers? Need we assume that all these people—whoever they are—turned immediately "to their affairs"? Does the ending of this poem seem to you callous or merely realistic? Would a more tearful and sentimental ending have made the poem better or worse?

3. What figure of speech is used in lines 21–22?

Allusions will vary widely in the amount of reliance that the poet puts on them to convey his meaning. Lord Chesterfield risked his whole meaning on his hearers' recognizing his allusion. Robert Frost in "Out, Out—" makes his meaning entirely clear even for the reader who does not recognize the allusion contained in his title. His theme is the uncertainty and unpredictability of life, which may be accidentally ended at any moment, and the tragic waste of human potentiality which takes place when such premature deaths occur. A boy who is already "doing a man's work" and gives every promise of having a useful life ahead of him is suddenly wiped out. There seems no rational explanation for either the accident or the death. The only comment to be made is, "No more to build on there."

Frost's title, however, is an allusion to one of the most famous passages in all English literature, and it offers a good illustration of how a poet may use allusion not only to reinforce emotion but also to help define his theme. The passage is that in *Macbeth*, in which Macbeth has just been informed of his wife's death. A good

many readers will recall the key phrase, "Out, out, brief candle!"
with its underscoring of the tragic brevity and uncertainty of life
which can be snuffed out at any moment. For some readers, however, the allusion will summon up the whole passage in which this
phrase occurs. Macbeth's words are:

> She should have died hereafter;
> There would have been a time for such a word.
> To-morrow, and to-morrow, and to-morrow
> Creeps in this petty pace from day to day
> To the last syllable of recorded time;   5
> And all our yesterdays have lighted fools
> The way to dusty death. Out, out, brief candle!
> Life's but a walking shadow, a poor player,
> That struts and frets his hour upon the stage
> And then is heard no more. It is a tale   10
> Told by an idiot, full of sound and fury,
> Signifying nothing.
>
> *Act V, Scene 5*

Macbeth's first words underscore the theme of premature death.
The boy also "should have died hereafter." The rest of the passage,
with its marvelous evocation of the vanity and meaninglessness of
life, expresses neither Shakespeare's philosophy nor, ultimately,
Frost's, but it is Macbeth's philosophy at the time of his bereave-
ment, and it is likely to express the feelings of us all when such
tragic accidents occur. Life does indeed seem cruel and meaningless, a tale told by an idiot, signifying nothing, when human life
and potentiality are thus without explanation so suddenly ended.

Allusions vary widely in the number of readers to whom they
will be familiar. The poet, in using an allusion as in using a figure
of speech, is always in danger of not being understood. In appealing powerfully to one reader, he may lose another reader altogether.
But the poet must assume a certain fund of common experience
with his readers. He could not even write about the ocean unless
he could assume that his reader had seen the ocean or a lake or
pictures thereof. In the same way he will assume a certain common
fund of literary experience. He is often justified in expecting a
rather wide range of literary experience in his readers, for the
people who read poetry for pleasure are generally people of good
minds and good education who have read widely. But, obviously,
beginning readers will not have this range, just as they will not
know the meanings of as many words as will maturer readers. The
student ought therefore to be prepared to look up certain allusions,
just as he should be eager to look up in his dictionary the meanings

of unfamiliar words. He will find that every increase in knowledge will broaden his base for understanding both literature and life.

• • •

IN JUST-[3]

> in Just-
> spring   when the world is mud-
> luscious the little
> lame balloonman
>
> whistles   far   and wee   5
>
> and eddieandbill come
> running from marbles and
> piracies and it's
> spring
>
> when the world is puddle-wonderful   10
>
> the queer
> old balloonman whistles
> far   and   wee
> and bettyandisbel come dancing
>
> from hop-scotch and jump-rope and   15
>
> it's
> spring
> and
>   the
>
>   goat-footed   20
>
> balloonMan   whistles
> far
> and
> wee

—*e. e. cummings [1894–1962]*

QUESTION

1. Why is the balloonman called *goat-footed?* How does the identification made by this mythological allusion enrich the meaning of the poem?

[3] Mr. Cummings recorded "in Just-" (78 rpm, Linguaphone Institute, HBC).

ON HIS BLINDNESS

When I consider how my light is spent
Ere half my days in this dark world and wide,
And that one talent which is death to hide
Lodged with me useless, though my soul more bent
To serve therewith my Maker, and present   5
My true account, lest he returning chide,
"Doth God exact day-labor, light denied?"
I fondly ask. But Patience, to prevent
That murmur, soon replies, "God doth not need
Either man's work or his own gifts. Who best   10
Bear his mild yoke, they serve him best. His state
Is kingly: thousands at his bidding speed,
And post o'er land and ocean without rest;
They also serve who only stand and wait."

—John Milton [1608–1674]

QUESTIONS

   1. Vocabulary: *spent* (1), *fondly* (8), *prevent* (8), *post* (13).
   2. What two meanings has *talent* (3)? What is Milton's "one talent"?
   3. The poem is unified and expanded in its dimensions by a Biblical allusion which Milton's original readers would have recognized immediately. What is it? If you do not know, look up Matthew 25:14–30. In what ways is the situation in the poem similar to that in the parable? In what ways is it different?
   4. What is the point of the poem?

NO SECOND TROY

Why should I blame her that she filled my days
With misery, or that she would of late
Have taught to ignorant men most violent ways,
Or hurled the little streets against the great,
Had they but courage equal to desire?   5
What could have made her peaceful with a mind
That nobleness made simple as a fire,
With beauty like a tightened bow, a kind
That is not natural in an age like this,
Being high and solitary and most stern?   10
Why, what could she have done, being what she is?
Was there another Troy for her to burn?

—William Butler Yeats [1865–1939]

1. Yeats, an Irish poet, as a young man fell hopelessly in love with an Irish beauty whose principal life interest was obtaining Irish freedom from English rule. Identify the figure of speech in line 4 and explain its appropriateness.

2. Explain the appropriateness of the similes in lines 6–7 and 8.

3. Explain the allusion in line 12.

4. State the idea of the poem in a sentence.

LEDA AND THE SWAN

A sudden blow: the great wings beating still
Above the staggering girl, her thighs caressed
By the dark webs, her nape caught in his bill,
He holds her helpless breast upon his breast.
How can those terrified vague fingers push   5
The feathered glory from her loosening thighs?
And how can body, laid in that white rush,
But feel the strange heart beating where it lies?
A shudder in the loins engenders there
The broken wall, the burning roof and tower   10
And Agamemnon dead.
                                    Being so caught up,
So mastered by the brute blood of the air,
Did she put on his knowledge with his power
Before the indifferent beak could let her drop?

—*William Butler Yeats [1865–1939]*

QUESTIONS

1. What is the connection between Leda and "the broken wall, the burning roof and tower/And Agememnon dead"? If you do not know, look up the myth of Leda, and, if necessary, the story of Agamemnon.

2. What is the significance of the question asked in the last two lines?

EPITAPH ON NEWTON

Nature and Nature's laws lay hid in night:
God said, "Let Newton be!" and all was light.

—*Alexander Pope [1688–1744]*

1. Besides formulating the law of gravitation and the laws of motion, Sir Isaac Newton discovered the composition of light and wrote an important book on optics. How does Pope use a Biblical allusion to pay Newton a graceful compliment?

2. In how many ways does Pope use the words *night* and *light?*

THE CARPENTER'S SON

"Here the hangman stops his cart:
Now the best of friends must part.
Fare you well, for ill fare I:
Live, lads, and I will die.

"Oh, at home had I but stayed   5
'Prenticed to my father's trade,
Had I stuck to plane and adze,
I had not been lost, my lads.

"Then I might have built perhaps
Gallow-trees for other chaps,   10
Never dangled on my own,
Had I but left ill alone.

"Now, you see, they hang me high,
And the people passing by
Stop to shake their fists and curse;   15
So 'tis come from ill to worse.

"Here hang I, and right and left
Two poor fellows hang for theft:
All the same's the luck we prove,
Though the midmost hangs for love.   20

"Comrades all, that stand and gaze,
Walk henceforth in other ways;
See my neck and save your own:
Comrades all, leave ill alone.

"Make some day a decent end,   25
Shrewder fellows than your friend.
Fare you well, for ill fare I:
Live, lads, and I will die."

—*A. E. Housman [1859–1936]*

1. With whom is the speaker being implicitly compared and contrasted? How do you know?
2. In what sense is the speaker being hanged "for love"? In what sense was his prototype?
3. What is the import of "Live, lads, and I will die" in the mouth of the speaker as contrasted with its traditional import in the story of his prototype?
4. What meaning has the speaker's advice to "leave ill alone" when transferred to the story of his prototype? What general meanings are implicit in the poem?

THE PARABLE OF THE OLD MEN AND THE YOUNG

So Abram rose, and clave the wood, and went,
And took the fire with him, and a knife.
And as they sojourned both of them together,
Isaac the first-born spake and said, "My Father,
Behold the preparations, fire and iron,   5
But where the lamb for this burnt-offering?"
Then Abram bound the youth with belts and straps,
And builded parapets and trenches there,
And stretchèd forth the knife to slay his son.
When lo! an angel called him out of heaven,   10
Saying, "Lay not thy hand upon the lad,
Neither do anything to him. Behold,
A ram, caught in a thicket by its horns;
Offer the Ram of Pride instead of him."
But the old man would not so, but slew his son,—   15
And half the seed of Europe, one by one.

—*Wilfred Owen [1893–1918]*

QUESTIONS

1. A parable is a form of allegory. The occasion for this parable was World War I, in which the poet himself was killed. What is the allegorical significance of Abraham, Isaac, the fire and iron, the belts and straps, the parapets and trenches, the angel, the ram?
2. Read Genesis 22:1–18 and explore the similarities and differences between Owen's version of the story and the Biblical original. What is the effect of the differences?

IN THE GARDEN

In the garden there strayed
A beautiful maid
As fair as the flowers of the morn;
The first hour of her life
She was made a man's wife,
And was buried before she was born.

—Anonymous

QUESTION

1. Resolve the paradox by identifying the allusion.

QUATRAIN

Jack, eating rotten cheese, did say,
Like Samson I my thousands slay;
I vow, quoth Roger, so you do.
And with the self-same weapon too.

—Benjamin Franklin [1706–1790]

9

Meaning and Idea

Little Jack Horner
Sat in a corner
Eating a Christmas pie.
He stuck in his thumb
And pulled out a plum
And said, "What a good boy am I!"

The meaning of a poem is the experience which it expresses—nothing less. But the reader who, baffled by a particular poem, asks perplexedly, "What does it *mean?*" is usually after something more specific than this. He wants something that he can grasp entirely with his mind. We may therefore find it useful to make a distinction between the TOTAL MEANING of a poem—that which it communicates (and which can be communicated in no other way)—and its PROSE MEANING—the ingredient which can be separated out in the form of a prose paraphrase. If we make this distinction, however, we must be careful not to confuse the two kinds of meaning. The prose meaning is no more the poem than a plum is a pie, or than a prune is a plum.

The prose meaning will not necessarily or perhaps even usually be an idea. It may be a story, it may be a description, it may be a statement of emotion, it may be a presentation of human character, or it may be some combination of these. "The Griesly Wife" (page 13) tells a story; "Cavalry Crossing a Ford" (page 67) is primarily descriptive; "Western Wind" (page 78) is a cry of emotion; "My Last Duchess" (page 109) is an account of human character; none of these poems is directly concerned with ideas. The message-hunter will be baffled and disappointed by poetry of this kind, for he will not find what he is looking for, and he may attempt to read some idea into the poem which is really not there. Yet ideas are also part of human experience, and therefore many poems will be concerned, at least partially, with presenting ideas. But with these poems message-hunting is an even more dangerous activity. For the message-hunter is likely to think that the whole object of reading the poem is to find the message—that the idea is really the only important thing in it. Like Little Jack Horner, he will reach in and pluck it out and say, "What a good boy am I!" as if the pie existed for the plum.

The idea in a poem is only part of the total experience which it communicates. The value and worth of the poem are determined by the value of the total experience, not by the truth or the nobility of the idea itself. This is not to say that the truth of the idea is unimportant, or that its validity should not be examined and appraised. But a good idea will not make a good poem, nor need an idea with which the reader does not agree ruin one. The good reader of poetry will be a reader receptive to all kinds of experience. He will be able to make that "willing suspension of disbelief" which Coleridge characterized as constituting poetic faith. When one attends a performance of *Hamlet* he is willing to forget for the time being that such a person as Hamlet never existed and that the events going on on the stage are fictions. The reader of poetry should also be willing to enter imaginatively, for the time being, into ideas which objectively he regards as untrue. It is one way of understanding these ideas better and of enlarging his own experience. The Christian should be able to enjoy a good poem expressing atheistic ideas, and the atheist a good poem in praise of God. The optimist by temperament should be able to find pleasure in pessimistic poetry, and the pessimist in optimistic poetry. The teetotaler should be able to enjoy "The Rubáiyát of Omar Khayyám," and the winebibber a good poem in praise of austerity. The primary value of a poem depends not so much on the truth of the idea presented as on the power with which it is communicated and on its being made a convincing part of a meaningful total experience. We must feel that the idea has been truly and deeply *felt* by the poet, and that he is doing something more than merely moralizing. The plum must be made part of a pie. If the plum is properly combined with other ingredients and if the pie is well cooked, it should be enjoyable even for persons who do not care for the brand of plums of which it is made. Let us consider, for instance, the following two poems:

BARTER

> Life has loveliness to sell,
>   All beautiful and splendid things,
> Blue waves whitened on a cliff,
>   Soaring fire that sways and sings,
> And children's faces looking up,   5
> Holding wonder like a cup.
>
> Life has loveliness to sell,
>   Music like a curve of gold,
> Scent of pine trees in the rain,
>   Eyes that love you, arms that hold,   10
> And for your spirit's still delight,
> Holy thoughts that star the night.
>
> Spend all you have for loveliness,
>   Buy it and never count the cost;
> For one white singing hour of peace   15
>   Count many a year of strife well lost,
> And for a breath of ecstasy
> Give all you have been, or could be.

—Sara Teasdale [1884–1933]

STOPPING BY WOODS ON A SNOWY EVENING [1]

> Whose woods these are I think I know.
> His house is in the village though;
> He will not see me stopping here
> To watch his woods fill up with snow.
>
> My little horse must think it queer   5
> To stop without a farmhouse near
> Between the woods and frozen lake
> The darkest evening of the year.

---

[1] Mr. Frost recorded "Stopping by Woods on a Snowy Evening" (LP, National Council of Teachers of English, RL 20–1; LP, Yale, YP 320; or LP, Library of Congress, PL 20).

He gives his harness bells a shake
To ask if there is some mistake.   10
The only other sound's the sweep
Of easy wind and downy flake.

The woods are lovely, dark and deep,
But I have promises to keep,
And miles to go before I sleep,   15
And miles to go before I sleep.

—*Robert Frost [1874–1963]*

QUESTIONS

1. How do these two poems differ in idea?
2. What contrasts are suggested between the speaker in the second poem
and (a) his horse, and (b) the owner of the woods?

Both of these poems present ideas, the first more or less explicitly, the second symbolically. Perhaps the best way to get at
the idea of the second poem is to ask two questions. First, why
does the speaker stop? Second, why does he go on? He stops, we
answer, to watch the woods fill up with snow—to observe a scene
of natural beauty. He goes on, we answer, because he has "promises" to keep, that is, he has obligations to fulfill. He is momen-
tarily torn between his love of beauty and these other various and
complex claims that life has upon him. The small conflict in the
poem is symbolical of a larger conflict in life. One part of the
sensitive, thinking man would like to give up his life to the enjoyment of beauty and art. But another part is aware of larger duties
and responsibilities—responsibilities owed, at least in part, to other
human beings. The speaker in the poem would like to satisfy both
impulses. But when the two come into conflict, he seems to suggest,
the "promises" must be given precedence.

The first poem also presents a philosophy, but an opposed one.
For this poet, beauty is of such a supreme value that any conflicting demand should be sacrificed to it. "Spend all you have for
loveliness,/Buy it and never count the cost . . . And for a breath
of ecstasy/Give all you have been, or could be." The reader, if he
is a thinking person, will have to choose between these two philoso-
phies—to commit himself to one or the other. But if he is a good
reader of poetry, this commitment should not destroy for him his

enjoyment of either poem. If it does, he is reading for plums and not for pies.

Nothing so far said in this chapter should be construed as meaning that the truth or falsity of the idea in a poem is a matter of no importance. *Other things being equal,* the good reader naturally will, and properly should, value more highly the poem whose idea he feels to be maturer and nearer to the heart of human experience. There may be some ideas, moreover, which he feels to be so vicious or so foolish or so beyond the pale of normal human decency as to discredit *by themselves* the poems in which he finds them. A rotten plum may spoil a pie. But a good reader will always be a person of considerable intellectual flexibility and tolerance, able to entertain sympathetically ideas other than his own. He will often like a poem with whose idea he disagrees better than one with an idea which he accepts. And, above all, he will not confuse the prose meaning of any poem with its total meaning. He will not mistake plums for pies.

• • •

SONG

The year's at the spring,
And day's at the morn;
Morning's at seven;
The hillside's dew-pearled;
The lark's on the wing;
The snail's on the thorn;
God's in his heaven—
All's right with the world!

—*Robert Browning [1812–1889]*

DIRGE

Rough wind, that moanest loud
Grief too sad for song;
Wild wind, when sullen cloud
Knells all the night long;
Sad storm, whose tears are vain,
Bare woods, whose branches strain,
Deep caves and dreary main,—
Wail, for the world's wrong!

—*Percy Bysshe Shelley [1792–1822]*

1. In what ways are these two poems alike? In what ways different?
2. How would you evaluate the two comments made on "the world"? Is it possible to justify both? Should you be surprised to learn that the first poet was a tremendous admirer of the second?

TO A WATERFOWL

Whither, midst falling dew,
While glow the heavens with the last steps of day,
Far, through their rosy depths, dost thou pursue
Thy solitary way?

Vainly the fowler's eye   5
Might mark thy distant flight to do thee wrong,
As, darkly seen against the crimson sky,
Thy figure floats along.

Seek'st thou the plashy brink
Of weedy lake, or marge of river wide,   10
Or where the rocking billows rise and sink
On the chafed ocean-side?

There is a Power whose care
Teaches thy way along that pathless coast—
The desert and illimitable air—   15
Lone wandering, but not lost.

All day thy wings have fanned,
At that far height, the cold, thin atmosphere,
Yet stoop not, weary, to the welcome land,
Though the dark night is near.   20

And soon that toil shall end;
Soon shalt thou find a summer home, and rest,
And scream among thy fellows; reeds shall bend,
Soon, o'er thy sheltered nest.

Thou'rt gone, the abyss of heaven   25
Hath swallowed up thy form; yet, on my heart
Deeply has sunk the lesson thou hast given,
And shall not soon depart.

He who, from zone to zone,
Guides through the boundless sky thy certain flight,   30
In the long way that I must tread alone,
Will lead my steps aright.

—William Cullen Bryant [1794–1878]

DESIGN [2]

I found a dimpled spider, fat and white,
On a white heal-all, holding up a moth
Like a white piece of rigid satin cloth—
Assorted characters of death and blight
Mixed ready to begin the morning right,   5
Like the ingredients of a witches' broth—
A snow-drop spider, a flower like a froth,
And dead wings carried like a paper kite.

What had that flower to do with being white,
The wayside blue and innocent heal-all?   10
What brought the kindred spider to that height,
Then steered the white moth thither in the night?
What but design of darkness to appall?—
If design govern in a thing so small.

—Robert Frost [1874–1963]

QUESTIONS

1. Vocabulary: *characters* (4).
2. The heal-all is a wildflower, usually blue or violet but occasionally
white, found blooming along roadsides in the summer. It was once supposed
to have healing qualities; hence its name. Of what significance, scientific and
poetic, is the fact that the spider, the heal-all, and the moth are all white?
Of what poetic significance is the fact that the spider is "dimpled" and "fat"
and like a "snow-drop," and that the flower is "innocent" and named "heal-
all"?
3. The "argument from design," as it was called, was a favorite eighteenth-
century argument for the existence of God. What twist does Frost give the
argument? What questions does the poem pose?
4. Contrast this poem in content with "To a Waterfowl." Is it possible to
admire both?

[2] Mr. Frost recorded "Design" (LP, Yale, YP 320).

OF A CONTENTED MIND

When all is done and said, in the end thus shall you find,
He most of all doth bathe in bliss that hath a quiet mind;
And, clear from worldly cares, to deem can be content
The sweetest time in all his life in thinking to be spent.

The body subject is to fickle fortune's power,   5
And to a million of mishaps is casual every hour;
And death in time doth change it to a clod of clay,
When as the mind, which is divine, runs never to decay.

Companion none is like unto the mind alone,
For many have been harmed by speech; through thinking, few or none. 10
Fear oftentimes restraineth words, but makes not thoughts to cease,
And he speaks best that hath the skill when for to hold his peace.

Our wealth leaves us at death, our kinsmen at the grave,
But virtues of the mind unto the heavens with us we have:
Wherefore, for virtue's sake, I can be well content   15
The sweetest time of all my life to deem in thinking spent.

—*Thomas Vaux [1510–1556]*

QUESTIONS

1. Vocabulary: *casual* (6), *skill* (12).
2. With what things is "a quiet mind" contrasted? What are its advantages over these other things?

AN ACRE OF GRASS

Picture and book remain,
An acre of green grass
For air and exercise,
Now strength of body goes;
Midnight, an old house   5
Where nothing stirs but a mouse.

My temptation is quiet.
Here at life's end
Neither loose imagination,
Nor the mill of the mind   10
Consuming its rag and bone,
Can make the truth known.

Grant me an old man's frenzy,
Myself must I remake
Till I am Timon and Lear   15
Or that William Blake
Who beat upon the wall
Till Truth obeyed his call;

A mind Michael Angelo knew
That can pierce the clouds,   20
Or inspired by frenzy
Shake the dead in their shrouds;
Forgotten else by mankind,
An old man's eagle mind.

—*William Butler Yeats [1865–1939]*

QUESTIONS

1. Timon and Lear (15) are both Shakespearean tragic heroes who lived
an unquiet, passionate old age. William Blake (16) and Michelangelo (19)
maintained turbulent, creative minds into old age. Why does Yeats wish for
"an old man's frenzy"? What, for him, is "Truth," and how does man achieve it?
2. Is the "mind" of line 10 the same as the "mind" of lines 19 and 24?
If not, what is the difference, and how is it established? What is a "loose
imagination" (9), and what is its opposite?
3. Is "quiet" (7) an adjective or a noun? What function is served by
"that" (16)?
4. Compare and contrast this poem with the preceding one. In what respects are Vaux and Yeats in agreement about old age? in what respects in
disagreement?

THE CAGED SKYLARK

As a dare-gale skylark scanted in a dull cage
    Man's mounting spirit in his bone-house, mean house, dwells—
    That bird beyond the remembering his free fells;
This in drudgery, day-laboring-out life's age.

Though aloft on turf or perch or poor low stage,   5
    Both sing sometimes the sweetest, sweetest spells,
    Yet both droop deadly sometimes in their cells
Or wring their barriers in bursts of fear or rage.

Not that the sweet-fowl, song-fowl, needs no rest—
Why, hear him, hear him babble and drop down to his nest,   10
    But his own nest, wild nest, no prison.

Man's spirit will be flesh-bound when found at best,
But uncumbered: meadow-down is not distressed
For a rainbow footing it nor he for his bones risen.

—*Gerard Manley Hopkins [1844–1889]*

QUESTIONS

1. Vocabulary: *scanted* (1), *fells* (3). What meanings of *mean* (2) are appropriate here?

2. This poem, written by a poet-priest, expresses his belief in the orthodox Roman Catholic doctrine of the resurrection of the body. According to this belief man's immortal spirit, after death, will be ultimately reunited with his body; this body, however, will be a weightless, perfected, glorified body, not the gross imperfect body of mortal life. Express the analogy in the poem as a pair of mathematical statements of proportion (in the form $a{:}b = c{:}d$, and $e{:}f = g{:}h = i{:}j$), using the following terms: caged skylark, mortal body, meadow-down, cage, rainbow, spirit-in-life, nest, immortal spirit, wild skylark, resurrected body.

3. Discuss the image of the last two lines as a figure for weightlessness. Why would not a shadow have been equally apt as a rainbow for this comparison?

THE IMMORTAL PART

When I meet the morning beam
Or lay me down at night to dream,
I hear my bones within me say,
"Another night, another day.

"When shall this slough of sense be cast,   5
This dust of thoughts be laid at last,
The man of flesh and soul be slain
And the man of bone remain?

"This tongue that talks, these lungs that shout,
These thews that hustle us about,   10
This brain that fills the skull with schemes,
And its humming hive of dreams,—

"These to-day are proud in power
And lord it in their little hour:
The immortal bones obey control   15
Of dying flesh and dying soul.

" 'Tis long till eve and morn are gone:
Slow the endless night comes on,

And late to fulness grows the birth
That shall last as long as earth.   20

"Wanderers eastward, wanderers west.
Know you why you cannot rest?
'Tis that every mother's son
Travails with a skeleton.

"Lie down in the bed of dust;   25
Bear the fruit that bear you must;
Bring the eternal seed to light,
And morn is all the same as night.

"Rest you so from trouble sore,
Fear the heat o' the sun no more,   30
Nor the snowing winter wild,
Now you labor not with child.

"Empty vessel, garment cast,
We that wore you long shall last.
—Another night, another day."   35
So my bones within me say.

Therefore they shall do my will
To-day while I am master still,
And flesh and soul, now both are strong,
Shall hale the sullen slaves along,   40

Before this fire of sense decay,
This smoke of thought blow clean away,
And leave with ancient night alone
The stedfast and enduring bone.

—*A. E. Housman [1859–1936]*

QUESTIONS

1. Vocabulary: *slough* (5), *thews* (10), *travails* (24), *hale* (40).
2. Discuss the figures of speech in lines 3–16, 12, 19–27, 41–42, 43.
3. Do you recognize the allusion in stanza 8? If not, refer to page 295. How is the allusion appropriate here?
4. Contrast the meaning of the word *soul* in this poem with its meaning in "The Caged Skylark." How do the two poems differ in idea? Is there any pronounced difference between them in poetic merit?

ARS POETICA [3]

A poem should be palpable and mute
As a globed fruit,

Dumb
As old medallions to the thumb,

Silent as the sleeve-worn stone   5
Of casement ledges where the moss has grown—

A poem should be wordless
As the flight of birds.

      *

A poem should be motionless in time
As the moon climbs,   10

Leaving, as the moon releases
Twig by twig the night-entangled trees,

Leaving, as the moon behind the winter leaves,
Memory by memory the mind—

A poem should be motionless in time   15
As the moon climbs.

      *

A poem should be equal to:
Not true.

For all the history of grief
An empty doorway and a maple leaf.   20

For love
The leaning grasses and two lights above the sea—

A poem should not mean
But be.

—*Archibald MacLeish* [1892–   ]

QUESTIONS

1. How can a poem be "wordless"? How can it be "motionless in time"?
2. The Latin title, literally translatable as "The Art of Poetry," is a traditional title for works on the philosophy of poetry. What is *this* poet's philosophy of poetry? What does he mean by saying that a poem should not "mean"
and should not be "true"?

[3] Mr. MacLeish has recorded "Ars Poetica" (78 rpm, Harvard Vocarium, P–1220).

10

Tone

TONE, in literature, may be defined as the writer's or speaker's attitude toward his subject, his audience, or himself. It is the emotional coloring, or the emotional meaning, of the work, and is an extremely important part of the full meaning. In spoken language it is indicated by the inflections of the speaker's voice. If, for instance, a friend tells us, "I'm going to get married today," the facts of his statement are entirely clear. But the emotional meaning of his statement may vary widely according to the tone of voice with which he utters it. He may be ecstatic ("Hooray! I'm going to get married today!"); he may be incredulous ("I can't believe it! I'm going to get married today"); he may be resigned ("Might as well face it. I'm going to get married today"); he may be in despair ("Horrors! I'm going to get married today!"). Obviously, a correct interpretation of his tone will be an important part of understanding his full meaning. It may even have rather important consequences. If someone calls us a crazy ox, our interpretation of his tone may determine whether we take off our coat for a fight or buy him a double malted. If a girl says "No" to our proposal of marriage, our interpretation of her tone may determine whether we ask her again and win her, or lose heart and remain single.

In poetry tone is likewise important. We have not really understood a poem unless we have accurately sensed whether the attitude it manifests is playful or solemn, mocking or reverent, calm or excited. But the correct determination of tone in literature is a much more delicate matter than it is with spoken language, for we do not have the speaker's voice to guide us. We must learn to recognize tone by other means. Almost all the elements of poetry go into indicating its tone: connotation, imagery, and metaphor; irony and understatement; rhythm, sentence construction, and formal pattern. There is therefore no simple formula for recognizing tone. It is an end product of all the elements in a poem. The best we can do is illustrate:

Robert Frost's "Stopping by Woods" (page 125) seems a simple poem, but it has always afforded trouble to beginning readers. A very good student, asked to interpret it, once wrote this: "The poem means that we are forever passing up pleasures to go onward to what we wrongly consider our obligations. We would like to watch the snow fall on the peaceful countryside, but we always have to rush home to supper and other engagements. Mr. Frost feels that the average man considers life too short to stop and take time to appreciate true pleasures." This student did a good job in recognizing the central conflict of the poem. He went astray in recognizing its tone. Let's examine why:

In the first place, the fact that the speaker in the poem *does* stop to watch the snow fall in the woods immediately establishes him as a human being with more sensitivity and feeling for beauty than most. He is not one of the people of Wordsworth's sonnet (page 34) who, "getting and spending," have laid waste their powers and lost the capacity to be stirred by nature. Frost's speaker is contrasted with his horse, who, as a creature of habit and an animal, without esthetic perception, cannot understand the speaker's reason for stopping. There is also a suggestion of contrast with the "owner" of the woods, who, if he saw the speaker stopping, might be as puzzled as the horse. (Who most truly "profits" from the woods—its absentee owner or the person who can enjoy its beauty?) The speaker goes on because he has "promises" to keep. But the word *promises*, though it may here have a wry ironic undertone of regret, has a favorable connotation: people almost universally agree that promises ought to be kept. If the poet had used a different term, say, *things to do*, or *business to attend to*, or *financial affairs to take care of*, or *money to make*, the connotations would have been quite different. As it is, the tone of the poem tells us that the poet is sympathetic to the speaker, is endorsing rather than censuring his action. Perhaps we may go even further. In the concluding two lines, because of their climatic position, because they are repeated, and because *sleep* in poetry is often used figura-

tively to refer to death, there is a suggestion of symbolical interpretation: "And many years to live before I die." If we accept this
interpretation, it poses a parallel between giving oneself up to con-
templation of the woods, and dying. Beauty, the poet's total im-
plication would seem to be, is a distinctively human value which
deserves its place in a full life; but to devote one's life to its pursuit, at the expense of other obligations and duties, is tantamount
to one's death as a responsible being. The poet therefore accepts
the choice the speaker makes, though not without a touch of regret.

Differences in tone, and their importance, can perhaps be
studied best in poems with similar content. Consider, for instance,
the following pair:

THE VILLAIN

While joy gave clouds the light of stars,
    That beamed where'er they looked;
And calves and lambs had tottering knees,
    Excited, while they sucked;
While every bird enjoyed his song,   5
Without one thought of harm or wrong—
I turned my head and saw the wind,
    Not far from where I stood,
Dragging the corn by her golden hair,
    Into a dark and lonely wood.   10

—*W. H. Davies [1871–1940]*

QUESTIONS

    1. Vocabulary: *corn* (9).

    2. From what realm of experience is the image in the title and the last
two lines taken? What implications does your answer have for the way this
image should be taken, i.e., its relation to reality?

APPARENTLY WITH NO SURPRISE

Apparently with no surprise
To any happy flower,
The frost beheads it at its play
In accidental power.
The blond assassin passes on,
The sun proceeds unmoved

To measure off another day
For an approving God.

—Emily Dickinson [1830–1886]

QUESTIONS

1. What is the "blond assassin"?
2. What ironies are involved in this poem?

Both of these poems are concerned with nature; both use contrast as their basic organizing principle—a contrast between innocence and evil, joy and tragedy. But in tone the two poems are
sharply different. The first is light and fanciful; its tone is one of
delight or delighted surprise. The second, though superficially fanciful, is basically grim, almost savage; its tone is one of horror. Let's
examine the difference:

In "The Villain" the images of the first six lines all suggest
joy and innocence. The last four introduce the sinister. The poet,
on turning his head, sees a villain dragging a beautiful maiden
toward a dark wood to commit there some unmentionable deed, or
so his metaphor tells us. But our response is one not of horror but of
delight, for we realize that the poet does not mean us to take his
metaphor seriously. He has actually seen only the wind blowing
through the wheat and bending its golden tops gracefully toward
a shady wood. The beauty of the scene has delighted him, and he
has been further delighted by the fanciful metaphor which he has
found to express it. The reader shares his delight both in the scene
and in the metaphor.

The second poem makes the same contrast of joyful innocence
(the "happy flower . . . at its play") with the sinister ("the blond
assassin"). The chief difference would seem to be that the villain
is this time the frost rather than the wind. But this time the poet,
though her metaphor is no less fanciful, is earnest in what she is
saying. For the frost actually *does* kill the flower. What makes the
horror of the killing even worse is that nothing else in nature is
disturbed over it or seems even to notice it. The sun "proceeds unmoved" to measure off another day. Nothing in nature stops or
pauses. The flower itself is not surprised. And even God—the God
whom we have all been told is benevolent and concerned over the
least sparrow's fall—seems to approve of what has happened, for
he shows no displeasure, and it was he who created the frost as
well as the flower. Further irony lies in the fact that the "assassin"
(the word's connotations are of terror and violence) is not dark but

"blond," or white (the connotations here are of innocence and beauty). The destructive agent, in other words, is among the most exquisite creations of God's handiwork. The poet, then, is shocked at what has happened, and is even more shocked that nothing else in nature is shocked. What has happened seems inconsistent with a rule of benevolence in the universe. In her ironic reference to an "approving God," therefore, the poet is raising a dreadful question: Are the forces which created and govern the universe actually benevolent? And if we think that the poet is unduly disturbed over the death of a flower, we may consider that what is true for the flower is true throughout nature. Death—even early or accidental death, in terrible juxtaposition with beauty—is its constant condition; the fate that befalls the flower befalls us all.

These two poems then, though superficially similar, are basically as different as night and day. And the difference is primarily one of tone.

Accurate determination of tone, therefore, is extremely important, whether in the reading of poetry or the interpretation of a woman's "No." For the good reader it will be instinctive and automatic. For the beginning reader it will require study. But beyond the general suggestions for reading that have already been made, no specific instructions can be given. Recognition of tone requires an increasing familiarity with the meanings and connotations of words, alertness to the presence of irony and other figures, and, above all, careful reading. Poetry cannot be read as one would skim a newspaper or a mystery novel, looking merely for facts.

EXERCISES

1. Marvell's "To His Coy Mistress" (page 64), Herrick's "To the Virgins, to Make Much of Time" (page 76), and Housman's "Loveliest of Trees" (page 170) all treat a traditional poetic theme known as the *carpe diem* ("seize the day") theme. They differ, however, in tone. Characterize the tone of each, and point out the differences in poetic management which account for the difference in tone.
2. Shakespeare (page 11), Hopkins (page 50), and Nashe (page 288) have all written poems entitled "Spring." Describe and account for the differences in tone among them.
3. Describe and account for the differences of tone in each of the following pairs: (a) "Song" and "Dirge" (page 127); (b) "Ulysses" and "Curiosity" (pages 79, 81); (c) "The Unknown Citizen" and "Departmental" (pages 106, 107).

• • •

THE COMING OF WISDOM WITH TIME

Though leaves are many, the root is one;
Through all the lying days of my youth
I swayed my leaves and flowers in the sun;
Now I may wither into the truth.

—William Butler Yeats [1865–1939]

QUESTION

1. Is the poet exulting over a gain or lamenting over a loss?

SINCE THERE'S NO HELP

Since there's no help, come let us kiss and part.
Nay, I have done, you get no more of me;
And I am glad, yea, glad with all my heart,
That thus so cleanly I myself can free.
Shake hands for ever, cancel all our vows,   5
And when we meet at any time again,
Be it not seen in either of our brows
That we one jot of former love retain.
Now at the last gasp of Love's latest breath,
When, his pulse failing, Passion speechless lies,   10
When Faith is kneeling by his bed of death,
And Innocence is closing up his eyes,
  Now, if thou wouldst, when all have given him over,
  From death to life thou mightst him yet recover.

—Michael Drayton [1563–1631]

QUESTIONS

1. What difference in tone do you find between the first eight lines and the last six? What differences in rhythm and the kind of language used help to establish this difference in tone?

2. How many figures are there in the allegorical scene in lines 9–12? Why is "Love" dying?

3. Define the dramatic situation as precisely as possible, taking into consideration both the man's attitude and the woman's.

THIS SIDE OF CALVIN

The Reverend Dr. Harcourt, folk agree,
 Nodding their heads in solid satisfaction,
Is just the man for this community.
 Tall, young, urbane, but capable of action,

He pleases where he serves. He marshals out   5
    The younger crowd, lacks trace of clerical unction,
Cheers the Kiwanis and the Eagle Scout,
    Is popular at every public function.

And in the pulpit eloquently speaks
    On divers matters with both wit and clarity.   10
Art, Education, God, the Early Greeks,
    Psychiatry, Saint Paul, true Christian charity,
Vestry repairs that shortly must begin,
    All things but Sin. He seldom mentions Sin.

—Phyllis McGinley [1905–   ]

QUESTIONS

1. Vocabulary: *unction* (6), *divers* (10).
2. What is the poet's attitude toward Dr. Harcourt?
3. Can you explain the significance of the allusion in the title?

EPILOGUE TO *ASOLANDO*

At the midnight in the silence of the sleep-time,
    When you set your fancies free,
Will they pass to where—by death, fools think, imprisoned—
Low he lies who once so loved you, whom you loved so—
        Pity me?   5

Oh, to love so, be so loved, yet so mistaken!
    What had I on earth to do
With the slothful, with the mawkish, the unmanly?
Like the aimless, helpless, hopeless, did I drivel—
        Being—who?   10

One who never turned his back but marched breast forward,
    Never doubted clouds would break,
Never dreamed, though right were worsted, wrong would triumph,
Held we fall to rise, are baffled to fight better,
        Sleep to wake.   15

No, at noonday in the bustle of man's work-time,
    Greet the unseen with a cheer!
Bid him forward, breast and back as either should be,
"Strive and thrive!" cry, "Speed—fight on, fare ever
        There as here!"   20

—Robert Browning [1812–1889]

141

QUESTIONS

1. This poem, the last ever written by Browning, is the "epilogue" to a volume of poems entitled *Asolando,* published on the day of Browning's death. Who is the speaker and to whom is he speaking?
2. Why does he think that he should not be pitied?
3. What is his conception of immortality?

EPITAPH

Mr. Heath-Stubbs as you must understand
Came of a gentleman's family out of Staffordshire
Of as good blood as any in England
But he was wall-eyed and his legs too spare.

His elbows and finger-joints could bend more ways than one   5
And in frosty weather would crack audibly
As to delight his friends he would give demonstration
Which he might have done in public for a small fee.

Amongst the more learned persons of his time
Having had his schooling in the University of Oxford   10
In anglo-saxon latin ornithology and crime
Yet after four years he was finally not preferred.

Orthodox in beliefs as following the English Church
Barring some heresies he would have for recreation
Yet too often left these sound principles (as I am told) in   15
    the lurch
Being troubled with idleness lechery pride and dissipation.

In his youth he would compose poems in prose and verse
In a classical romantic manner which was pastoral
To which the best judges of the Age were not averse
And the public also but his profit was not financial.   20

Now having outlived his friends and most of his reputation
He is content to take his rest under these stones and grass
Not expecting but hoping that the Resurrection
Will not catch him unawares whenever it takes place.

                    —*John Heath-Stubbs* [1918–]

QUESTIONS

1. Vocabulary: *wall-eyed* (4), *ornithology* (11). *Preferred* (12), in this context, probably means given a fellowship or teaching appointment.
2. "Epilogue to *Asolando*" and "Epitaph" have a number of points in

common. In each the poet, as part of the dramatic framework, imagines that he is dead. In each the poet is writing about himself and his life, making, in effect, a self-evaluation, and making some indication about his expectation for the future. Define as precisely as possible the difference in tone between the two poems. What accounts for the difference? Which poem do you find more worthy of respect?

A SONNET OF THE MOON

> Look how the pale Queen of the silent night
> Doth cause the ocean to attend upon her,
> And he, as long as she is in his sight,
> With his full tide is ready her to honor;
> But when the silver waggon of the Moon   5
> Is mounted up so high he cannot follow,
> The sea calls home his crystal waves to moan,
> And with low ebb doth manifest his sorrow.
>
> So you, that are the sovereign of my heart,
> Have all my joys attending on your will,   10
> My joys low-ebbing when you do depart,
> When you return, their tide my heart doth fill.
> So as you come and as you do depart,
> Joys ebb and flow within my tender heart.

> —*Charles Best*
> (*poem written c. 1608*)

QUESTION

1. The relationship of the speaker and his beloved is compared, by simile and metaphor, to two other relationships—one scientific, the other social. Supply the paired terms for each of the three relationships, and discuss the development of each comparison.

TARGET

> The moon holds nothing in her arms;
>   She is as empty as a drum.
> She is a cipher, though she charms;
>   She is delectable but dumb.
> She has no factories or farms,   5
> Or men to sound the fire-alarms
>   When the marauding missiles come.

We have no cause to spare that face
Suspended fatly in the sky.
She does not help the human race.   10
    Surely, she shines when bats flit by
And burglars seek their burgling-place
And lovers in a soft embrace
    Among the whispering bushes lie—

But that is all. Dogs still will bark   15
    When cottage doors are lightly knocked,
And poachers crawl about the park
    Cursing the glint on guns halfcocked;
None of the creatures of the dark
Will, in their self-absorption, mark   20
    That visage growing slightly pocked.

                              —*R. P. Lister* [*1914*–]

1. The primary subject of Charles Best's poem is love; of Lister's, the
moon—or shooting missiles at the moon. Best talks also about the moon, however, and Lister about love. By an analysis of the tone of each, determine
whether their attitudes toward love and toward the moon are similar or different.

2. Comment on the rimes employed in the last stanza.

YES; I WRITE VERSES

Yes; I write verses now and then,
But blunt and flaccid is my pen,
No longer talked of by young men
    As rather clever;
In the last quarter are my eyes,   5
You see it by their form and size;
Is it not time then to be wise?
    Or now or never.

Fairest that ever sprang from Eve!
While Time allows the short reprieve,   10
Just look at me! would you believe
    'Twas once a lover?
I cannot clear the five-bar gate,
But, trying first its timbers' state,
Climb stiffly up, take breath, and wait   15
    To trundle over.

Through gallopade I cannot swing
The entangling blooms of Beauty's spring;
I cannot say the tender thing,
    Be't true or false,   20
And am beginning to opine
Those girls are only half-divine
Whose waists yon wicked boys entwine
    In giddy waltz.

I fear that arm above that shoulder,   25
I wish them wiser, graver, older,
Sedater, and no harm if colder,
    And panting less.
Ah! people were not half so wild
In former days, when, starchly mild,   30
Upon her high-heeled Essex smiled
    The brave Queen Bess.

—Walter Savage Landor [1775–1864]

QUESTIONS

1. Vocabulary: *flaccid* (2), *trundle* (16), *gallopade* (17).
2. Identify and explain the figures of speech in lines 2, 5, 9, and 18, and the allusion in lines 31–32.

TO AGE

Welcome, old friend! These many years
    Have we lived door by door;
The Fates have laid aside their shears
    Perhaps for some few more.

I was indocile at an age   5
    When better boys were taught,
But thou at length hast made me sage,
    If I am sage in aught.

Little I know from other men,
    Too little they from me,   10
But thou hast pointed well the pen
    That writes these lines to thee.

Thanks for expelling Fear and Hope,
    One vile, the other vain;
One's scourge, the other's telescope,   15
    I shall not see again.

Rather what lies before my feet
My notice shall engage—
He who hath braved Youth's dizzy heat
Dreads not the frost of Age.   20

—Walter Savage Landor [1775–1864]

QUESTIONS

1. Vocabulary: *indocile* (5), *scourge* (15).
2. Identify and explain the figures of speech in lines 1–2, 11, 13–16, and 19–20, and the allusion in lines 3–4.
3. Define the poet's attitude toward himself and advancing old age in this poem and in the preceding one. (He was 71 when "Yes; I Write Verses" was published, 78 when "To Age" was published.) What are the apparent differences? Try to account for them.
4. Describe the difference in tone between the two poems.

LOVE

There's the wonderful love of a beautiful maid,
    And the love of a staunch true man,
And the love of a baby that's unafraid—
    All have existed since time began.
But the most wonderful love, the Love of all loves,
    Even greater than the love for Mother,
Is the infinite, tenderest, passionate love
    Of one dead drunk for another.

—Anonymous

QUESTION

1. The radical shift in tone makes "Love" come off. If such a shift were unintentional in a poem, what would our view be?

11

Musical Devices

It is obvious to the most uninitiated reader that poetry makes a greater use of the "music" of language than does language which is not poetry. The poet, unlike the man who uses language to convey only information, chooses his words for sound as well as for meaning, and he uses the sound as a means of reinforcing his meaning. So prominent is this musical quality of poetry that some writers have made it the distinguishing term in their definitions of poetry. Edgar Allan Poe, for instance, describes poetry as "music . . . combined with a pleasurable idea." Whether or not it deserves this much importance, verbal music, like connotation, imagery, and figurative language, is one of the important resources which enable the poet to do something more than communicate mere information. The poet may sometimes indeed pursue verbal music for its own sake; more often, at least in first-rate poetry, it is an adjunct to the total meaning or communication of the poem.

There are two broad ways by which the poet achieves his musical quality: by his choice and arrangement of sounds, and by his arrangement of accents. In this chapter we will consider one aspect of the first of these.

An essential element in all music is repetition. In fact, we might say that all art consists of giving structure to two elements: repetition and variation. All things we enjoy greatly and lastingly, indeed, have these two elements. We enjoy the sea endlessly because it is always the same, yet always different. We enjoy a baseball game because it contains the same complex combination of pattern and variation. Our love of art, then, is rooted in human psychology. We like the familiar, we like variety, but we like them combined. If we get too much sameness, the result is monotony and tedium; if we get too much variety, the result is bewilderment and confusion. The composer of music, therefore, repeats certain musical tones; repeats them in certain combinations, or chords; and repeats them in certain patterns, or melodies. The poet likewise repeats certain sounds in certain combinations and arrangements, and thus gives organization and structure to his verse. Consider the following short example:

THE TURTLE

The turtle lives 'twixt plated decks
Which practically conceal its sex.
I think it clever of the turtle
In such a fix to be so fertile.

—*Ogden Nash* [1902–   ]

Here is a little joke, a paradox of animal life to which the author has cleverly drawn our attention. An experiment will show us, however, that much of its appeal lies not so much in what it says as in the manner in which it says it. If, for instance, we recast the verse as prose: "The turtle lives in a shell which almost conceals its sex. It is ingenious of the turtle, in such a situation, to be so prolific," the joke falls flat. Some of its appeal must lie in its metrical form. So now we cast it in unrimed verse:

Because he lives between two decks,
It's hard to tell a turtle's gender.
The turtle is a clever beast
In such a plight to be so fertile.

Here, perhaps, is *some* improvement, but still the piquancy of the original is missing. Much of that appeal must have consisted in the use of rime—the repetition of sound in *decks* and *sex, turtle* and *fertile*. So we try once more:

> The turtle lives 'twixt plated decks
> Which practically conceal its sex.
> I think it clever of the turtle
> In such a plight to be so fertile.

But for the perceptive reader there is still something missing—he does not at first see what—but some little touch that makes the difference between a good piece of verse and a little masterpiece in its kind. And then he sees it: *plight* has been substituted for *fix*.

But why should *fix* make such a difference? Its meaning is little different from that of *plight;* its only important difference is in sound. But there we are. The final *x* in *fix* catches up the concluding consonant sound in *sex*, and its initial *f* is repeated in the initial consonant sound of *fertile*. Not only do these sound recurrences provide a subtle gratification to the ear, but they also give the verse structure; they emphasize and draw together the key words of the piece: *sex, fix,* and *fertile*.

The poet may repeat any unit of sound from the smallest to the largest. He may repeat individual vowel and consonant sounds, whole syllables, words, phrases, lines, or groups of lines. In each instance, in a good poem, the repetition will serve several purposes: it will please the ear; it will emphasize those words in which the repetition occurs; and it will give structure to the poem. The popularity and initial impressiveness of such repetitions is evidenced by their becoming in many instances embedded in the language as clichés like "wild and woolly"; "first and foremost"; "footloose and fancy-free"; "penny-wise, pound-foolish"; "dead as a doornail"; "might and main"; "sink or swim"; "do or die"; "pell-mell"; "helter-skelter"; "harum-scarum"; "hocus-pocus." Some of these kinds of repetition have names, as we will see.

A syllable consists of a vowel sound which may be preceded or followed by consonant sounds. Any of these sounds may be repeated. The repetition of initial consonant sounds, as in "tried and true," "safe and sound," "fish or fowl," "rime or reason," is ALLITERATION. The repetition of vowel sounds, as in "mad as a hatter," "time out of mind," "free and easy," "slapdash," is ASSONANCE. The repetition of final consonant sounds, as in "first and last," "odds and ends," "short and sweet," "a stroke of luck," or Shakespeare's "struts and frets" (page 116) is CONSONANCE.[1]

[1] There is no established terminology for these various repetitions. *Alliteration* is used

Repetitions may be used alone or in combination. Alliteration and assonance are combined in such phrases as "time and tide," "thick and thin," "kith and kin," "alas and alack," "fit as a fiddle," and Edgar Allan Poe's famous line, "The viol, the violet, and the vine." Alliteration and consonance are combined in such phrases as "crisscross," "last but not least," "lone and lorn," "good as gold," or Rossetti's "gleams and glooms" (page 295) and Swinburne's "rains and ruins" (page 153). The combination of assonance and consonance is rime.

RIME (or rhyme) is the repetition of the accented vowel sound and all succeeding sounds. It is called MASCULINE when the rime sounds involve only one syllable, as in *decks* and *sex*, or *support* and *retort*. It is FEMININE when the rime sounds involve two or more syllables, as in *turtle* and *fertile*, or *spitefully* and *delightfully*. It is referred to as INTERNAL RIME when one or both riming words are *within* the line, and as END RIME when both riming words are at the *ends* of lines. End rime is probably the most frequently used and most consciously sought-after sound repetition employed in English poetry. Because it comes at the end of the line, it receives emphasis as a musical effect and perhaps contributes more than any other musical resource except rhythm and meter to give poetry its musical effect as well as its structure. There exists, however, a large body of poetry which does not employ rime, and for which rime would not be appropriate. Also, there has always been a tendency, especially noticeable in modern poetry, to substitute approximate rimes for perfect rimes at the ends of lines. APPROXIMATE RIMES include words with any kind of sound similarity, from close to fairly remote. Under approximate rime we include alliteration, assonance, and consonance or their combinations when used at the end of the line; half-rime (feminine rimes in which only half of the word rimes—the accented half, as in *lightly* and *frightful*, or the unaccented half, as in *yellow* and *willow*); and other similarities too elusive to name. The poems "Mary Hynes" (page 101), "Epitaph" (page 142), "Poem in October" (page 206), "Lord Randal" (page 211), and "Vergissmeinicht" (page 270) employ various kinds of approximate rime.

by some writers to mean any repetition of consonant sounds. *Assonance* has been used to mean the similarity as well as the identity of vowel sounds, or even the similarity of any sounds whatever. *Consonance* has often been reserved for words in which both the initial *and* final consonant sounds correspond, as in *green* and *groan*, *moon* and *mine*. *Rime* has been used to mean any sound repetition, including alliteration, assonance, and consonance. In the absence of clear agreement on the meanings of these terms, the terminology chosen has appeared most useful, with support in usage. Labels are useful in analysis. The student, however, should learn to recognize the devices, and, more important, to see their function, without worrying too much over nomenclature.

THAT NIGHT WHEN JOY BEGAN

That night when joy began
Our narrowest veins to flush,
We waited for the flash
Of morning's levelled gun.

But morning let us pass,   5
And day by day relief
Outgrew his nervous laugh,
Grows credulous of peace.

As mile by mile is seen
No trespasser's reproach,   10
And love's best glasses reach
No fields but are his own.

—*W. H. Auden* [1907–]

QUESTIONS

1. What has been the past experience with love of the two people in the poem? What is their present experience? What precisely is the tone of the poem?

2. What basic metaphor underlies the poem? Work it out stanza by stanza. What is "the flash of morning's levelled gun"? Does line 10 mean that no trespasser reproaches the lovers or that no one reproaches the lovers for being trespassers? Does *glasses* (11) refer to spectacles, tumblers, or field glasses? Point out three personifications.

3. The rime pattern in this poem is intricate and exact. Work it out, considering alliteration, assonance, and consonance.

In addition to the repetition of individual sounds and syllables, the poet may repeat whole words, phrases, lines, or groups of lines. When such repetition is done according to some fixed pattern, it is called a REFRAIN. The refrain is especially common in songlike poetry. Examples are to be found in Shakespeare's "Winter" (page 6) and "Spring" (page 11).

It is not to be thought that we have exhausted the possibilities of sound repetition by giving names to a few of the more prominent kinds. The complete study of possible kinds of sound repetition in poetry would be so complex that it would break down under its own machinery. Some of the subtlest and loveliest effects, indeed, escape our net of names. In as short a phrase as this from the prose of John Ruskin—"ivy as light and lovely as the vine"—

we notice alliteration in *light* and *lovely,* assonance in *ivy, light,* and *vine,* and consonance in *ivy* and *lovely,* but we have no name to connect the *v* in *vine* with the *v*'s in *ivy* and *lovely,* or the second *l* in *lovely* with the first *l,* or the final syllables of *ivy* and *lovely* with each other; but these are all an effective part of the music of the line. Also contributing to the music of poetry is the use of related rather than identical sounds, such as *m* and *n,* or *p* and *b,* or the vowel sounds in *boat, boot,* and *book.*

These various musical repetitions, for a trained reader, will ordinarily make an almost subconscious contribution to his reading of the poem: the reader will feel their effect without necessarily being aware of what has caused it. There is value, however, in occasionally analyzing a poem for these devices in order to increase awareness of them. A few words of caution are necessary. First, these repetitions are entirely a matter of sound; spelling is irrelevant. *Bear* and *pair* are rimes, but *through* and *rough* are not. *Cell* and *sin, folly* and *philosophy* alliterate, but *sin* and *sugar, gun* and *gem* do not. Second, alliteration, assonance, consonance, and masculine rime are matters which ordinarily involve only stressed or accented syllables; for only such syllables ordinarily make enough impression on the ear to be significant in the sound pattern of the poem. We should hardly consider *which* and *its* in the second line of "The Turtle," for instance, as an example of assonance, for neither word is stressed enough in the reading to make it significant as a sound. Third, the words involved in these repetitions must be close enough together that the ear retains the sound, consciously or subconsciously, from its first occurrence to its second. This distance will vary according to circumstances, but for alliteration, assonance, and consonance the words will ordinarily have to be in the same line or adjacent lines. End rime will bridge a longer gap.

WHEN THE HOUNDS OF SPRING

When the hounds of spring are on winter's traces,
 The mother of months in meadow or plain
Fills the shadows and windy places
 With lisp of leaves and ripple of rain;
And the brown bright nightingale amorous   5
Is half assuaged for Itylus,
For the Thracian ships and the foreign faces,
 The tongueless vigil, and all the pain.

Come with bows bent and with emptying of quivers,
  Maiden most perfect, lady of light,   10
With a noise of winds and many rivers,
  With a clamor of waters, and with might;
Bind on thy sandals, O thou most fleet,
Over the splendor and speed of thy feet;
For the faint east quickens, the wan west shivers,   15
  Round the feet of the day and the feet of the night.

Where shall we find her, how shall we sing to her,
  Fold our hands round her knees, and cling?
O that man's heart were as fire and could spring to her,
  Fire, or the strength of the streams that spring!   20
For the stars and the winds are unto her
As raiment, as songs of the harp-player;
For the risen stars and the fallen cling to her,
  And the southwest-wind and the west-wind sing.

For winter's rains and ruins are over,   25
  And all the season of snows and sins;
The days dividing lover and lover,
  The light that loses, the night that wins;
And time remembered is grief forgotten,
And frosts are slain and flowers begotten,   30
And in green underwood and cover
  Blossom by blossom the spring begins.

The full streams feed on flower of rushes,
  Ripe grasses trammel a traveling foot,
The faint fresh flame of the young year flushes   35
  From leaf to flower and flower to fruit;
And fruit and leaf are as gold and fire,
And the oat is heard above the lyre,
And the hoofèd heel of a satyr crushes
  The chestnut-husk at the chestnut-root,   40

And Pan by noon and Bacchus by night,
  Fleeter of foot than the fleet-foot kid,
Follows with dancing and fills with delight
  The Maenad and the Bassarid;
And soft as lips that laugh and hide   45
The laughing leaves of the trees divide,
And screen from seeing and leave in sight
  The god pursuing, the maiden hid.

The ivy falls with the Bacchanal's hair
   Over her eyebrows hiding her eyes;   50
The wild vine slipping down leaves bare
   Her bright breast shortening into sighs;
The wild vine slips with the weight of its leaves,
But the berried ivy catches and cleaves
To the limbs that glitter, the feet that scare   55
   The wolf that follows, the fawn that flies.

—*Algernon Charles Swinburne [1837–1909]*

QUESTIONS

1. Vocabulary: *assuaged* (6), *trammel* (34), *satyr* (39), *kid* (42).
2. What is the subject of the poem? What is its tone?
3. The poet views the coming of spring in terms of Greek mythology. Can you suggest reasons why? The "mother of months" (2) is Artemis, goddess of the moon and of wild nature, usually pictured as a virgin huntress with bow, arrows, and hounds. Lines 5–8 refer to the legend of Philomela, whose brother-in-law, the king of Thrace, violated her and cut out her tongue. In revenge, she and her sister served the king's son Itylus to him as food, and fled. Later she was changed into a nightingale. Bacchus (41) is the god of wine, and the Maenad and Bassarid (44) and Bacchanal (49) are female worshippers of Bacchus. What characteristics of spring does Swinburne describe? What activities of the gods does he recount? What is meant by "The light that loses, the night that wins" (28)?
4. Copy stanzas 1 and 5 (double space if you typewrite), and, using different-colored pencils, encircle and tie together all examples of alliteration, assonance, consonance, and rime. Do these exhaust the kinds of musical repetition which Swinburne uses in the poem?
5. Swinburne has been criticized because the "music" of many of his poems distracts from, rather than contributes to, their meaning. Do you think this criticism applicable to this poem?

We should not leave the impression that the use of these musical devices is necessarily or always valuable. Like the other resources of poetry, they can be judged only in the light of the poem's total intention. Many of the greatest works of English poetry—for instance, *Hamlet* and *King Lear* and *Paradise Lost*—do not employ end rime. Both alliteration and rime, especially feminine rime, if used excessively or unskillfully, become humorous or silly. If the intention is humorous, the result is delightful; if not, fatal. Shakespeare, who knew how to use all these devices to the utmost advantage, parodied their unskillful use in lines like "The preyful princess pierced and pricked a pretty pleasing pricket" in *Love's Labor's Lost* and

> Whereat with blade, with bloody, blameful blade,
> He bravely broached his boiling bloody breast

in *Midsummer Night's Dream.* Swinburne parodied his own highly alliterative style in "Nephelidia" with lines like "Life is the lust of a lamp for the light that is dark till the dawn of the day when we die." Used skillfully and judiciously, however, musical devices provide a palpable and delicate pleasure to the ear and, even more important, add dimension to meaning.

EXERCISE

Discuss the various ways in which the following poems make use of refrain: (a) "Winter" (page 6); (b) "Spring" (page 11); (c) "The House on the Hill" (page 88); (d) "Fine Flowers in the Valley" (page 104); (e) "Oh Who Is That Young Sinner" (page 174); (f) "The Barrel-Organ" (page 176); (g) "The Bench of Boors" (page 195); (h) "I sing of a maiden" (page 205); (i) "Edward" (page 209); (j) "Lord Randal" (page 211); (k) "Cha Till Maccruimein" (page 225); (l) "The Shield of Achilles" (page 257); (m) "Spring" (page 288); (n) "Doctor, doctor, a little of your love" (page 297); (o) "Do not go gentle into that good night" (page 303).

● ● ●

GOD'S GRANDEUR

> The world is charged with the grandeur of God.
> It will flame out, like shining from shook foil;
> It gathers to a greatness, like the ooze of oil
> Crushed. Why do men then now not reck his rod?
> Generations have trod, have trod, have trod;   5
> And all is seared with trade; bleared, smeared with toil;
> And wears man's smudge and shares man's smell: the soil
> Is bare now, nor can foot feel, being shod.
>
> And for all this, nature is never spent;
> There lives the dearest freshness deep down things;   10
> And though the last lights off the black West went
> Oh, morning, at the brown brink eastward, springs—
> Because the Holy Ghost over the bent
> World broods with warm breast and with ah! bright wings.

—Gerard Manley Hopkins [1844–1889]

1. What is the theme of this sonnet? How can it be compared with the theme of Wordsworth's sonnet "The World Is Too Much with Us" (page 34)?

2. The image in lines 3-4 refers probably to olive oil being collected in great vats from crushed olives. Explain the simile in line 2 and the symbols in lines 7-8 and 11-12.

3. Explain *reck his rod* (4), *spent* (9), *bent* (13).

4. Using different-colored pencils, encircle and connect examples of alliteration, assonance, consonance, and internal rime. Do these help to carry the meaning?

THE HARBOR

Passing through huddled and ugly walls,
By doorways when women haggard
Looked from their hunger-deep eyes,
Haunted with shadows of hunger-hands,
Out from the huddled and ugly walls,   5
I came sudden, at the city's edge,
On a blue burst of lake—
Long lake waves breaking under the sun
On a spray-flung curve of shore;
And a fluttering storm of gulls,   10
Masses of great gray wings
And flying white bellies
Veering and wheeling free in the open.

—*Carl Sandburg [1878–]*

QUESTIONS

1. Define as precisely as possible the contrast in content between the first five and the last seven lines of the poem. What qualities are symbolized by the gulls? What judgment is made by means of the contrast?

2. This poem is in free verse (without meter), and does not rime. But you should be able to find examples of assonance in almost every line. Underline or draw circles around the repeated vowels. What vowel sound dominates the first six lines? Does the pattern change in the last seven? If so, what function is served by this change?

3. What consonant sounds are most prominent in the first six lines? Is there a change in the last seven? Why?

PARTING, WITHOUT A SEQUEL

She has finished and sealed the letter
At last, which he so richly has deserved,
With characters venomous and hatefully curved,
And nothing could be better.

But even as she gave it   5
Saying to the blue-capped functioner of doom,
"Into his hands," she hoped the leering groom
Might somewhere lose and leave it.

Then all the blood
Forsook the face. She was too pale for tears,   10
Observing the ruin of her younger years.
She went and stood

Under her father's vaunting oak
Who kept his peace in wind and sun, and glistened
Stoical in the rain; to whom she listened   15
If he spoke.

And now the agitation of the rain
Rasped his sere leaves, and he talked low and gentle
Reproaching the wan daughter by the lintel;
Ceasing and beginning again.   20

Away went the messenger's bicycle,
His serpent's track went up the hill forever,
And all the time she stood there hot as fever
And cold as any icicle.

—*John Crowe Ransom* [1888–   ]

QUESTIONS

1. Identify the figures of speech in lines 3 and 22 and discuss their effectiveness. Are there traces of dramatic irony in the poem? Where?

2. Is the oak literal or figurative? Neither? Both? Discuss the meanings of *vaunting* (13), *stoical* (15), *sere* (18), and *lintel* (19).

3. Do you find any trite language in the poem? Where? What does it tell us about the girl's action?

4. W. H. Auden has defined poetry as "the clear expression of mixed feelings." Discuss the applicability of the definition to this poem. Try it out on other poems.

5. A feminine rime which involves two syllables is known also as a DOUBLE RIME. Find examples in the poem of both perfect and approximate double rimes. A feminine rime which involves three syllables is a TRIPLE

RIME. Find one example of a triple rime. Which lines employ masculine or SINGLE RIMES, either perfect or approximate?

COUNTING-OUT RHYME

Silver bark of beech, and sallow
Bark of yellow birch and yellow
Twig of willow.

Stripe of green in moosewood maple,
Color seen in leaf of apple,   5
Bark of popple.

Wood of popple pale as moonbeam,
Wood of oak for yoke and barn-beam
Wood of hornbeam.

Silver bark of beech, and hollow   10
Stem of elder, tall and yellow
Twig of willow.

—Edna St. Vincent Millay [1892–1950]

QUESTIONS

1. List all instances of alliteration, assonance, consonance, half-rime, internal rime, and word repetition.
2. How serious is the purpose of this poem?
3. What is a "counting-out rhyme"? Can you remember any from your childhood? What here is being counted?

SONG

The pints and the pistols, the pike-staves and pottles,
   The trooper's fierce shout and the toper's bold song;
O! theirs is such friendship that battles and bottles
   When going together can never go wrong.

The wine of the vintner, the blood of the Roundhead,   5
   The Cavalier taps them with equal delight;
And we are the boys for whom always abounded
   Good casks for the table, good casques for the fight.

Then thus do we drink to the flag and the flagon,
   The two stoutest allies the world ever saw;   10
For war without wine would so wearily drag on
   That none but a blockhead the bilbo would draw.

The can and the cannon sure never can bicker,
   Full quarts and free quarters shall still be our cry;
One hand draws the blade and the other the liquor,   15
   And grape is the best of all shot—when we're dry.

Drink sack and sack cities—whet swords and wet gullets,
   Nor blush, jolly boys, when we make it our boast
That friends as we are both to bowls and to bullets,
   We're not always fond of the charge of the host.   20

Who like not both swilling and killing are asses,
   For Bacchus was surely the brother of Mars;
So shrink not to charge to the muzzles your glasses
   And fire off a salvo for wine-cups and wars.

        —Attributed to *Winthrop Mackworth Praed* [1802–1839]

QUESTIONS

   1. Vocabulary: *pottles* (1), *toper* (2), *casques* (9), *bilbo* (12).
   2. In a drinking song we expect high spirits and jollity rather than profundity. How do the high spirits express themselves here in the very language itself? How many of the devices discussed in this chapter can you identify? How many puns do you count?

THE CHANGELING

Toll no bell for me, dear Father, dear Mother,
   Waste no sighs;
There are my sisters, there is my little brother
   Who plays in the place called Paradise,
Your children all, your children for ever;   5
   But I, so wild,
Your disgrace, with the queer brown face, was never,
   Never, I know, but half your child!

In the garden at play, all day, last summer,
   Far and away I heard   10
The sweet "tweet-tweet" of a strange new-comer,
   The dearest, clearest call of a bird.
It lived down there in the deep green hollow,
   My own old home, and the fairies say
The word of a bird is a thing to follow,   15
   So I was away a night and a day.

One evening, too, by the nursery fire,
   We snuggled close and sat round so still,
When suddenly as the wind blew higher,
   Something scratched on the window-sill.   20

A pinched brown face peered in—I shivered;
No one listened or seemed to see;
The arms of it waved and the wings of it quivered,
Whoo—I knew it had come for me;
Some are as bad as bad can be!   25
All night long they danced in the rain,
Round and round in a dripping chain,
Threw their caps at the window-pane,
Tried to make me scream and shout
And fling the bedclothes all about: 30
I meant to stay in bed that night,
And if only you had left a light
They would never have got me out!

Sometimes I wouldn't speak, you see,
Or answer when you spoke to me,   35
Because in the long, still dusks of Spring
You can hear the whole world whispering:
The shy green grasses making love,
The feathers grow on the dear, grey dove,
The tiny heart of the redstart beat,   40
The patter of the squirrel's feet,
The pebbles pushing in the silver streams,
The rushes talking in their dreams,
The swish-swish of the bat's black wings,
The wild-wood bluebell's sweet ting-tings,   45
Humming and hammering at your ear,
Everything there is to hear
In the heart of hidden things,
But not in the midst of the nursery riot.
That's why I wanted to be quiet,   50
Couldn't do my sums, or sing,
Or settle down to anything.
And when, for that, I was sent upstairs
I *did* kneel down to say my prayers;
But the King who sits on your high church steeple   55
Has nothing to do with us fairy people!

'Times I pleased you, dear Father, dear Mother,
Learned all my lessons and liked to play,
And dearly I loved the little pale brother
Whom some other bird must have called away.   60
Why did They bring me here to make me
Not quite bad and not quite good,
Why, unless They're wicked, do They want, in spite, to take me
Back to their wet, wild wood?

Now, every night I shall see the windows shining,   65
    The gold lamp's glow, and the fire's red gleam,
While the best of us are twining twigs and the rest of us are whining
        In the hollow by the stream.
Black and chill are Their nights on the wold;
    And They live so long and They feel no pain: 70
I shall grow up, but never grow old,
I shall always, always be very cold,
        I shall never come back again!

—*Charlotte Mew [1869–1928]*

QUESTIONS

1. Vocabulary: *redstart* (40), *wold* (69).

2. In fairy lore a changeling is a fairy child, usually defective in some way, which has been left in place of a stolen human baby. What kind of child is the speaker? What characteristics denote him as a changeling?

3. Two kinds of world are juxtaposed in the poem: the human world, and the fairy world. What kind of world is each? Does the contrast of the two, even though the fairy world is imaginary, help to illuminate the quality of the human world?

4. How does the speaker feel toward his family, the human world, and the fairy world? Which world does he prefer?

5. Take any ten or twelve lines of the poem and analyze them for internal rime, alliteration, assonance, consonance, masculine end rime, and feminine end rime. How is the effect of these devices different from their effect in the preceding poem?

AUTUMNUS

When the leaves in autumn wither,
    With a tawny tannèd face,
Warped and wrinkled-up together,
    The year's late beauty to disgrace:

There thy life's glass may'st thou find thee,
    Green now, gray now, gone anon;
    Leaving (worldling) of thine own,
Neither fruit, nor leaf behind thee.

—*Joshua Sylvester [1563–1618]*

QUESTIONS

1. To whom is the poem addressed? What is the *glass* (5)?

2. Discuss the contribution of musical devices to the structure and meaning of the poem.

12

Rhythm and Meter

Our love of rhythm and meter is rooted even deeper in us than our love for musical repetition. It is related to the beat of our hearts, the pulse of our blood, the intake and outflow of air from our lungs. Everything that we do naturally and gracefully we do rhythmically. There is rhythm in the way we walk, the way we swim, the way we ride a horse, the way we swing a golf club or a baseball bat. So native is rhythm to us that we read it, when we can, into the mechanical world around us. Our clocks go tick-tick-tick-tick, but we hear them go tick-tock, tick-tock in an endless trochaic. The click of railway wheels beneath us patterns itself into a tune in our heads. There is a strong appeal for us in language which is rhythmical.

The term RHYTHM refers to any wavelike recurrence of motion or sound. In speech it is the natural rise and fall of language. All language is to some degree rhythmical, for all language involves some kind of alternation between accented and unaccented syllables. Language varies considerably, however, in the degree to which it exhibits rhythm. In some forms of speech the rhythm is so unobtrusive or so unpatterned that we are scarcely, if at all, aware of it. In other forms of speech the rhythm is so pronounced that we may be tempted to tap our foot to it.

METER is the kind of rhythm we can tap our foot to. In lan-

162

guage which is metrical the accents are so arranged as to occur at apparently equal intervals of time, and it is this interval which we mark off with the tap of our foot. Metrical language is called VERSE. Nonmetrical language is PROSE. Not all poetry is metrical, nor is all metrical language poetry. *Verse* and *poetry* are not synonymous terms, nor is a *versifier* necessarily a *poet.*

The study of meter is a fascinating but highly complex subject. It is by no means an absolute prerequisite to an enjoyment, even a rich enjoyment, of poetry. But a knowledge of its fundamentals does have certain values. It can make the beginning reader more aware of the rhythmical effects of poetry and of how poetry should be read. It can enable the more advanced reader to analyze how certain effects are achieved, to see how rhythm is adapted to thought, and to explain what makes one poem (in this respect) better than another. The beginning student ought to have at least an elementary knowledge of the subject. It is not so difficult as its terminology might suggest.

In every word of more than one syllable, one syllable is *accented* or *stressed*, that is, given more prominence in pronunciation than the rest.[1] We say to*day*, to*mor*row, *yes*terday, *dai*ly, inter*vene.* If words of even one syllable are arranged into a sentence, we give certain words, or syllables, more prominence in pronunciation than the rest. We say: "He *went* to the *store,*" or "*Jack* is *driv*ing his *car.*" There is nothing mysterious about this; it is the normal process of language. The only difference between prose and verse is that in prose these accents occur more or less haphazardly; in verse the poet has arranged them to occur at regular intervals.

The word *meter* comes from a word meaning "measure." To measure something we must have a unit of measurement. For measuring length we use the inch, the foot, and the yard; for measuring time we use the second, the minute, and the hour. For measuring verse we use the foot, the line, and (sometimes) the stanza.

The basic metrical unit, the FOOT, consists normally of one accented syllable plus one or two unaccented syllables, though occasionally there may be no unaccented syllables, and very rarely there may be three. For diagramming verse, various systems of

---

[1] Though the words *accent* and *stress* are generally used interchangeably, as here, a distinction is sometimes made between them in technical discussions. *Accent,* the relative prominence given a syllable in relation to its neighbors, is then said to result from one or more of four causes: *stress,* or force of utterance, producing loudness; *duration; pitch;* and *juncture,* the manner of transition between successive sounds. Of these, *stress,* in English verse, is most important.

visual symbols have been invented. In this book we shall use a short curved line to indicate an unaccented syllable, a short horizontal line to indicate an accented syllable, and a vertical bar to indicate the division between feet. The basic kinds of feet are thus as follows:

Example	Name of Foot	Name of Meter[a]	
tŏ-dāy	Iamb	Iambic	⎫ Duple meters
dāi-lў	Trochee	Trochaic	⎭
ĭn-tĕr-vēne	Anapest	Anapestic	⎫ Triple meters
yēs-tĕr-dăy	Dactyl	Dactylic	⎭
dāy-brēak	Spondee	(Spondaic)	
dāy	Monosyllabic foot		

[a] In the spondee the accent is thought of as being distributed equally or almost equally over the two syllables and is sometimes referred to as a hovering accent. No whole poems are written in spondees or monosyllabic feet; hence there are only four basic meters: iambic, trochaic, anapestic, and dactylic. Iambic and trochaic are DUPLE METERS (because they employ two-syllable feet); anapestic and dactylic are TRIPLE METERS (because they employ three-syllable feet).

The secondary unit of measurement, the LINE, is measured by naming the number of feet in it. The following names are used:

Monometer	one foot	Pentameter	five feet
Dimeter	two feet	Hexameter	six feet
Trimeter	three feet	Heptameter	seven feet
Tetrameter	four feet	Octameter	eight feet

The third unit, the STANZA, consists of a group of lines whose metrical pattern is repeated throughout the poem. Since not all verse is written in stanzas, we shall save our discussion of this unit till a later chapter.

The process of measuring verse is referred to as SCANSION. To scan any specimen of verse, we do three things: (1) we identify the prevailing foot, (2) we name the number of feet in a line—if this length follows any regular pattern, and (3) we describe the stanza pattern—if there is one. Suppose we try out our skill on the poem "To Lucasta, Going to the Wars" (page 99).

The first step in scanning a poem is to read it normally, listening to where the accents fall, and perhaps keeping time with our hand. In "To Lucasta" we immediately run into difficulty, for the first line is highly irregular and may leave us uncertain as to just where the accents fall. Let us pass over it, then, and look for easier lines. Though the second stanza, we discover, is more regular than the first, the third stanza is most regular of the three. So let us begin with it. Lines 9, 11, and 12 go regularly, and we mark them as follows:

> ˘　—｜˘　—｜˘　—｜˘　—｜
> Yet this in-con-stan-cy is such
>
> As you too shall a-dore;　　　　　　　　　　10
>
> ˘　—｜˘　—｜˘　—｜˘　—｜
> I could not love thee, Dear, so much,
>
> 　　˘　—｜˘　—｜˘　—｜
> Loved I not Hon-or more.

Line 10 might also be marked regularly, but if we listen carefully we shall probably detect a slightly stronger stress on *too*, though it comes in an unstressed position, than on either of the adjacent syllables. So we'll mark it thus:

> ˘　—｜—　—｜˘　—｜
> As you too shall a-dore.

We now see that this stanza is written in lines of alternating iambic tetrameter and iambic trimeter. Knowing this, we return to the first and second stanzas, expecting them, since they look similar, to conform to a similar pattern.

In the second stanza, lines 7 and 8 are perfectly regular, so we mark them confidently, but lines 5 and 6 offer some variation. Here is what we hear:

> —　˘　—　˘　—　˘　—
> True, a new mis-tress now I chase,　　　　　　5
>
> ˘　—　—　˘　˘　—
> The first foe in the field;
>
> ˘　—｜˘　—｜˘　—｜˘　—｜
> And with a strong-er faith em-brace
>
> ˘　—｜˘　—｜˘　—｜
> A sword, a horse, a shield.

Since we are expecting lines 5 and 6 to conform to the established pattern, we shall assume that they are respectively a tetrameter and a trimeter line, and we shall mark the divisions between the feet in such a way as to yield the maximum number of iambs. The result is as follows:

$$\bar{\ }\ \ \smile | \ \bar{\ }\ \ \bar{\ } | \smile \ \bar{\ } | \smile \ \bar{\ } |$$
True, a new mis-tress now I chase,   5

$$\smile \ \bar{\ } | \bar{\ }\ \smile | \smile \ \bar{\ } |$$
The first foe in the field.

We are now ready for the difficult first stanza. Following the same process of, first, marking the accents where we hear them, and then dividing the feet so as to yield tetrameter and trimeter lines with the maximum possible number of iambic feet, we get something like the following:

$$\bar{\ }\ \ \smile | \ \bar{\ }\ \ \bar{\ } | \bar{\ }\ \smile | \smile \ \bar{\ } |$$
Tell me not, Sweet, I am un-kind,

$$\smile \ \bar{\ } | \smile \ \bar{\ } | \smile \ \bar{\ } |$$
That from the nun-ner-y   2

$$\smile \ \bar{\ } | \ \bar{\ }\ \ \bar{\ } | \smile \ \bar{\ } | \smile | \ \bar{\ } |$$
Of thy chaste breast and qui-et mind

$$\smile \ \bar{\ } | \smile \ \bar{\ } | \smile | \ \bar{\ } |$$
To war and arms I fly.

We are now ready to make a few generalizations about scansion:

(1) A good reader will not ordinarily stop to scan a poem he is reading, and certainly will not read a poem with the exaggerated emphasis on accented syllables that we sometimes give them in order to make the scansion more apparent. However, occasional scansion of a poem does have value. We hope to make this more apparent in the next chapter.

(2) Scansion is at best a gross way of describing the rhythmical quality of a poem. It depends on classifying all syllables into either accented or unaccented categories, and in ignoring the sometimes considerable difference between degrees of accent. Actually "accented" and "unaccented" are relative terms, and seldom will two syllables have exactly the same degree of accent. Whether we call a syllable accented or unaccented depends, moreover, on its degree of accent relative to the syllables on either side of it. In line 7 of "To Lucasta," for instance, the accent on *with* is not nearly so great as the accent on *strong*, and in line 2 the accent on the final *y* in *nunnery* is *lighter* than that on the *un*accented *thee* in line 11. Scansion therefore is incapable of dealing with the subtlest rhythmical effects in poetry. It is nevertheless a useful device, and probably any device more sensitive would be so complicated as to be no longer useful.

(3) Scansion is not an altogether exact science. Within certain

limits we may say that a certain scansion is right or wrong, but
beyond these limits there is legitimate room for personal interpretation and disagreement between qualified readers. Lines 11 and 12
of "To Lucasta," for instance, have been scanned above as perfectly
regular. But a different reader might read line 11 thus:

I could not love thee, Dear, so much,

or line 12 thus:

Loved I not Hon-or more.

The divisions between feet, moreover, are highly arbitrary and
have little meaning except to help us name the meter of the poem.
They correspond to no real divisions in the reading of the line,
coming often, as they do, in the middle of a word. They are placed
where they are usually only for the purpose of yielding the most
possible of a single kind of foot. Accordingly, line 6 has been
marked:

The first foe in the field,

though it might more plausibly have been marked:

The first foe in the field.

(4) Finally—and this is the most important generalization
of all—perfect regularity of meter is no criterion of merit. Beginning students sometimes get this notion. If the meter is smooth
and perfectly regular, they feel that the poet has handled his meter
successfully and deserves all credit for it. Actually there is nothing
easier than for any moderately talented versifier to make language
go ta-*dum* ta-*dum* ta-*dum*. But there are two reasons why this is
not generally desirable. The first is that, as we have said, all art
consists essentially of repetition and variation. If a meter alter-
nates too regularly between light and heavy beats, the result is to
banish variation; the meter becomes mechanical and, for any sensitive reader, monotonous. The second is that, once a basic meter
has been established, any deviations from it become highly significant and are the means by which the poet can use meter to reinforce meaning. If a meter is too perfectly regular, the probability
is that the poet, instead of adapting rhythm to meaning, has simply
forced his meaning into a metrical strait jacket.

Actually what gives the skillful use of meter its greatest effectiveness is that it consists, not of one rhythm, but of two. One of

167

these is the *expected* rhythm. The other is the *heard* rhythm. Once we have determined the basic meter of a poem, say, iambic tetrameter, we have an expectation that this rhythm will continue. Thus a silent drumbeat is set up in our minds, and this drumbeat constitutes the expected rhythm. But the actual rhythm of the words —the heard rhythm—will sometimes confirm this expected rhythm and sometimes not. Thus the two rhythms are counterpointed against each other, and the appeal of the verse is magnified just as when two melodies are counterpointed against each other in music, or as when we see two swallows flying together and around each other, following the same general course but with individual variations, and making a much more eye-catching pattern than one swallow flying alone. If the heard rhythm conforms too closely to the expected rhythm, the meter becomes dull and uninteresting. If it departs too far from the expected rhythm, there ceases to be an expected rhythm. If the irregularity is too great, meter disappears, and the result is prose rhythm or free verse.

There are several ways by which variation can be introduced into the poet's use of meter. The most obvious way is by the substitution of different kinds of feet for regular feet. In our scansion of "To Lucasta," for instance, we noted one spondaic and two trochaic substitutions in the very first line. A less obvious but equally important means of variation is through simple phrasing and variation of degrees of accent. Lines 2, 4, 8, and 12 of "To Lucasta" have all been marked as regular, but actually there is considerable difference between them. Line 4 is quite regular, for the phrasing corresponds with the metrical pattern, and the line can be read ta-*dum* ta-*dum* ta-*dum*. Line 8 is even more regular, for the unaccented syllables are all *very* light, the accented syllables are all *very* strong, and the divisions between the feet are marked off by grammatical pauses indicated in the punctuation. This line goes ta-*dumm!* ta-*dumm!* ta-*dumm!* Line 12, on the other hand, is less regular, because the word *Honor* cuts across the division between two feet. We should read it ta-*dum* ta-*dum*pty *dum.* And line 2 is even less regular because not only does *nunnery* cut across the division between two feet, but its final syllable is so lightly stressed as hardly to be accented at all. We should read this line something like ta-*dum* ta-*dum*pteree. Finally, variation can be introduced by grammatical and rhetorical pauses. Line 11 of "To Lucasta," though scanned as regular, actually introduces variation because of the pause indicated by the commas around *Dear.*

The uses of rhythm and meter are several. Like the musical

repetitions of sound, the musical repetitions of accent can be pleasing for their own sake. In addition, rhythm works as an emotional stimulus and serves, when used skillfully, to heighten our attention and awareness to what is going on in a poem. Finally, by his choice of meter, and by his skillful use of variation within the metrical framework, the poet can adapt the sound of his verse to its content and thus make meter a powerful reinforcement of meaning. We should avoid, however, the notion that there is any mystical correspondence between certain meters and certain emotions. There are no "happy" meters and no "melancholy" ones. The poet's choice of meter is probably less important than how he handles it after he has chosen it. However, some meters are swifter than others, some slower; some are more lilting than others, some more dignified. The poet can choose a meter that is appropriate or one that is inappropriate to his content, and by his handling of it can increase the appropriateness or inappropriateness. If he chooses a swift, lilting meter for a serious and grave subject, the meter will probably act to keep the reader from feeling any really deep emotion. But if he chooses a more dignified meter, it will intensify the emotion. In all great poetry meter works intimately with the other elements of the poem to produce the appropriate total effect.

We must not forget, of course, that poetry need not be metrical at all. Like alliteration and rime, like metaphor and irony, like even imagery, meter is simply one resource which the poet may or may not use. His job is to employ his resources to the best advantage for the object he has in mind—the kind of experience he wishes to express. And on no other basis can we judge him.

EXERCISES

1. Two additional terms which every student should be familiar with and should be careful to discriminate between are *blank verse* and *free verse*. BLANK VERSE is a very specific meter: *iambic pentameter, unrimed*. It has a special name because it is the principal English meter, that is, the meter that has been used for a large proportion of the greatest English poetry, including the tragedies of Shakespeare and the epics of Milton. Iambic pentameter in English seems especially suitable for the serious treatment of serious themes. The natural movement of the English language tends to be iambic. Lines shorter than pentameter tend to be songlike, not suited to *sustained* treatment of serious material. Lines longer than pentameter tend to break up into shorter units, the hexameter line being read as two three-foot units, the heptameter line as a four-foot and a three-foot unit, and so on. Rime, while highly appropriate to most short poems, often proves a handicap for a long and lofty work. (The word *blank* implies that the end

169

of the line is "blank," i.e., bare of rime.) The above generalizations, of course, represent tendencies, not laws.

FREE VERSE, by our definition, is not verse at all; that is, it is not metrical. It may be rimed or unrimed. The word *free* means that it is free of metrical restrictions. The only difference between free verse and rhythmical prose is that free verse introduces one additional rhythmical unit, the line. The arrangement into lines divides the material into rhythmical units or cadences. Beyond its line arrangement there are no necessary differences between it and rhythmical prose.

Of the following poems, some are in free verse (*F*), some in blank verse (*B*), and some in other (*O*) meters. Determine into which category each belongs, and indicate by putting an *F*, *B*, or *O* in the blank space: "Dulce et Decorum Est" (page 8) ...., "Cavalry Crossing a Ford" (page 67) ...., "Exspecto Resurrectionem" (page 77) ...., "Ulysses" (page 79) ...., "Patterns" (page 82) ...., " 'Out, Out—' " (page 114) ...., "A Christmas Tree" (page 213) ...., "The Trees in the Garden" (page 264) ...., "Days" (page 271) ...., "City Life" (page 283) .....

2. Another useful distinction is that between end-stopped lines and run-on lines. An END-STOPPED LINE is one in which the end of the line corresponds with a natural speech pause; a RUN-ON LINE is one in which the sense of the line hurries on into the next line. (There are, of course, all degrees of end-stop and run-on. A line ending with a period or semicolon is heavily end-stopped. A line without punctuation at the end but representing a slight pause between phrases or sense units would be lightly end-stopped.) The use of run-on lines is one way the poet can make use of grammatical or rhetorical pauses to vary his basic meter. Examine, for instance, Swift's "A Description of the Morning" (page 51) and Browning's "My Last Duchess" (page 109). Both of these poems are written in the same meter: iambic pentameter, rimed in couplets. Is their general rhythmical effect quite similar or markedly different? What accounts for the difference? Does this contrast support our statement that the poet's choice of meter is probably less important than the way he handles it?

• • •

LOVELIEST OF TREES

Loveliest of trees, the cherry now
Is hung with bloom along the bough,
And stands about the woodland ride
Wearing white for Eastertide.

Now, of my threescore years and ten,   5
Twenty will not come again,
And take from seventy springs a score,
It only leaves me fifty more.

And since to look at things in bloom
Fifty springs are little room,   10
About the woodlands I will go
To see the cherry hung with snow.

—A. E. Housman [1859–1936]

QUESTIONS

1. Very briefly, this poem presents a philosophy of life. In a sentence, what is it?
2. How old is the speaker? Why does he assume that his life will be seventy years in length? What is surprising about the words *only* (8) and *little* (10)?
3. A good deal of ink has been spilt over whether *snow* (12) is literal or figurative. What do you say? Justify your answer.
4. Scan the poem, identify its meter, and point out the principal variations from the expected rhythm.

THE OAK

Live thy Life,
    Young and old,
Like yon oak,
Bright in spring,
    Living gold;   5

Summer-rich
    Then; and then
Autumn-changed,
Soberer-hued
    Gold again.   10

All his leaves
    Fall'n at length,
Look, he stands,
Trunk and bough,
    Naked strength.   15

—Alfred, Lord Tennyson [1809–1892]

QUESTIONS

1. Scan the poem without putting in the bar divisions. Should this poem be regarded as iambic or trochaic? Or could it be either? Some metrists have discarded the traditional distinction between iambic and trochaic and between anapestic and dactylic as being artificial. The only real distinction, they feel,

is between duple and triple meters. Does this poem support their claim?

2. With the above question in mind, turn to Donne's "Song" in Part Two (page 269) and scan it. How would you classify it?

THE "JE NE SAIS QUOI"

Yes, I'm in love, I feel it now,
　And Celia has undone me;
And yet I'll swear I can't tell how
　The pleasing plague stole on me.

'Tis not her face that love creates,　　　　　　　　5
　For there no Graces revel;
'Tis not her shape, for there the Fates
　Have rather been uncivil.

'Tis not her air, for sure in that,
　There's nothing more than common;　　　　　　10
And all her sense is only chat,
　Like any other woman.

Her voice, her touch, might give the alarm—
　'Tis both perhaps, or neither;
In short, 'tis that provoking charm　　　　　　　15
　Of Celia altogether.

—William Whitehead [1715–1785]

QUESTIONS

1. *Je ne sais quoi* is a French expression meaning "I do not know what" —an indefinable something. Does the use of approximate rimes rather than perfect rimes in the even lines of this poem help to establish the quality of uncertainty which is the subject of the poem?

2. Find examples of *oxymoron* (page 112) in the first and last stanzas. What broad paradox underlies the whole poem?

3. What is the reason for the capitalization and pluralization of grace and fate in the second stanza? What is the image here conveyed? Is *love* (5) the subject or object of the verb?

4. Because of the feminine rimes of the even-numbered lines, you will find, on scanning the poem, that there is an extra unaccented syllable left over in these lines. For instance, the first two lines may be scanned as follows:

$$\breve{}\ -\ |\breve{}\ -\ |\breve{}\ -|\breve{}\ -\ |$$
Yes, I'm in love, I feel it now,

$$\breve{}\ -|\breve{}\ -|\breve{}\ -\ |\breve{}$$
And Cel-ia has un-done me.

It will often happen that one or two unaccented syllables are left over—at the end of the line with iambic and anapestic meter, at the beginning of the line with trochaic and dactylic meter. Although we ignore these unaccented extras in naming the meter (the above poem is written in alternating iambic tetrameter and iambic trimeter), they make considerable difference in the rhythmical effect. They are another way in which the poet can vary his basic meter.

5. All the lines of Tennyson's "The Oak" begin and end with accented syllables (the rimes are masculine); half of the lines of "The 'Je Ne Sais Quoi'" begin and end with unaccented syllables (and have feminine rimes). Do you see any correlation between this metrical difference of the two poems and their difference of subject? Could the subject matter of either poem be treated as successfully in the meter of the other?

IF EVERYTHING HAPPENS THAT CAN'T BE DONE

if everything happens that can't be done
(and anything's righter
than books
could plan)
the stupidest teacher will almost guess   5
(with a run
skip
around we go yes)
there's nothing as something as one

one hasn't a why or because or although   10
(and buds know better
than books
don't grow)
one's anything old being everything new
(with a what   15
which
around we come who)
one's everyanything so

so world is a leaf so tree is a bough
(and birds sing sweeter   20
than books
tell how)
so here is away and so your is a my
(with a down
up   25
around again fly)
forever was never till now

now i love you and you love me
(and books are shuter
than books   30
can be)
and deep in the high that does nothing but fall
(with a shout
each
around we go all)   35
there's somebody calling who's we

we're anything brighter than even the sun
(we're everything greater
than books
might mean)   40
we're everyanything more than believe
(with a spin
leap
alive we're alive)
we're wonderful one times one   45

—*e. e. cummings* [1894–1962]

QUESTIONS

1. Explain the last line. Of what very familiar idea is this poem a fresh treatment?

2. The poem is based on a contrast between heart and mind, or love and learning. Which does the poet prefer? What symbols does he use for each?

3. What is the tone of the poem?

4. Which lines of each stanza regularly rime with each other (either perfect or approximate rime)? How does the poet link the stanzas together?

5. What is the basic metrical scheme of the poem?

6. Can you suggest any reason why the poet prints lines 2–4 and 6–8 of each stanza as three lines rather than one? What metrical variations does the poet use in lines 6–8 of each stanza, and with what effect?

OH WHO IS THAT YOUNG SINNER

Oh who is that young sinner with the handcuffs on his wrists?
And what has he been after that they groan and shake their fists?
And wherefore is he wearing such a conscience-stricken air?
Oh they're taking him to prison for the color of his hair.

'Tis a shame to human nature, such a head of hair as his;   5
In the good old time 'twas hanging for the color that it is;
Though hanging isn't bad enough and flaying would be fair
For the nameless and abominable color of his hair.

Oh a deal of pains he's taken and a pretty price he's paid
To hide his poll or dye it of a mentionable shade;   10
But they've pulled the beggar's hat off for the world to see and stare,
And they're taking him to justice for the color of his hair.

Now 'tis oakum for his fingers and the treadmill for his feet,
And the quarry-gang on Portland in the cold and in the heat,
And between his spells of labor in the time he has to spare   15
He can curse the God that made him for the color of his hair.

—A. E. Housman [1859–1936]

QUESTIONS

1. Vocabulary: *poll* (10), *oakum* (13). *Portland* (14), an English penin-
sula, is the site of a famous criminal prison.
2. What kind of irony does the poem exhibit? Explain.
3. What symbolical meanings are suggested by "the color of his hair"?
4. This poem represents a kind of meter that we have not yet discussed.
It *may* be scanned as iambic heptameter:

Oh who is that young sin-ner with the hand-cuffs on his wrists?

But you will probably find yourself reading it as a four-beat line:

Oh who is that young sin-ner with the hand-cuffs on his wrists?

Although the meter is duple insofar as there is an alternation between unaccented and accented syllables, there is also an alternation in the degree of
stress on the accented syllables: the first, third, fifth, and seventh stresses being heavier than the second, fourth, and sixth; the result is that the two-
syllable feet tend to group themselves into larger units. We may scan it as
follows, using a short line for a light accent, a longer one for a heavy accent:

Oh who is that young sin-ner with the hand-cuffs on his wrists?
And what has he been af-ter that they groan and shake their fists?
And where-fore is he wear-ing such a con-science-strick-en air?
Oh they're tak-ing him to pris-on for the col-or of his hair.

This kind of meter, in which there is an alternation between heavy and light
stresses, is known as DIPODIC (two-footed) VERSE. The alternation may not be
perfect throughout, but it will be frequent enough to establish a pattern in the
reader's mind. Now scan the last three stanzas.
5. For other examples of dipodic verse, see "John Gorham (page 30) and
"America for Me" (page 230).

THE BARREL-ORGAN

There's a barrel-organ carolling across a golden street
    In the City as the sun sinks low,
With a silvery cry of linnets in its dull mechanic beat,
    As it dies into the sunset glow;
And it pulses through the pleasures of the City and the pain   5
    That surround the singing organ like a large eternal light;
And they've given it a glory and a part to play again
    In the Symphony that rules the day and night.

And now it's marching onward through the realms of old romance,
    And trolling out a fond familiar tune,   10
And now it's roaring cannon down to fight the King of France,
    And now it's prattling softly to the moon,
And all around the organ there's a sea without a shore
    Of human joys and wonders and regrets,
To remember and to recompense the music evermore   15
    For what the cold machinery forgets. . . .

        Yes; as the music changes,
            Like a prismatic glass,
        It takes the light and ranges
            Through all the moods that pass;   20
        Dissects the common carnival
            Of passions and regrets,
        And gives the world a glimpse of all
            The colors it forgets.

        And there *La Traviata* sighs   25
            Another sadder song;
        And there *Il Trovatore* cries
            A tale of deeper wrong;
        And bolder knights to battle go
            With sword and shield and lance,   30
        Than ever here on earth below
            Have whirled into—*a dance!*—

Go down to Kew in lilac-time, in lilac-time, in lilac-time;
    Go down to Kew in lilac-time (it isn't far from London!)
And you shall wander hand in hand with love in summer's wonderland;   35
    Go down to Kew in lilac-time (it isn't far from London!)

The cherry-trees are seas of bloom and soft perfume and sweet perfume,
    The cherry-trees are seas of bloom (and oh, so near to London!)
And there they say, when dawn is high and all the world's a blaze of sky
    The cuckoo, though he's very shy, will sing a song for London.   40

The Dorian nightingale is rare and yet they say you'll hear him there
   At Kew, at Kew in lilac-time (and oh, so near to London!)
The linnet and the throstle, too, and after dark the long halloo
   And golden-eyed *tu-whit, tu-whoo* of owls that ogle London.

For Noah hardly knew a bird of any kind that isn't heard   45
   At Kew, at Kew in lilac-time (and oh, so near to London!)
And when the rose begins to pout and all the chestnut spires are out
   You'll hear the rest without a doubt, all chorusing for London:—

Come down to Kew in lilac-time, in lilac-time, in lilac-time;
   Come down to Kew in lilac-time (it isn't far from London!)   50
And you shall wander hand in hand with love in summer's wonderland;
   Come down to Kew in lilac-time (it isn't far from London!)

And then the troubadour begins to thrill the golden street,
   In the City as the sun sinks low;
And in all the gaudy busses there are scores of weary feet   55
Marking time, sweet time, with a dull mechanic beat,
And a thousand hearts are plunging to a love they'll never meet,
Through the meadows of the sunset, through the poppies and the wheat,
   In the land where the dead dreams go.

             .   .   .   .   .

              So it's Jeremiah, Jeremiah,   60
                  What have you to say
              When you meet the garland girls
                  Tripping on their way?

              All around my gala hat
                  I wear a wreath of roses
              (A long and lonely year it is
                  I've waited for the May!)
              If any one should ask you,
                  The reason why I wear it is—
              My own love, my true love   70
                  Is coming home to-day.

And it's buy a bunch of violets for the lady
   (*It's lilac-time in London; it's lilac-time in London!*)
Buy a bunch of violets for the lady
   While the sky burns blue above: 75

On the other side the street you'll find it shady
   (*It's lilac-time in London; it's lilac-time in London!*)
But buy a bunch of violets for the lady,
   And tell her she's your own true love.

                                                        177

There's a barrel-organ carolling across a golden street   **80**
    In the City as the sun sinks glittering and slow;
And the music's not immortal; but the world has made it sweet
And enriched it with the harmonies that make a song complete
In the deeper heavens of music where the night and morning meet,
    As it dies into the sunset-glow;   **85**
And it pulses through the pleasures of the City and the pain
    That surround the singing organ like a large eternal light,
And they've given it a glory and a part to play again
    In the Symphony that rules the day and night.

           And there, as the music changes,   **90**
              The song runs round again.
           Once more it turns and ranges
              Through all its joy and pain,
           Dissects the common carnival
              Of passions and regrets;   **95**
           And the wheeling world remembers all
              The wheeling song forgets.

           Once more *La Traviata* sighs
              Another sadder song:
           Once more *Il Trovatore* cries   **100**
              A tale of deeper wrong;
           Once more the knights to battle go
              With sword and shield and lance
           Till once, once more, the shattered foe
              Has whirled into—*a dance!*   **105**

Come down to Kew in lilac-time, in lilac time, in lilac-time;
    Come down to Kew in lilac-time (it isn't far from London!)
And you shall wander hand in hand with love in summer's wonderland;
    Come down to Kew in lilac-time (it isn't far from London!)

                                   —*Alfred Noyes [1880–1958]*

QUESTIONS

1. A barrel-organ is a mechanical hand organ played by turning a crank.
The City is the business section of London. Kew, a suburb of London, is
famous for its large public gardens. *La Traviata* and *Il Trovatore* are popular
operas by Verdi. What precisely is the hour of the day in the poem?
2. The poem describes the music of the barrel-organ and its effect on the
people on the street. Lines 17–52, 60–79, and 90–109 represent melodies played
by the organ. How many different melodies are metrically indicated? What effect does the music have on the people? Do the people have any effect on the
music?

3. The four-line refrain with which the poem ends is about as appealing for pure melodiousness as anything in poetry. Analyze the musical devices which it makes use of and try to account for its effectiveness.

4. The narrative stanzas and two of the songs are in dipodic verse and illustrate additional varieties of dipodic feet. Notice that a dipodic foot (like a spondee in duple meter) *may* have no unaccented syllables at all:

> — ⌣ —|⌣ — ⌣ —|⌣ — ⌣— ⌣ — ⌣ — |
> There's a bar-rel-or-gan car-ol-ling a-cross a gold-en street
>
> ⌣ ⌣ —|⌣ — ⌣ — | — — |
> In the Cit-y as the sun sinks low.

An additional variation is the metrical pause or rest. Unlike grammatical and rhetorical pauses, the metrical pause affects the scansion. If you beat out the rhythm of lines 72–75 with your hand, you will find that some of the beats fall *between* syllables. The METRICAL PAUSE, then, is a pause which replaces an accented syllable. It is usually found in verse that has a pronounced lilt or swing. We have represented it in the scansion with an *x*:

> ⌣ ⌣ — | ⌣ — ⌣ —|⌣ ⌣ — ⌣ —|⌣ x
> And it's buy a bunch of vi-o-lets for the la-dy
>
> ⌣⌣ —|⌣ — ⌣ —| ⌣ x⌣ —|⌣ — ⌣ —| ⌣ x
> (*It's li-lac-time in Lon-don; it's li-lac-time in Lon-don!*)
>
> —|⌣ — ⌣—|⌣ ⌣ — ⌣ —|⌣ x
> Buy a bunch of vi-o-lets for the la-dy
>
> ⌣ ⌣ —| — —|x⌣ — |
> While the sky burns blue a-bove.

Scan the rest of this song, and also the song before it, looking out for metrical pauses.

METRICAL FEET

> — ⌣ — ⌣ — ⌣ —
> Trochee trips from long to short.
>
> From long to long in solemn sort
>
> — — — — — —
> Slow Spondee stalks; strong foot! yet ill able
>
> — ⌣ ⌣ — ⌣ ⌣ — ⌣ ⌣ —⌣ ⌣
> Ever to come up with Dactyl trisyllable.
>
> ⌣ — ⌣ — ⌣ — —
> Iambics march from short to long.
>
> ⌣ ⌣ — ⌣ ⌣ — ⌣ ⌣ — ⌣⌣ —
> With a leap and a bound the swift Anapests throng.

> —*Samuel Taylor Coleridge [1772–1834]*

QUESTION

1. If you have trouble remembering the metrical feet, memorize this.

179

13

Sound and Meaning

Rhythm and sound co-operate to produce what we call the music of poetry. This music, as we have pointed out, may serve two general functions: first it may be enjoyable in itself; second, it may be used to reinforce meaning and intensify the communication.

Pure pleasure in sound and rhythm exists from a very early age in the human being—probably from the age the baby first starts cooing in its cradle, certainly from the age that children begin chanting nursery rimes and skipping rope. The appeal of the following verse, for instance, depends almost entirely on its "music":

$$- \mid - \quad \smile \mid - \mid$$
Pease por-ridge hot,
$$- \mid - \quad \smile \mid - \mid$$
Pease por-ridge cold,
$$- \mid - \quad \smile \mid - \quad \smile \mid - \mid$$
Pease por-ridge in the pot
$$- \mid - \mid - \mid$$
Nine days old.

There is very little sense here; the attraction comes from the emphatic rhythm, the emphatic rimes (with a strong contrast between the short vowel and short final consonant of *hot-pot* and the long vowel and long final consonant combination of *cold-old*), and the heavy alliteration (exactly half the words begin with *p*).

From nonsense rimes such as this, many of us graduate into a love of more meaningful poems whose appeal resides largely in the sound they make. Much of the pleasure that we find in Swinburne's "When the Hounds of Spring" (page 152) lies in its musical quality. Other famous examples are Vachel Lindsay's "The Congo," Edgar Allan Poe's "The Bells," and Alfred Noyes's "The Barrel-Organ."

The peculiar function of poetry as distinguished from music, however, is to convey, not sounds, but meaning or experience *through* sounds. In third- and fourth-rate poetry sound and rhythm sometimes distract attention from sense. In first-rate poetry the sound exists, not for its own sake, not for mere decoration, but as a medium of meaning. Its function is to support the leading player, not to steal the scene.

There are numerous ways in which the poet may reinforce meaning through sound. Without claiming to exhaust them, perhaps we can include most of the chief means under four general headings.

First, the poet can choose words whose sound in some degree suggests their meaning. In its narrowest sense this is called onomatopoeia. ONOMATOPOEIA, strictly defined, means the use of words which, at least supposedly, sound like what they mean, such as *hiss, snap,* and *bang.*

SONG

> Hark, hark!
>   Bow-wow.
> The watch-dogs bark!
>   Bow-wow.
> Hark, hark! I hear
> The strain of strutting chanticleer
> Cry, "Cock-a-doodle-doo!"

—William Shakespeare [1564–1616]

In this lyric, *bark, bow-wow,* and *cock-a-doodle-doo* are onomatopoetic words. In addition Shakespeare has reinforced the onomatopoetic effect with the repeated use of *hark,* which sounds like *bark.* The usefulness of onomatopoeia, of course, is strictly limited, because it can be used only where the poet is describing sound, and most poems do not describe sound. And the use of pure onomatopoeia, as in the above example, is likely to be fairly trivial except as it forms an incidental part of a more complex poem. But by combining onomatopoeia with other devices which help convey

181

meaning, the poet can achieve subtle and beautiful effects whose recognition is one of the keenest pleasures in reading poetry.

In addition to onomatopoetic words there is another group of words, sometimes called PHONETIC INTENSIVES, whose sound, by a process as yet obscure, to some degree suggests their meaning. An initial *fl-* sound, for instance, is often associated with the idea of moving light, as in *flame, flare, flash, flicker, flimmer;* an initial *gl-* also frequently accompanies the idea of light, usually unmoving, as in *glare, gleam, glint, glow, glisten.* An initial *sl-* often introduces words meaning "smoothly wet," as in *slippery, slick, slide, slime, slop, slosh, slobber, slushy.* Short *-i-* often goes with the idea of smallness, as in *inch, imp, thin, slim, little, bit, chip, sliver, chink, slit, sip, whit, tittle, snip, wink, glint, glimmer, flicker, pigmy, midge, chick, kid, kitten, minikin, miniature.* Long *-o-* or *-oo-* may suggest melancholy or sorrow, as in *moan, groan, woe, mourn, forlorn, toll, doom, gloom, moody.* Medial and final *-are* sometimes goes with the idea of a big light or noise, as *flare, glare, stare, blare.* Medial *-att-* suggests some kind of particled movement, as in *spatter, scatter, shatter, chatter, rattle, prattle, clatter, batter.* Final *-er* and *-le* indicate repetition, as in *glitter, flutter, shimmer, whisper, jabber, chatter, clatter, sputter, flicker, twitter, mutter,* and *ripple, bubble, twinkle, sparkle, rattle, rumble, jingle.* None of these various sounds is invariably associated with the idea which it seems to suggest, and, in fact, a short *-i-* is found in *thick* as well as *thin,* in *big* as well as *little.* Language is a complex phenomenon. But there is enough association between these sounds and ideas to suggest some sort of intrinsic if obscure relationship, and a word like *flicker,* though not onomatopoetic, for it does not refer to sound, would seem somehow to suggest its sense, the *fl-* suggesting moving light, the *-i-* suggesting smallness, the *-ck-* suggesting sudden cessation of movement (as in *crack, peck, pick, hack,* and *flick*), and the *-er* suggesting repetition. The above list of sound-idea correspondences is only a very partial one. A complete list, though it would involve only a small proportion of words in the language, would probably be a longer list than that of the more strictly onomatopoetic words, to which they are related.

SPLINTER

> The voice of the last cricket
> across the first frost
> is one kind of good-by.
> It is so thin a splinter of singing.

> —*Carl Sandburg [1878–]*

1. Why is "so thin a splinter" a better choice of metaphor than "so small an atom" or "so meager a morsel"?

2. How does the poet intensify the effect of the two phonetic intensives in line 4?

Second, the poet can choose sounds and group them so that the effect is smooth and pleasant sounding (*euphonious*) or rough and harsh sounding (*cacophonous*). The vowels, for instance, are in general more pleasing than the consonants, for the vowels are musical tones, whereas the consonants are merely noises. A line with a high percentage of vowel sounds in proportion to consonant sounds will therefore tend to be more melodious than one in which the proportion is low. The vowels and consonants themselves differ considerably in quality. The "long" vowels, such as those in *fate, reed, rime, coat, food,* and *dune* are fuller and more resonant than the "short" vowels, as in *fat, red, rim, cot, foot,* and *dun.* Of the consonants, some are fairly mellifluous, such as the "liquids," *l, m, n,* and *r;* the soft *v* and *f* sounds; the semi-vowels *w* and *y;* and such combinations as *th* and *wh.* Others, such as the "explosives," *b, d, g, k, p,* and *t,* are harsher and sharper in their effect. These differences in sound are the poet's materials. He will not necessarily seek out those sounds which are pleasing, however, and attempt to combine them in melodious combinations. Rather, he will use euphonious and cacophonous combinations as they are appropriate to his content. Consider, for instance, the following poem:

UPON JULIA'S VOICE

So smooth, so sweet, so silv'ry is thy voice,
As, could they hear, the Damned would make no noise,
But listen to thee (walking in thy chamber)
Melting melodious words to Lutes of Amber.

—*Robert Herrick [1591–1674]*

1. Literally, an amber lute is as nonsensical as a silver voice. What connotations do *amber* and *silv'ry* have which contribute to the meaning of this poem?

There are no strictly onomatopoetic words in this poem, and yet the sound seems marvelously adapted to the sense. Especially remarkable are the first and last lines, those most directly concerned with Julia's voice. In the first line the sounds which most strike the ear are the unvoiced *s*'s and the soft *v*'s, supported by *th*: "So *smooth*, so *sweet*, so *silv'ry* is thy *voice*." In the fourth line the predominating sounds are the liquid consonants *m*, *l*, and *r*, supported by a *w*: "*Melting melodious words* to *lutes* of *amber*." The least euphonious line in the poem, on the other hand, is the second, where the subject is the tormented in hell, not Julia's voice. Here the prominent sounds are the *d*'s, supported by a voiced *s* (a voiced *s* buzzes, unlike the unvoiced *s*'s in line 1), and two *k* sounds: "As, *could* they hear, the *damned* would *make* no noi*s*e." Throughout the poem there is a remarkable correspondence between the pleasant-sounding and the pleasant in idea, the unpleasant-sounding and the unpleasant in idea.

A third way in which a poet can reinforce meaning through sound is by controlling the speed and movement of his lines by his choice and use of meter, by his choice and arrangement of vowel and consonant sounds, and by his disposition of pauses. In meter the unaccented syllables go faster than the accented syllables; hence the triple meters are swifter than the duple. But the poet can vary the tempo of any meter by the use of substitute feet. Whenever two or more unaccented syllables come together, the effect will be to speed up the pace of the line; when two or more accented syllables come together, the effect will be to slow it down. This pace will also be affected by the vowel lengths and by whether the sounds are easily run together. The long vowels take longer to pronounce than the short ones. Some words are easily run together, while others demand that the position of the mouth be re-formed before the next word is uttered. It takes much longer, for instance, to say, "Watch dogs catch much meat" than to say, "My aunt is away," though the number of syllables is the same. And finally the poet can slow down the speed of a line through the introduction of grammatical and rhetorical pauses. Consider lines 54–56 from Tennyson's "Ulysses" (page 80):

The lights be-gin to twin-kle from the rocks;

The long day wanes; the slow moon climbs; the deep   55

Moans round with man-y voi-ces. . . .

In these lines Tennyson wished the movement to be slow, in accordance with the slow waning of the long day and the slow climbing of the moon. His meter is iambic pentameter. This is not a swift meter, but in lines 55–56 he slows it down, first, by introducing three spondaic feet, thus bringing three accented syllables together in three separate places; second, by choosing for his accented syllables words which have long vowel sounds or diphthongs which the voice hangs on to: *long, day, wanes, slow, moon, climbs, deep, moans, round;* third, by choosing words which are not easily run together (except for *day* and *slow,* each of these words begins and ends with consonant sounds which demand varying degrees of readjustment of the mouth before pronunciation is continued); fourth, by introducing two grammatical pauses, after *wanes* and *climbs,* and a rhetorical pause after *deep.* The result is an extremely effective use of the movement of the verse to accord with the movement suggested by the words.[1]

A fourth way for a poet to fit sound to sense is to control both sound and meter in such a way as to put emphasis on words that are important in meaning. He can do this by marking out such words by alliteration, assonance, consonance, or rime; by placing them before a pause; or by skillfully placing or displacing them in the metrical pattern. Look again at Shakespeare's "Spring" (page 11):

When dai-sies pied and vio-lets blue

And la-dy-smocks all sil-ver-white

And cuck-oo-buds of yel-low hue

Do paint the mea-dows with de-light,

The cuck-oo then, on ev-ery tree,   5

Mocks mar-ried men; for thus sings he,

"Cuckoo!

Cuckoo, cuckoo!" O, word of fear,

Unpleasing to a married ear!

The scansion is regular until the beginning of the sixth line: there we find a spondaic substitution in the first foot. In addition, the first three words in this line are heavily alliterated, all beginning with *m.* And further, each of these words ends in a consonant, thus preventing their being run together. The result is to throw heavy emphasis on these three words: to give them, one might almost say,

---

[1] In addition, Tennyson uses one onomatopoetic word (*moans*) and one phonetic intensive (*twinkle*).

a tone of solemnity, or mock-solemnity. Whether or not the solemnity is in the sound, the emphasis on these three words is appropriate, for it serves to signal the shift in tone that takes place at this point. The first five lines have contained nothing but delightful images; the concluding four introduce the note of irony.

Just as Shakespeare uses metrical irregularity, plus alliteration, to give emphasis to important words, Tennyson, in the concluding line of "Ulysses," uses marked regularity, plus skillful use of grammatical pause, to achieve the same effect:

> �‿ ‒ |‿ ‒|‿ ‒ |‿ ‒ | ‿ ‒ |
> Though much is ta-ken, much a-bides; and though   65
>
> �‿ ‒| ‿ ‒ | ‿ ‒ | ‿ ‿ ‒| ‒ |
> We are not now that strength which in old days
>
> ‒ ‒| ‿ ‒| ‿ ‒| ‿ ‿ ‒| ‿ ‒ |
> Moved earth and hea-ven, that which we are, we are:
>
> ‒ ‒| ‿ ‒ | ‿ ‒|‿ ‒|‿ ‒ |
> One e-qual tem-per of he-ro-ic hearts,
>
> ‒ ‒|‿ ‒| ‿ ‒| ‿ ‒ |‿ ‒|
> Made weak by time and fate, but strong in will
>
> ‿ ‒ | ‿ ‒| ‿ ‒| ‿ ‒| ‿ ‒ |
> To strive, to seek, to find, and not to yield.   70

The blank verse rhythm throughout "Ulysses" is remarkably subtle and varied, but the last line is not only regular in its scansion but heavily regular, for a number of reasons: first, all the words are monosyllables: no words cross over the divisions between feet; second, the unaccented syllables are all very small and unimportant words—four *to*'s and one *and*, whereas the accented syllables consist of four important verbs and a very important *not*; third, each of the verbs is followed by a grammatical pause pointed off by a mark of punctuation. The result is to cause a pronounced alternation between light and heavy syllables that brings the accent down on the four verbs and the *not* with sledge-hammer blows. The line rings out like a challenge, which it is.

THE SPAN OF LIFE

> The old dog barks backward without getting up.
> I can remember when he was a pup.

> —*Robert Frost [1874–1963]*

QUESTIONS

1. Is the dog a dog only or also a symbol?
2. The first line presents a visual and auditory image; the second line

makes a comment. But does the second line *call up* images? Does it suggest more than it says? Would the poem have been more or less effective if the second line had been, "He was frisky and lively when he was a pup"?

We may well conclude our discussion of the adaptation of sound to sense by analyzing this very brief poem. It consists of one riming anapestic tetrameter couplet. Its content is a contrast between the decrepitude of an old dog and his friskiness as a pup. The scansion is as follows:

$$\breve{\ } \ \_ \mid \_ \quad \_ \quad \_ \mid \breve{\ } \quad \breve{\ } \quad \_ \mid \breve{\ } \quad \breve{\ } \quad \_ \mid$$
The old dog barks back-ward with-out get-ting up.
$$\_ \mid \breve{\ } \quad \breve{\ } \quad \_ \mid \breve{\ } \quad \breve{\ } \quad \_ \mid \breve{\ } \quad \breve{\ } \ \_ \mid$$
I can re-mem-ber when he was a pup.

How is sound fitted to sense? In the first place, the triple meter chosen by the poet is a swift meter, but in the first line he has jammed it up in a remarkable way by substituting a kind of foot so rare that we do not even have a name for it. It might be called a triple spondee: at any rate it is a foot in which the accent is distributed over three syllables. This foot, following the accented syllable in the first foot, creates a situation where four accented syllables are pushed up together. In addition, each of these accented syllables begins and ends with a strong consonant sound or cluster of consonant sounds, so that they cannot be run together in pronunciation: the mouth must be re-formed between each syllable: "The *old dog barks back*ward." The result is to slow down the line drastically, to almost destroy its rhythmical quality, and to make it difficult to utter. Indeed, the line is as decrepit as the old dog who turns his head but does not get up. When we get to the second line, however, the contrast is startling. The rhythm is swift and regular, the syllables end in vowels or liquid consonants and are easily run together, the whole line ripples fluently off the tongue. In addition, where the first line has a high proportion of explosive and cacophonous consonants—"The ol*d dog b*arks *back*ward withou*t g*etting u*p*"—the second line contains predominantly consonants which are smoother and more graceful—"I ca*n* re*member when he was* a pup." Thus the motion and the sound of the lines are remarkably in accord with the visual images which they suggest. In addition, in the first line the poet has supported the onomatopoetic word *barks* with a near echo *back*, so that the sound reinforces the auditory image. If the poem does a great deal in just two lines, this skillful adaptation of sound to sense is one very important reason.

In analyzing verse for correspondence between sound and sense, we need to be very cautious not to make exaggerated claims. A great deal of nonsense has been written about the moods of certain meters and the effects of certain sounds, and it is easy to suggest correspondences that exist really only in our imaginations. Nevertheless, the first-rate poet has nearly always an instinctive tact about handling his sound so that it in some degree supports his meaning; the inferior poet is usually obtuse to these correspondences. One of the few absolute rules which can be applied to the judgment of poetry is that the form should be adequate to the content. This rule does not mean that there must always be a close and easily demonstrable correspondence. It does mean that there will be no glaring discrepancies. Poor poets, and even good poets in their third-rate work, sometimes go horribly wrong.

The two selections which we have introduced into this chapter to illustrate, first, the use of sound in verse almost purely for its own sake ("Pease porridge hot"), and second, the use of sound in verse almost purely to *imitate* meaning ("Hark, hark! Bow-wow"), are, as significant poetry, perhaps the most trivial pieces in this whole book. But in between these extremes there is an abundant range of poetic possibilities where sound is pleasurable for itself without violating meaning, and where sound to varying degrees corresponds with and corroborates meaning; and in this rich middle range, for the reader who can learn to perceive them, lie many of the greatest pleasures of reading poetry.

EXERCISE

In which of the following pairs of quotations is sound more successfully adapted to sense? As precisely as possible, explain why. (The poet whose name is given is in each case the author of the superior version.)

1. a. Go forth—and Virtue, ever in your sight,
      Shall be your guide by day, your guard by night.
   b. Go forth—and Virtue, ever in your sight,
      Shall point your way by day, and keep you safe at night.
      —*Charles Churchill*

2. a. How charming is divine philosophy!
      Not harsh and rough as foolish men suppose
      But musical as is the lute of Phoebus.
   b. How charming is divine philosophy!
      Not harsh and crabbed as dull fools suppose
      But musical as is Apollo's lute.—*Milton*

3. a. Dress! arm! mount!—away!
      Save my castle before the day
      Turns to blue from silver gray.
      Dress! arm! mount!—away!
   b. Boot, saddle, to horse, and away!
      Rescue my castle before the hot day
      Brightens to blue from its silvery gray,
      Boot, saddle, to horse, and away!—*Browning*

4. a. Your talk attests how bells of singing gold
      Would sound at evening over silent water.
   b. Your low voice tells how bells of singing gold
      Would sound at twilight over silent water.—*Edwin Arlington Robinson*

5. a. A thousand streamlets flowing through the lawn,
      The moan of doves in gnarled ancient oaks,
      And quiet murmuring of countless bees.
   b. Myriads of rivulets hurrying through the lawn,
      The moan of doves in immemorial elms,
      And murmuring of innumerable bees.—*Tennyson*

6. a. It is the lark that sings so out of tune,
      Straining harsh discords and unpleasing sharps.
   b. It is the lark that warbles out of tune
      With harsh discordant voice and hateful flats.—*Shakespeare*

7. a. "Artillery" and "armaments" and "implements of war"
      Are phrases too severe to please the gentle Muse.
   b. Bombs, drums, guns, bastions, batteries, bayonets, bullets,—
      Hard words, which stick in the soft Muses' gullets.—*Byron*

8. a. The hands of the sisters Death and Night incessantly softly wash again,
      and ever again, this soiled world.
   b. The hands of the soft twins Death and Night repeatedly wash again,
      and ever again, this dirty world.—*Whitman*

9. a. The curfew sounds the knell of parting day,
      The lowing cattle slowly cross the lea,
      The plowman goes wearily plodding his homeward way,
      Leaving the world to the darkening night and me.
   b. The curfew tolls the knell of parting day,
      The lowing herd wind slowly o'er the lea,
      The plowman homeward plods his weary way,
      And leaves the world to darkness and to me.—*Thomas Gray*

10. a. Let me chastise this odious, gilded bug,
       This painted son of dirt, that smells and bites.
    b. Yet let me flap this bug with gilded wings,
       This painted child of dirt, that stinks and stings.—*Pope*

SOUND AND SENSE

True ease in writing comes from art, not chance,
As those move easiest who have learned to dance.
'Tis not enough no harshness gives offense,
The sound must seem an echo to the sense:
Soft is the strain when Zephyr gently blows,   5
And the smooth stream in smoother numbers flows;
But when loud surges lash the sounding shore,
The hoarse, rough verse should like the torrent roar;
When Ajax strives some rock's vast weight to throw,
The line too labors, and the words move slow;   10
Not so, when swift Camilla scours the plain,
Flies o'er the unbending corn, and skims along the main.
Hear how Timotheus' varied lays surprise,
And bid alternate passions fall and rise!

—*Alexander Pope [1688–1744]*
(*from* An Essay on Criticism)

QUESTIONS

1. Vocabulary: *numbers* (6), *lays* (13).
2. This excerpt is from a long poem on the arts of writing and judging poetry. Which line is the topic sentence of the passage?
3. There are four classical allusions: *Zephyr* (5) was god of the west wind; *Ajax* (9), a Greek warrior noted for his strength; *Camilla* (11), a legendary queen reputedly so fleet of foot that she could run over a field of corn without bending the blades or over the sea without wetting her feet; *Timotheus* (13), a famous Greek rhapsodic poet. Does the use of these allusions enable Pope to achieve greater economy?
4. Copy the passage and scan it. Then, considering both meter and sounds, show how Pope practices what he preaches. (Incidentally, on which syllable should *alternate* in line 14 be accented?)

I LIKE TO SEE IT LAP THE MILES

I like to see it lap the miles,
And lick the valleys up,
And stop to feed itself at tanks;
And then, prodigious, step

Around a pile of mountains,   5
And, supercilious, peer
In shanties by the sides of roads;
And then a quarry pare

To fit its ribs,
And crawl between,   10
Complaining all the while
In horrid, hooting stanza;
Then chase itself down hill

And neigh like Boanerges;
Then, punctual as a star,   15
Stop—docile and omnipotent—
At its own stable door.

—Emily Dickinson [1830–1886]

QUESTIONS

1. Vocabulary: *prodigious* (4), *supercilious* (6). *Boanerges* (13), literally "Sons of Thunder," was possibly the name of a famous horse at the time this poem was written. It commonly refers to a declamatory or vociferous preacher, from Christ's having used it of James and John (Mark 3:17).

2. What basic metaphor underlies the poem? What additional figures do you find in lines 8, 12, 15, 16, and 17? Explain their appropriateness. Is this poem about a locomotive only or a whole train?

3. Point out examples of alliteration, assonance, and consonance. Does this poem have a rime scheme?

4. Considering such matters as sounds and sound repetitions, grammatical pauses, run-on lines monosyllabic and polysyllabic words, onomatopoeia, and meter, explain in detail how sound is fitted to sense in this poem.

ENGLAND IN 1819

An old, mad, blind, despised, and dying king,—
Princes, the dregs of their dull race, who flow
Through public scorn,—mud from a muddy spring,—
Rulers who neither see, nor feel, nor know,
But leech-like to their fainting country cling,   5
Till they drop, blind in blood, without a blow,—
A people starved and stabbed in the untilled field,—
An army, which liberticide and prey
Makes as a two-edged sword to all who wield;
Golden and sanguine laws which tempt and slay;   10
Religion Christless, Godless—a book sealed;
A Senate,—Time's worst statute unrepealed,—
Are graves, from which a glorious Phantom may
Burst, to illumine our tempestuous day.

—Percy Bysshe Shelley [1792–1822]

1. Vocabulary: *liberticide* (8), *sanguine* (10). Does *sanguine* in this context have one meaning or two?

2. In 1819 King George III (whose abuses had gone far to inspire the American Declaration of Independence in 1776) was 81 years old, blind, and insane. The Prince Regent and the other sons of the King were scandalously profligate. The ministers were reactionary. The standing army was a menace to oppressor and oppressed alike. Parliament had defeated a motion to repeal the laws excluding Roman Catholics from holding office ("Time's worst statute" [12]). And on August 16 occurred the Peterloo Massacre, in which the army attacked a peaceable rally of Manchester citizens for parliamentary reforms, and killed several people. This massacre (7) was the immediate stimulus for the poem. All this is past history. Is the poem, therefore, only historically interesting, or does it have a more lasting relevance? What?

3. List the figures of speech and discuss their appropriateness. (The "Phantom" [13] is usually explained as Freedom or Liberty.)

4. Point out examples of alliteration and consonance and explain their function. What consonant sounds predominate in the first seven lines? Discuss the contribution made by the sound pattern to the feelings of scorn and disgust expressed by the poem.

5. Do you detect any metrical difference between the last two lines and the previous twelve? If so, what function does it serve?

THE DARK HILLS

Dark hills at evening in the west,
Where sunset hovers like a sound
Of golden horns that sang to rest
Old bones of warriors under ground,
Far now from all the bannered ways
Where flash the legions of the sun,
You fade—as if the last of days
Were fading, and all wars were done.

—*Edwin Arlington Robinson* [1869–1935]

QUESTIONS

1. This poem consists of one sentence; analyze it grammatically. What is its skeleton? Is the poem primarily narrative, descriptive, or philosophical? What is the poem about?

2. Point out and explain the figures of speech in the poem. What are "the bannered ways" (5) and "the legions of the sun" (6)? What unity of idea does the figurative language have? What overtones of suggestion does the poem have?

3. Analyze the poem for musical devices. How is sound fitted to sense?

HEAVEN-HAVEN

A Nun Takes the Veil

I have desired to go
        Where springs not fail,
To fields where flies no sharp and sided hail
        And a few lilies blow.

And I have asked to be
        Where no storms come,
Where the green swell is in the havens dumb,
        And out of the swing of the sea.

—*Gerard Manley Hopkins [1844–1889]*

QUESTIONS

1. Who is the speaker and what the situation? Explain the metaphors which form the substance of the poem. What things are being compared?

2. Comment on the meaning of *springs* (2) and on the effectiveness of the poet's choice of *lilies* (4).

3. How do the sound repetitions of the title reinforce the meaning? Are there other instances in the poem where sound reinforces meaning?

4. Scan the poem. (The meter is basically iambic, but there is a great deal of variation.) How does the meter reinforce meaning, especially in the last line? What purpose is served by the displacement of *not* (2) from its normal order?

ON THE LATE MASSACRE IN PIEMONT

Avenge, O Lord, thy slaughtered Saints, whose bones
Lie scattered on the Alpine mountains cold;
Even them who kept thy truth so pure of old,
When all our fathers worshiped stocks and stones,
Forget not: in thy book record their groans   5
Who were thy sheep, and in their ancient fold
Slain by the bloody Piemontese, that rolled
Mother with infant down the rocks. Their moans
The vales redoubled to the hills, and they
To heaven. Their martyred blood and ashes sow   10
O'er all the Italian fields, where still doth sway
The triple Tyrant; that from these may grow
A hundredfold, who, having learnt thy way,
Early may fly the Babylonian woe.

—*John Milton [1608–1674]*

1. This poem has for its background the bitter religious struggles between Protestants and Roman Catholics during the late Reformation. When, in 1655, the soldiers of an Italian Catholic duke massacred a group of Waldensian Protestants in Piedmont (in Northern Italy), Milton, a Puritan poet, wrote this sonnet. The "stocks and stones" (4) refer to wooden and stone images in English churches before England turned Protestant. The "triple Tyrant" (12) refers to the pope, who wore a triple crown. "Babylonian" (14) is a Biblical allusion: Babylon in the Bible is associated with idolatry, pagan luxury, and abuse of power. What is the tone of this poem? How does the language contribute to the tone?

2. How do the rhythm and sound patterns of the poem reinforce its tone? In this respect discuss the meter, the use of run-on lines, the contribution of alliteration, etc. What is unusual about the rime pattern of this sonnet? What part is played by onomatopoeia and phonetic intensives?

EIGHT O'CLOCK

He stood, and heard the steeple
  Sprinkle the quarters on the morning town.
One, two, three, four, to market-place and people
  It tossed them down.

Strapped, noosed, nighing his hour,
  He stood and counted them and cursed his luck;
And then the clock collected in the tower
  Its strength, and struck.

            —A. E. Housman [1859–1936]

QUESTIONS

1. Vocabulary: *quarters* (2).

2. Eight A.M. is the traditional hour in England for putting condemned men to death. Discuss the force of *morning* (2) and *struck* (8). Discuss the appropriateness of the image of the clock collecting its strength. Can you suggest any reason for the use of *nighing* (5) rather than *nearing?*

3. Scan the poem and note its musical devices. Comment on the adaptation of sound to sense.

ALL DAY I HEAR

All day I hear the noise of waters
  Making moan,
Sad as the sea-bird is, when going
  Forth alone,
He hears the winds cry to the waters'
  Monotone.   5

The grey winds, the cold winds are blowing
Where I go.
I hear the noise of many waters
    Far below.   10
All day, all night, I hear them flowing
    To and fro.

—*James Joyce [1882–1941]*

QUESTIONS

1. What is the central purpose of the poem? Is it primarily descriptive?
2. What kinds of imagery does the poem contain?
3. Discuss the adaptation of sound to meaning, commenting on the use of onomatopoeia, phonetic intensives, alliteration, consonance, rime, vowel quality, stanzaic structure, the counterpointing of the rhythmically varied long lines with the rhythmically regular short lines.

THE BENCH OF BOORS

In bed I muse on Tenier's boors,
Embrowned and beery losels all:
    A wakeful brain
    Elaborates pain:
Within low doors the slugs of boors   5
Laze and yawn and doze again.

In dreams they doze, the drowsy boors,
Their hazy hovel warm and small:
    Thought's ampler bound
    But chill is found: 10
Within low doors the basking boors
Snugly hug the ember-mound.

Sleepless, I see the slumberous boors
Their blurred eyes blink, their eyelids fall:
    Thought's eager sight   15
    Aches—overbright!
Within low doors the boozy boors
Cat-naps take in pipe-bowl light.

—*Herman Melville [1819–1891]*

QUESTIONS

1. Vocabulary: *boors* (1), *losels* (2), *slugs* (5).
2. David Teniers, the Younger, a seventeenth-century Flemish painter,

was famous for his genre paintings of peasant life. What was the essential characteristic of this life according to the poem? What symbolism do you find in the fifth line of each stanza?

3. What is the relation of the third and fourth lines of each stanza to the speaker? to the boors? How does the form of the stanza emphasize the contrast in thought?

4. Comment on other correspondences between sound and meaning.

THE DANCE [2]

In Breughel's great picture, The Kermess,
the dancers go round, they go round and
around, the squeal and the blare and the
tweedle of bagpipes, a bugle and fiddles
tipping their bellies (round as the thick-   5
sided glasses whose wash they impound)
their hips and their bellies off balance
to turn them. Kicking and rolling about
the Fair Grounds, swinging their butts, those
shanks must be sound to bear up under such   10
rollicking measures, prance as they dance
in Breughel's great picture, The Kermess.

—*William Carlos Williams [1883–1963]*

QUESTIONS

1. Peter Breughel, the Elder, was a sixteenth-century Flemish painter of peasant life. A kermess is an annual outdoor festival or fair. How do the form, the meter, and the sounds of this poem reinforce its content?

2. Explore the similarities and differences between this poem and the preceding, both as to form and content.

---

[2] Dr. Williams has recorded "The Dance" (LP, *Pleasure Dome*, Columbia ML–4259).

14

Pattern

Art, ultimately, is organization. It is a searching after order, after form. The primal artistic act was God's creation of the universe out of chaos, shaping the formless into form; and every artist since, on a lesser scale, has sought to imitate Him—by selection and arrangement to reduce the chaotic in experience to a meaningful and pleasing order. For this reason we evaluate a poem partially by the same criteria which an English instructor uses to evaluate a theme—by its unity, its coherence, and its proper placing of emphasis. In a well-constructed poem there is neither too little nor too much; every part of the poem belongs where it is and could be placed nowhere else; any interchanging of two stanzas, two lines, two words, or even two accents, would to some extent damage the poem and make it less effective than it is. We come to feel, with a truly first-rate poem, that the choice and placement of every word is inevitable, that it could not be otherwise.

In addition to the internal ordering of his materials, of images, ideas, and sounds, the poet may also impose some external pattern on his poem, may give it not only an inside logical order but an outside symmetry. In doing so, he appeals to the human instinct for design: the instinct that makes primitive men tattoo and paint their bodies, later men to decorate their swords and shields with beautiful and complex designs, and modern men to choose patterned ties and dresses, carpets, curtains, and wallpapers. The poet appeals to our love of the shapely.

In general, there are three broad kinds of form into which the poet may cast his work: continuous form, stanzaic form, and a fixed form.

In CONTINUOUS FORM, as illustrated by "Patterns" (page 82), "Dover Beach" (page 256), "Ulysses" (page 79), and "My Last Duchess" (page 109), the element of formal design is slight. The lines follow each other without formal grouping, the only breaks being dictated by units of meaning, as paragraph breaks are in prose. Even here there are degrees of formal pattern. The free verse "Patterns" has neither regular meter nor regular rime. "Dover Beach," on the other hand, is metrical; it has no regularity in length of line, but the meter is prevailingly iambic. "Ulysses" is regular in both meter and length of line; it is unrimed iambic pentameter, or blank verse. And to these regularities "My Last Duchess" adds regularity of rime, for it is written in riming iambic pentameter couplets. Thus, in increasing degrees, the authors of "Dover Beach," "Ulysses," and "My Last Duchess" have chosen a predetermined pattern in which to cast their work.

In STANZAIC FORM the poet writes in a series of STANZAS, that is, repeated units having the same number of lines, the same metrical pattern, and often an identical rime scheme. The poet may choose some traditional stanza pattern (for poetry, like college, is rich in tradition), or invent his own. The traditional stanza patterns (for example, terza rima, ballad meter, rime royal, Spenserian stanza) are many, and the student specializing in literature will wish to familiarize himself with some of them; the general student should know that they exist. Often the use of one of these traditional stanza forms constitutes a kind of literary allusion. The reader who is conscious of its traditional use or of its use by a previous great poet will be aware of subtleties in the communication that a less well-read reader may miss.

As with continuous form, there are degrees of formal pattern in stanzaic form. In "Poem in October" (page 206), for instance, the stanzas are alike in length of line but are without a regular pattern of rime. In "To Lucasta" (page 99), a rime pattern is added to a metrical pattern. In Shakespeare's "Winter" (page 6) and "Spring" (page 11), a refrain is employed in addition to the patterns of meter and rime. The following poem illustrates additional elements of design:

O WHERE ARE YOU GOING?

"O where are you going?" said reader to rider,
"That valley is fatal when furnaces burn,
Yonder's the midden whose odours will madden,
That gap is the grave where the tall return."

"O do you imagine," said fearer to farer,   5
"That dusk will delay on your path to the pass,
Your diligent looking discover the lacking
Your footsteps feel from granite to grass?"

"O what was that bird," said horror to hearer,
"Did you see that shape in the twisted trees?   10
Behind you swiftly the figure comes softly,
The spot on your skin is a shocking disease?"

"Out of this house"—said rider to reader,
"Yours never will"—said farer to fearer,
"They're looking for you"—said hearer to horror,   15
As he left them there, as he left them there.

—*W. H. Auden* [1907–]

QUESTIONS

1. Vocabulary: *midden* (3).
2. In addition to the metrical and rime pattern of the first three stanzas, they have a rhetorical pattern. Each asks a question combined with a warning. The first lines begin with the same word and end with the same formula: "said X to Y." Where are the answers to these questions?
3. How many people are involved in this dialogue—six? four? two? or one? What types of character do they symbolize? With which does the poet sympathize?
4. What does the journey to the pass symbolize?
5. Besides the elements of pattern mentioned in question 2, what patterns of musical repetition do you find in the first three stanzas?

A stanza form may be described by designating four things: the rime scheme (if there is one), the position of the refrain (if there is one), the prevailing metrical foot, and the number of feet in each line. Rime scheme is traditionally designated by using letters of the alphabet to indicate the riming lines, and *x* for unrimed lines. Refrain lines may be indicated by a capital letter, and the number of feet in the line by a numerical exponent after the letter.

Thus the stanza pattern of Browning's "Meeting at Night" (page 46) is iambic tetrameter *abccba* (or iambic *abccba*^{4}); that of Cummings' "if everything happens that can't be done" (page 173) is anapestic $a^4x^2x^1a^1b^4x^1x^1b^2a^3$; that of Shakespeare's "Spring" (page 11) is iambic $ababcc^4X^1DD^4$.

A FIXED FORM is a traditional pattern which applies to a whole poem. In French poetry many fixed forms have been widely used: rondeaus, roundels, villanelles, triolets, sestinas, ballades, double ballades, and others. In English poetry, though most of these have been experimented with, perhaps only two—the limerick and the sonnet—have really taken hold.

The LIMERICK, though really a subliterary form, will serve to illustrate the fixed form in general. Its pattern is anapestic $aa^3bb^2a^3$:

There was a young la-dy of Ni-ger

Who smiled as she rode on a ti-ger;

They re-turned from the ride

With the la-dy in-side,

And the smile on the face of the ti-ger.

—*Anonymous*

The limerick form is used exclusively for humorous and nonsense verse, for which, with its swift catchy meter, its short lines and emphatic rimes, it is particularly suitable. By trying to recast these little jokes and bits of nonsense in a different meter and pattern or into prose, we may discover how much of their effect they owe particularly to the limerick form. There is, of course, no magical or mysterious identity between certain forms and certain types of content, but there may be more or less correspondence. A form may be appropriate or inappropriate. The limerick form is apparently inappropriate for the serious treatment of serious material.

The SONNET is less rigidly prescribed than the limerick. It must be fourteen lines in length, and it must be iambic pentameter, but in structure and rime scheme there may be considerable leeway. Most sonnets, however, conform more or less closely to one of two general models or types, the Italian and the English.

The ITALIAN or *Petrarchan* SONNET (so called because the Italian poet Petrarch originated it) is divided usually between eight lines called the octave, using two rimes arranged *abbaabba*, and six lines called the sestet, using any arrangement of either two or three rimes: *cdcdcd* and *cdecde* are common patterns. Usually in the Italian sonnet, corresponding to the division between octave and sestet indicated by the rime scheme (and sometimes marked off in printing by a space), there is a division in thought. The octave will present a situation and the sestet a comment, or the octave an idea and the sestet an example, or the octave a question and the sestet an answer.

ON FIRST LOOKING INTO CHAPMAN'S HOMER

Much have I travelled in the realms of gold,
And many goodly states and kingdoms seen;
Round many western islands have I been
Which bards in fealty to Apollo hold.
Oft of one wide expanse had I been told   5
That deep-browed Homer ruled as his demesne;
Yet did I never breathe its pure serene
Till I heard Chapman speak out loud and bold:
Then felt I like some watcher of the skies
When a new planet swims into his ken;   10
Or like stout Cortez when with eagle eyes
He stared at the Pacific—and all his men
Looked at each other with a wild surmise—
Silent, upon a peak in Darien.

—*John Keats [1795–1821]*

QUESTIONS

1. Vocabulary: *fealty* (4), *Apollo* (4), *demesne* (6), *ken* (10), *Darien* (14).

2. John Keats, at twenty-one, could not read Greek, and was probably acquainted with Homer's *Iliad* and *Odyssey* only through the translations of Alexander Pope, which to him would have seemed prosy and stilted. Then one day he and a friend found a vigorous poetic translation by the Elizabethan poet George Chapman. Keats and his friend, enthralled, sat up late at night excitedly reading aloud to each other from Chapman's book. Toward morning Keats walked home and, before going to bed, wrote the above sonnet and sent it to his friend. What common ideas underlie the three major figures of speech in the poem?

3. What is the rime scheme? What division of thought corresponds to the division between octave and sestet?

4. Balboa, not Cortez, discovered the Pacific. Does this mistake seriously detract from the value of the poem? Why or why not?

The ENGLISH or *Shakespearean* SONNET (invented by the English poet Surrey and made famous by Shakespeare) is composed of three quatrains and a concluding couplet, riming *abab cdcd efef gg*. Again, there is usually a correspondence between the units marked off by the rimes and the development of the thought. The three quatrains, for instance, may present three examples and the couplet a conclusion, or (as in the following example) three metaphorical statements of one idea plus an application.

THAT TIME OF YEAR

That time of year thou mayst in me behold
When yellow leaves, or none, or few, do hang
Upon those boughs which shake against the cold,
Bare ruined choirs where late the sweet birds sang.
In me thou see'st the twilight of such day   5
As after sunset fadeth in the west,
Which by and by black night doth take away,
Death's second self, that seals up all in rest.
In me thou see'st the glowing of such fire,
That on the ashes of his youth doth lie   10
As the deathbed whereon it must expire,
Consumed with that which it was nourished by.
   This thou perceivest, which makes thy love more strong,
   To love that well which thou must leave ere long.

—*William Shakespeare [1564–1616]*

QUESTIONS

1. What are the three major images introduced by the three quatrains? What do they have in common? Can you see any reason for presenting them in this particular order, or might they be rearranged without loss?

2. Each of the images is to some degree complicated rather than simple. For instance, what additional image is introduced by "bare ruined choirs" (4)? Explain its appropriateness.

3. What additional comparisons are introduced in the second and third quatrains?

4. Explain line 12.

At first glance it may seem absurd that a poet should choose to confine himself in an arbitrary fourteen-line mold with prescribed meter and rime scheme. He does so partly from the desire to carry on a tradition, as all of us carry out certain traditions for their own sake, else why should we bring a tree indoors at Christmas time? But, in addition, the tradition of the sonnet has proved a useful one, for like the limerick, it seems effective for certain types of subject matter and treatment. Though this area cannot be as narrowly limited or as rigidly described as for the limerick, the sonnet is usually most effective when used for the serious treatment of love, but has also been used for the discussion of death, religion, political situations, and related subjects. Again, there is no magical affinity between form and subject, or treatment, and excellent sonnets have been written outside these traditional areas. The sonnet tradition has also proved useful because it has provided a challenge to the poet. The inferior poet, of course, is often defeated by that challenge: he will use unnecessary words to fill out his meter or inappropriate words for the sake of his rime. The good poet is inspired by the challenge: it will call forth ideas and images that might not otherwise have come. He will subdue his form rather than be subdued by it; he will make it do his will. There is no doubt that the presence of a net makes good tennis players more precise in their shots than they otherwise would be. And finally, there is in all form the pleasure of form itself.

EXERCISES

1. There are two examples in this book of the French fixed form known as the villanelle. After reading "The House on the Hill" (page 88) and "Do not go gentle into that good night" (page 303), frame a definition for the villanelle.

2. How many sonnets can you find in this book? List them by page number and designate each as English or Italian, noting any irregularities. Can you make any generalizations from them about the nature or subject matter of sonnets?

● ● ●

A HANDFUL OF LIMERICKS [1]

I sat next the Duchess at tea.
It was just as I feared it would be:
    Her rumblings abdominal
    Were simply abominable,
And everyone thought it was me.

[1] Most limericks are anonymous. If not written anonymously, they soon become so, unfortunately for the glory of their authors, because of repeated oral transmission and reprinting without accreditation.

There was a young lady of Lynn
Who was so uncommonly thin
    That when she essayed
    To drink lemonade
She slipped through the straw and fell in.

A tutor who tooted the flute
Tried to tutor two tooters to toot.
    Said the two to the tutor,
    "Is it harder to toot or
To tutor two tooters to toot?"

There was a young maid who said, "Why
Can't I look in my ear with my eye?
    If I put my mind to it,
    I'm sure I can do it.
You never can tell till you try."

There was a young woman named Bright,
Whose speed was much faster than light.
    She set out one day
    In a relative way
And returned on the previous night.

There was an old man of Peru
Who dreamt he was eating his shoe.
    He awoke in the night
    In a terrible fright,
And found it was perfectly true!

A decrepit old gas man named Peter,
While hunting around for the meter,
    Touched a leak with his light.
    He arose out of sight,
And, as anyone can see by reading this, he
    also destroyed the meter.

TO DAFFODILS

    Fair daffodils, we weep to see
        You haste away so soon;
    As yet the early-rising sun
        Has not attained his noon.
        Stay, stay,
        Until the hasting day
        Has run

5

But to the evensong;
And, having prayed together, we
Will go with you along.   10

We have short time to stay as you;
    We have as short a spring;
As quick a growth to meet decay
    As you, or anything.
        We die   15
    As your hours do, and dry
        Away
Like to the summer's rain;
Or as the pearls of morning's dew
    Ne'er to be found again.   20

—Robert Herrick [1591–1674]

QUESTIONS

1. Vocabulary: *evensong* (8).
2. What do the daffodils symbolize? What does "the hasting day"?
3. Describe the stanza pattern. Does it seem to you in any way to support the content?

I SING OF A MAIDEN

I sing of a maiden
    That is mateless:
King of all kings
    To her son she chose.

He came all so still   5
    Where his mother was
As dew in April
    That falleth on the grass.

He came all so still
    To his mother's bower   10
As dew in April
    That falleth on the flower.

He came all so still
    Where his mother lay,
As dew in April   15
    That falleth on the spray.

Mother and maiden
  Was never none but she;
Well may such a lady
  God's mother be.   20

—Anonymous [15th century]

QUESTION

1. The language in this lyric has been slightly modernized. *Mateless* (2)
—in the original, *makeless*—means both *without a mate* and *matchless*. What
do the repetitions add to the effect of the poem?

POEM IN OCTOBER [2]

It was my thirtieth year to heaven
Woke to my hearing from harbor and neighbor wood
    And the mussel-pooled and the heron-
      Priested shore
    The morning beckon   5
With water praying and call of seagull and rook
And the knock of sailing boats on the net-webbed wall
    Myself to set foot
      That second
In the still sleeping town and set forth.   10

My birthday began with the water-
Birds and the birds of the winged trees flying my name
    Above the farms and the white horses
      And I rose
    In rainy autumn   15
And walked abroad in a shower of all my days.
High tide and the heron dived when I took the road
    Over the border
      And the gates
Of the town closed as the town awoke.   20

A springful of larks in a rolling
Cloud and the roadside bushes brimming with whistling
    Blackbirds and the sun of October
      Summery
    On the hill's shoulder,   25
Here were fond climates and sweet singers suddenly
Come in the morning where I wandered and listened
    To the rain-wringing
      Wind blow cold
In the woods faraway under me.   30

[2] Dylan Thomas recorded "Poem in October" (LP, *Pleasure Dome*, Columbia, ML-
4259).

Pale rain over the dwindling harbor
And over the sea-wet church the size of a snail
  With its horns through mist and the castle
    Brown as owls
    But all the gardens   35
Of spring and summer were blooming in the tall tales
Beyond the border and under the lark-full cloud.
  There could I marvel
    My birthday
Away but the weather turned around.   40

It turned away from the blithe country
And down the other air and the blue altered sky
  Streamed again a wonder of summer
    With apples
    Pears and red currants   45
And I saw in the turning so clearly a child's
Forgotten mornings when he walked with his mother
  Through the parables
    Of sunlight
And the legends of the green chapels   50

And the twice-told fields of infancy
That his tears burned my cheeks and his heart moved in mine.
  These were the woods the river and sea
    Where a boy
    In the listening   55
Summertime of the dead whispered the truth of his joy
To the trees and the stones and the fish in the tide.
  And the mystery
    Sang alive
Still in the water and singingbirds.   60

And there could I marvel my birthday
Away but the weather turned around. And the true
  Joy of the long dead child sang burning
    In the sun.
    It was my thirtieth   65
Year to heaven stood there then in the summer noon
Though the town below lay leaved with October blood.
  O may my heart's truth
    Still be sung
On this high hill in a year's turning.   70

                   —Dylan Thomas [1914–1953]

1. The setting is a small fishing village on the coast of Wales. The poet's first name in Welsh means "water" (12). Trace the poet's walk in relation to the village, the weather, and the time of day.

2. "The weather turned around" is an expression indicating a change in the weather or the direction of the wind. In what psychological sense does the weather turn around during the poet's walk? Who is "the long dead child" (63), and what kind of child was he? With what wish does the poem close?

3. Explain "thirtieth year to heaven" (1), "horns" (33), "tall tales" (36), "green chapels" (50), "October blood" (67).

4. The elaborate stanza pattern in this poem is based not on the meter (which is very free) but on a syllable count. How many syllables are there in each line of the stanza? (In line 1 *thirtieth* is counted as only two syllables.) Notice that the stanzas 1 and 3 consist of exactly one sentence each.

5. The poem makes a considerable use of approximate rime, though not according to a regular pattern. Point out examples.

THE SONNET

A Sonnet is a moment's monument—
Memorial from the Soul's eternity
To one dead deathless hour. Look that it be,
Whether for lustral rite or dire portent,
Of its own arduous fullness reverent;   5
Carve it in ivory or in ebony,
As Day or Night may rule; and let Time see
Its flowering crest impearled and orient.

A Sonnet is a coin: its face reveals
The soul—its converse, to what Power 'tis due—   10
Whether for tribute to the august appeals
Of Life, or dower in Love's high retinue,
It serve; or, 'mid the dark wharf's cavernous breath,
In Charon's palm it pay the toll to Death.

     —Dante Gabriel Rossetti [1828–1882]

1. Vocabulary: *lustral* (4), *portent* (4), *arduous* (5), *orient* (8), *retinue* (12), *Charon* (14). Note: The Greeks buried their dead with coins over their eyes or in their mouths to pay for their passage to the underworld.

2. Rossetti "defines" the sonnet and gives advice about writing it. What characteristics of the Italian sonnet does Rossetti bring out?

3. What is Rossetti's advice for writing the sonnet? Keats once advised poets to "rift every vein with ore." Is Rossetti's advice similar or different?

4. This sonnet consists essentially of two extended metaphors, one in the

octave and one in the sestet. Trace the development and implications of each. Which is the more consistently and remarkably worked out?

FROM *ROMEO AND JULIET*

ROMEO. If I profane with my unworthiest hand
This holy shrine, the gentle sin is this;
My lips, two blushing pilgrims, ready stand
To smooth that rough touch with a tender kiss.
JULIET. Good pilgrim, you do wrong your hand too much,   5
Which mannerly devotion shows in this;
For saints have hands that pilgrims' hands do touch,
And palm to palm is holy palmers' kiss.
ROMEO. Have not saints lips, and holy palmers too?
JULIET. Ay, pilgrim, lips that they must use in prayer.   10
ROMEO. O! then, dear saint, let lips do what hands do;
They pray, Grant thou, lest faith turn to despair.
JULIET. Saints do not move,° though grant for prayers' sake.   propose,
ROMEO. Then move not, while my prayers' effect I take.   instigate

—William Shakespeare [1564–1616]

QUESTIONS

1. These fourteen lines have been lifted out of Act I, Scene 5, of Shakespeare's play. They are the first words exchanged between Romeo and Juliet, who are meeting for the first time, at a masquerade ball given by her father. Romeo is dressed as a pilgrim. Struck by Juliet's beauty, he has come up to greet her. What stage action accompanies this passage?
2. What is the basic metaphor employed? How does it affect the tone of the relationship between Romeo and Juliet?
3. What play on words do you find in lines 8 and 13–14? What two meanings has line 11?
4. By meter and rime scheme, these lines form a sonnet. Do you think this was coincidental or intentional on Shakespeare's part? Discuss.

EDWARD

"Why dois° your brand° sae drap wi bluid,   does; sword
    Edward, Edward,
Why dois your brand sae drap wi bluid,
    And why sae sad gang° yee O?"   go
"O I hae killed my hauke sae guid,   5
    Mither, mither,
O I hae killed my hauke sae guid,
    And I had nae mair bot hee O."

"Your haukis bluid was nevir sae reid,
　　　Edward, Edward,　　　　　　　　　　　　10
Your haukis bluid was nevir sae reid,
　　My deir son I tell thee O."
"O I hae killed my reid-roan steid,
　　　Mither, mither,
O I hae killed my reid-roan steid,　　　　　　15
　　That erst° was sae fair and frie° O."　　　　formerly; spirited

"Your steid was auld, and ye hae got mair,
　　　Edward, Edward,
Your steid was auld, and ye hae got mair,
　　Sum other dule° ye drie° O."　　　　　　grief; suffer　20
"O I hae killed my fadir deir,
　　　Mither, mither,
O I hae killed my fadir deir,
　　Alas, and wae is mee O!"

"And whatten penance wul ye drie for that,　　　　25
　　　Edward, Edward,
And whatten penance wul ye drie for that?
　　My deir son, now tell me O."
"Ile set my feit in yonder boat,
　　　Mither, mither,　　　　　　　　　　　　30
Ile set my feit in yonder boat,
　　And Ile fare ovir the sea O."

"And what wul ye doe wi your towirs and your ha,°　　hall
　　　Edward, Edward,
And what wul ye doe wi your towirs and your ha,　　35
　　That were sae fair to see O?"
"Ile let thame stand tul they doun fa,°　　　　　fall
　　　Mither, mither,
Ile let thame stand tul they doun fa,　　　　　　40
　　For here nevir mair maun° I bee O."　　　　must

"And what wul ye leive to your bairns° and your wife,　children
　　　Edward, Edward,
And what wul ye leive to your bairns and your wife,
　　Whan ye gang ovir the sea O?"　　　　　　44
"The warldis° room, late them beg thrae° life,　　world's;
　　　Mither, mither,　　　　　　　　　　　　through
The warldis room, late them beg thrae life,
　　For thame nevir mair wul I see O."

"And what wul ye leive to your ain mither deir,
    Edward, Edward?   50
And what wul ye leive to your ain mither deir?
    My deir son, now tell me O."
"The curse of hell frae me sall ye beir,
    Mither, mither,
The curse of hell frae me sall ye beir,   55
    Sic° counseils ye gave to me O."   Such

—*Anonymous*

QUESTIONS

1. What has Edward done, and why? Where do the two climaxes of the poem come?

2. Tell as much as you can about Edward and his feelings toward what he has done. From what class of society is he? Why does he at first give false answers to his mother's questions? What reversal of feelings and loyalties has he undergone? Do his answers about his hawk and steed perhaps indicate his present feelings toward his father? How do you explain his behavior to his wife and children? What are his present feelings toward his mother?

3. Tell as much as you can about Edward's mother. Why does she ask what Edward has done—doesn't she already know? Is there any clue as to the motivation of her deed? How skillful is she in her questioning? What do we learn about her from her dismissal of Edward's steed as "auld" and only one of many (17)? from her asking Edward what penance *he* will do for his act (25)? from her reference to herself as Edward's "ain mither deir" (49)?

4. Structure and pattern are both important in this poem. Could any of the stanzas be interchanged without loss, or do they build up steadily to the two climaxes? What effect has the constant repetition of the two short refrains, "Edward, Edward" and "Mither, mither"? What is the effect of the final "O" at the end of each speech? Does the repetition of each question and answer simply waste words or does it add to the suspense and emotional intensity? (Try reading the poem omitting the third and seventh lines of each stanza. Is it improved or weakened?)

5. Much of what happened is implied, much is omitted. Does the poem gain anything in power from what is *not* told?

LORD RANDAL

"O where ha' you been, Lord Randal, my son?
And where ha' you been, my handsome young man?"
"I ha' been at the greenwood, mother, mak my bed soon,
For I'm wearied wi' hunting and fain wad lie down."

"And wha met ye there, Lord Randal, my son?   5
And wha met you there, my handsome young man?"
"O I met wi' my true-love, mother, mak my bed soon,
For I'm wearied wi' hunting an fain wad lie down."

"And what did she give you, Lord Randal, my son?
And what did she give you, my handsome young man?"
"Eels fried in a pan, mother, mak my bed soon,
For I'm wearied wi' hunting and fain wad lie down."

"And wha gat your leavins,° Lord Randal, my son?   leavings
And wha gat your leavins, my handsome young man?"
"My hawks and my hounds, mother, mak my bed soon,   15
For I'm wearied wi' hunting and fain wad lie down."

"And what becam of them, Lord Randal, my son?
And what becam of them, my handsome young man?"
"They stretched their legs out an died, mother, mak my bed soon,
For I'm wearied wi' hunting and fain wad lie down."   20

"O I fear you are poisoned, Lord Randal, my son.
I fear you are poisoned, my handsome young man."
"O yes, I am poisoned, mother, mak my bed soon,
For I'm sick at the heart and I fain wad lie down."

"What d' ye leave to your mother, Lord Randal, my son?   25
What d' ye leave to your mother, my handsome young man?"
"Four and twenty milk kye,° mother, mak my bed soon,   cows
For I'm sick at the heart and I fain wad lie down."

"What d' ye leave to your sister, Lord Randal, my son?
What d' ye leave to your sister, my handsome young man?"   30
"My gold and my silver, mother, mak my bed soon,
For I'm sick at the heart an I fain wad lie down."

"What d' ye leave to your brother, Lord Randal, my son?
What d' ye leave to your brother, my handsome young man?"
"My houses and my lands, mother, mak my bed soon,   35
For I'm sick at the heart and I fain wad lie down."

"What d' ye leave to your true-love, Lord Randal, my son?
What d' ye leave to your true-love, my handsome young man?"
"I leave her hell and fire, mother, mak my bed soon,
For I'm sick at the heart and I fain wad lie down."   40

—*Anonymous*

1. Compare this ballad with "Edward" in form and content. Which is more dramatically effective, and why?

ESCAPIST'S SONG

The first woman I loved, he said—
Her skin was satin and gold.
The next woman I loved, he said—
Her skin was satin and gold.
The third woman I loved, he said—   5
Was made in a different mold.
She was deeper than me, and said so;
She was stronger than me, and said so;
She was wiser than me, and proved it;
I shivered, and grew cold.   10
The fourth woman I loved, he said—
Her skin was satin and gold.

—*Theodore Spencer [1902–1949]*

A CHRISTMAS TREE

Star,
If you are
A love compassionate,
You will walk with us this year.
We face a glacial distance, who are here
Huddld
At your feet.

—*William Burford [1927   ]*

QUESTION

1. Why do you think the author misspelled "huddled" in line 6?

15

Bad Poetry and Good

The attempt to evaluate a poem should never be made before it is understood; and, unless you have developed the capacity to feel some poetry deeply, any judgments you make will be worthless. A person who likes no wines can hardly be a judge of them. The ability to make judgments, to discriminate between good and bad, great and good, good and half-good, is surely a primary object of all liberal education, and one's appreciation of poetry is incomplete unless it includes discrimination. Of the mass of verse that appears each year in print, as of all literature, most is "flat, stale, and unprofitable"; a very, very little is of any enduring value.

In judging a poem, as in judging any work of art, we need to ask three basic questions: (1) *What is its central purpose?* (2) *How fully has this purpose been accomplished?* (3) *How important is this purpose?* The first question we need to answer in order to understand the poem. The last two questions are those by which we evaluate it. The first of these measures the poem on a scale of perfection. The second measures it on a scale of significance. And, just as the area of a rectangle is determined by multiplying its measurements on two scales, breadth and height, so the greatness of a poem is determined by multiplying its measurements on two scales, perfection and significance. If the poem measures well on the first of these scales, we call it a good poem, at least of its kind. If it measures well on both scales, we call it a great poem.[1]

The measurement of a poem is a much more complex process, of course, than is the measurement of a rectangle. It cannot be done as exactly. Agreement on the measurements will never be complete. Yet over a period of time the judgments of qualified readers[2] tend to coalesce: there comes to be more agreement than disagreement. There is almost universal agreement, for instance, that Shakespeare is the greatest of English poets. Although there might be sharp disagreements among qualified readers as to whether Donne or Keats is the superior poet, or Wordsworth or Chaucer, or Shelley or Pope, there is almost universal agreement among them that each of these is superior to Kipling or Longfellow. And there is almost universal agreement that Kipling and Longfellow are superior to James Whitcomb Riley and Edgar Guest.

But your problem is to be able to discriminate, not between already established reputations, but between poems—poems which you have not seen before and of which, perhaps, you do not even know the author. Here, of course, you will not always be right— even the most qualified readers occasionally go badly astray—but you should, we hope, be able to make broad distinctions with a higher average of success than you could when you began this book. And, unless you allow yourself to petrify, your ability to do this should improve throughout your college years, and beyond.

For answering the first of our evaluative questions, *How fully has the poem's purpose been accomplished?* there are no easy yardsticks that we can apply. We cannot ask, Is the poem melodious? Does it have smooth meter? Does it use good grammar? Does it contain figures of speech? Are the rimes perfect? Excellent poems exist without any of these attributes. We can judge any element in a poem only as it contributes or fails to contribute to the achievement of the central purpose; and we can judge the total

---

[1] As indicated in the footnote on page 22, some objection has been made to the use of the term "purpose" in literary criticism. For the two criteria suggested above these two may be substituted. (1) How thoroughly are the materials of the poem integrated or unified? (2) How many and how diverse are the materials that it integrates? Thus a poem becomes successful in proportion to the tightness of its organization, that is, according to the degree to which all its elements work together and require each other to produce the total effect; and it becomes great in proportion to its scope, that is, according to the amount and the diversity of the material that it amalgamates into unity.

[2] Throughout this discussion the term "qualified reader" is of utmost importance. By a qualified reader we mean briefly a person with considerable experience of literature and considerable experience of life: a person of intelligence, sensitivity, and knowledge. Without these qualities a person is no more qualified to judge literature than a color-blind man would be to judge painting, or a tone-deaf man to judge music, or a man who had never seen a horse before to judge a horse.

poem only as these elements work together to form an integrated whole. But we can at least attempt a few generalizations. In a perfect poem there will be no excess words, no words that do not bear their full weight in contributing to the total meaning, and no words just to fill out the meter. Each word will be the best word for expressing the total meaning: there will be no inexact words forced by the rime scheme or the metrical pattern. The word order will be the best order for expressing the author's total meaning; distortions or departures from normal order will be for emphasis or some other meaningful purpose. The diction, the images, and the figures of speech will be fresh, not trite (except, of course, when the poet uses trite language deliberately for purposes of irony). There will be no clashes between the sound of the poem and its sense, or its form and its content; and in general the poet will use both sound and pattern in such a way as to support his meaning. The organization of the poem will be the best possible organization: images and ideas will be so effectively arranged that any rearrangement would be harmful to the poem. We will always remember, however, that a good poem may have flaws. We should never damn a poem for its flaws if these flaws are amply compensated for by positive excellence.

If a poem is to have true excellence, it must be in some sense a "new" poem; it must exact a fresh response from the qualified reader—make him respond in a new way. It will not be merely imitative of previous literature, nor appeal to stock, pre-established ways of thinking and feeling which in some readers are automatically stimulated by words like *mother, baby, home, country, faith,* or *God,* as a coin put into a slot always gets an expected reaction.

And here, perhaps, may be discussed the kinds of poems which most frequently "fool" poor readers (and occasionally a few good ones) and achieve sometimes a tremendous popularity without winning the respect of most good readers. These are the poems which are found pasted in great numbers in the scrapbooks of sweet old ladies, and which appear in anthologies entitled *Poems of Inspiration, Poems of Courage,* or *Heart-Throbs.* The people who write such poems and the people who like them are often the best of people, but they are not poets or lovers of poetry in any genuine sense. They are lovers of conventional ideas or sentiments or feelings, which they like to see expressed with the adornment of rime and meter, and which, when so expressed, they respond to in predictable ways.

Of the several varieties of inferior poetry, we shall concern ourselves with three: the sentimental, the rhetorical, and the purely didactic. All three are perhaps unduly dignified by the name of poetry. They might more aptly be described as verse.

SENTIMENTALITY is indulgence in emotion for its own sake, or expression of more emotion than an occasion warrants. A sentimental *person* is gushy, stirred to tears by trivial or inappropriate causes; he weeps at all weddings and all funerals; he is made ecstatic by manifestations of young love; he clips locks of hair, gilds baby shoes, and talks baby talk; he grows compassionate over hardened criminals when he hears of their being punished. His opposite is the callous or unfeeling person. The ideal is the person who responds sensitively on appropriate occasions and feels deeply on occasions that deserve deep feeling, but who has nevertheless a certain amount of emotional reserve, a certain command over his feelings. Sentimental *literature* is "tear-jerking" literature. It aims primarily at stimulating the emotions directly rather than at communicating experience truly and freshly; it depends on trite and well-tried formulas for exciting emotion; it revels in old oaken buckets, rocking chairs, mother love, and the pitter-patter of little feet; it oversimplifies; it is unfaithful to the full complexity of human experience. In our book the best example of sentimental verse is the first seven lines of the anonymous "Love" (page 146). If this verse had ended as it began, it would have been pure sentimentalism. The eighth line redeems it by making us realize that the writer is not serious and thus transfers the piece from the classification of sentimental verse to that of humorous verse. In fact, the writer is poking fun at sentimentality by showing that in its most maudlin form it is characteristic of drunks.

RHETORICAL poetry is poetry which uses a language more glittering and high flown than its substance warrants. It offers a spurious vehemence of language—language without a corresponding reality of emotion or thought underneath. It is oratorical, overelegant, artificially eloquent. It is superficial and, again, often basically trite. It loves rolling phrases like "from the rocky coast of Maine to the sun-washed shores of California" and "our heroic dead" and "Old Glory." It deals in generalities. At its worst it is bombast. In this book an example is offered by the two lines quoted from the play-within-a-play in Shakespeare's *Midsummer Night's Dream:*

> Whereat with blade, with bloody, blameful blade,
> He bravely broached his boiling bloody breast.

Another example may be found in the player's recitation in *Hamlet* (II, ii):

Out, out, thou strumpet Fortune! All you gods,
In general synod take away her power,
Break all the spokes and fellies from her wheel,
And bowl the round nave down the hill of heaven
As low as to the fiends!

DIDACTIC poetry is poetry that has as a primary purpose to teach or preach. It is probable that all the very greatest poetry teaches in subtle ways, without being expressly didactic; and much expressly didactic poetry ranks high in poetic excellence: that is, it accomplishes its teaching without ceasing to be poetry. But when the didactic purpose supersedes the poetic purpose, when the poem communicates information or moral instruction only, then it ceases to be didactic poetry and becomes didactic verse. Such verse appeals to people who go to poetry primarily for noble thoughts or inspiring lessons and like them prettily expressed. It is recognizable often by the flatness of its diction, the poverty of its imagery and figurative language, its emphasis on moral platitudes, its lack of poetic freshness. It is either very trite or has little to distinguish it from informational prose except rime or meter. Tennyson's "The Oak" (page 171) is an excellent example of didactic *poetry*. The familiar couplet

Early to bed and early to rise,
Makes a man healthy, wealthy, and wise

is more aptly characterized as didactic *verse*.

Undoubtedly, so far in this chapter, we have spoken too categorically, have made our distinctions too sharp and definite. All poetic excellence is a matter of degree. There are no absolute lines between sentimentality and true emotion, artificial and genuine eloquence, didactic verse and didactic poetry. Though the difference between extreme examples is easy to recognize, subtler discriminations are harder to make. But a primary distinction between the educated man and the ignorant man is the ability to make value judgments.

A final caution to students. In making judgments on literature, always be honest. Do not pretend to like what you really do not like. Do not be afraid to admit a liking for what you do like. A genuine enthusiasm for the second-rate is much better than false enthusiasm or no enthusiasm at all. Be neither hasty nor timorous in making your judgments. When you have attentively read a poem and thoroughly considered it, decide what you think. Do not hedge, equivocate, or try to find out others' opinions before forming your own. Having formed an opinion and expressed it, do not allow it to petrify. Compare your opinion *then* with the opinions of others;

allow yourself to change it when convinced of its error: in this way you learn. Honesty, courage, and humility are the necessary moral foundations for all genuine literary judgment.

In the poems for comparison at the end of this chapter, the distinction to be made is not always between black and white; it may be between varying degrees of poetic merit.

EXERCISE

Poetry is not so much a thing as a quality; it exists in varying degrees in different specimens of language. Though we cannot always say definitely, "This is poetry; that is not," we can often say, "This is more poetical than that." Rank the following passages from most poetical to least poetical or not-poetical-at-all:

a. Why should we be in such desperate haste to succeed and in such desperate enterprises? If a man does not keep pace with his companions, perhaps it is because he hears a different drummer. Let him step to the music which he hears, however measured or far away.

b. $(x - 12) (x - 2) = x^2 - 14x + 24.$

c. Thirty days hath September,
April, June, and November.
All the rest have thirty-one,
Except February alone,
To which we twenty-eight assign,
Till leap year makes it twenty-nine.

d. "Meeting at Night" (page 46).

e. Thus, through the serene tranquillities of the tropical sea, among waves whose handclappings were suspended by exceeding rapture, Moby Dick moved on, still withholding from sight the full terrors of his submerged trunk, entirely hiding the wrenched hideousness of his jaw. But soon the fore part of him slowly rose from the water; for an instant his whole marbleized body formed a high arch, like Virginia's Natural Bridge, and warningly waving his bannered flukes in the air, the grand god revealed himself, sounded, and went out of sight. Hoveringly halting, and dipping on the wing, the white sea fowls longingly lingered over the agitated pool that he left.

f. Nature in the abstract is the aggregate of the powers and properties of all things. Nature means the sum of all phenomena, together with the causes which produce them; including not only all that happens, but all that is capable of happening; the unused capabilities of causes being as much a part of the idea of Nature, as those which take effect.

● ● ●

SAY NOT THE STRUGGLE NOUGHT AVAILETH

Say not the struggle nought availeth,
   The labor and the wounds are vain,
The enemy faints not, nor faileth,
   And as things have been they remain.

If hopes were dupes, fears may be liars;   5
   It may be, in yon smoke concealed,
Your comrades chase e'en now the fliers,
   And, but for you, possess the field.

For while the tired waves, vainly breaking,
   Seem here no painful inch to gain,   10
Far back, through creeks and inlets making,
   Comes silent, flooding in, the main.

And not by eastern windows only,
   When daylight comes, comes in the light,
In front, the sun climbs slow, how slowly,   15
   But westward, look, the land is bright.

THE MAN WHO THINKS HE CAN

If you think you are beaten, you are;
   If you think you dare not, you don't.
If you'd like to win, but think you can't,
   It's almost a cinch you won't.
If you think you'll lose, you're lost,   5
   For out in the world we find
Success begins with a fellow's will;
   It's all in the state of mind.

If you think you're outclassed, you are;
   You've got to think high to rise.   10
You've got to be sure of yourself before
   You can ever win a prize.
Life's battles don't always go
   To the stronger or faster man;
But soon or late the man who wins   15
   Is the one who thinks he can.

QUESTION

   1. Which of the above poems has more poetic merit? Discuss.

A PRAYER IN SPRING

Oh, give us pleasure in the flowers today;
And give us not to think so far away
As the uncertain harvest; keep us here
All simply in the springing of the year.

Oh, give us pleasure in the orchard white,   5
Like nothing else by day, like ghosts by night;
And make us happy in the happy bees,
The swarm dilating round the perfect trees.

And make us happy in the darting bird
That suddenly above the bees is heard,   10
The meteor that thrusts in with needle bill,
And off a blossom in mid air stands still.

For this is love and nothing else is love,
The which it is reserved for God above
To sanctify to what far ends He will,   15
But which it only needs that we fulfill.

PRAY IN MAY

Today the birds are singing and
The grass and leaves are green,
And all the gentle earth presents
A bright and sunny scene.
It is the merry month of May   5
When flowers bloom once more,
And there are hopes and happy dreams
And promises in store.
What time could be more wisely spent
Than this the first of May   10
To say that we are thankful for
Our blessings every day?
To give our gratitude to God
In humbleness and prayer
And offer deeds of charity   15
As incense in the air?
Then let us love our neighbor and
Our rich and fruitful sod,
And let us go to church today
And thank almighty God.   20

1. Which poem treats its subject with greater truth, freshness, and technical skill?

GOD'S WILL FOR YOU AND ME

Just to be tender, just to be true,
Just to be glad the whole day through,
Just to be merciful, just to be mild,
Just to be trustful as a child,
Just to be gentle and kind and sweet,   5
Just to be helpful with willing feet,
Just to be cheery when things go wrong,
Just to drive sadness away with a song,
Whether the hour is dark or bright,
Just to be loyal to God and right,   10
Just to believe that God knows best,
Just in his promises ever to rest—
Just to let love be our daily key,
That is God's will for you and me.

PIED BEAUTY

Glory be to God for dappled things—
    For skies of couple-color as a brinded cow;
        For rose-moles all in stipple upon trout that swim;
Fresh-firecoal chestnut-falls; finches' wings;
    Landscape plotted and pieced—fold, fallow and plow;   5
    And all trades, their gear and tackle and trim.

All things counter, original, spare, strange;
    Whatever is fickle, freckled (who knows how?)
    With swift, slow; sweet, sour; adazzle, dim;
He fathers-forth whose beauty is past change: 10
        Praise him.

QUESTION

1. Which is the superior poem? Explain in full.

IF I CAN STOP ONE HEART FROM BREAKING

If I can stop one heart from breaking,
I shall not live in vain;
If I can ease one life the aching,
Or cool one pain,

Or help one fainting robin
Unto his nest again,
I shall not live in vain.

DEATH IS A DIALOGUE

Death is a dialogue between
The spirit and the dust.
"Dissolve," says Death. The Spirit, "Sir,
I have another trust."

Death doubts it, argues from the ground.
The Spirit turns away,
Just laying off, for evidence,
An overcoat of clay.

QUESTION

1. Both of these poems are by the American poet Emily Dickinson. Which more surely testifies to her poetic power? Why?

MY SON, MY EXECUTIONER

My son, my executioner,
    I take you in my arms,
Quiet and small and just astir,
    And whom my body warms.

Sweet death, small son, our instrument   5
    Of immortality,
Your cries and hungers document
    Our bodily decay.

We twenty-five and twenty-two,
    Who seemed to live forever,   10
Observe enduring life in you
    And start to die together.

I take into my arms the death
　　Maturity exacts,
And name with my imperfect breath　　　　15
　　The mortal paradox.

ONLY A BABY SMALL

Only a baby small,
　　Dropped from the skies,
Only a laughing face,
　　Two sunny eyes;
Only two cherry lips,　　　　　　　　　5
　　One chubby nose;
Only two little hands,
　　Ten little toes.

Only a golden head,
　　Curly and soft;　　　　　　　　　10
Only a tongue that wags
　　Loudly and oft;
Only a little brain,
　　Empty of thought;
Only a little heart,　　　　　　　　　15
　　Troubled with naught.

Only a tender flower
　　Sent us to rear;
Only a life to love
　　While we are here;　　　　　　　　20
Only a baby small,
　　Never at rest;
Small, but how dear to us,
　　God knoweth best.

QUESTIONS

1. What is the "mortal paradox" of the first poem? Upon what paradox
is the second poem based? Which paradox seems to you more arresting and
significant?

2. Which of these two poems is superior? Support your answer by referring to both form and content.

THE SEND-OFF

Down the close, darkening lanes they sang their way
　　To the siding-shed,
And lined the train with faces grimly gay.

Their breasts were stuck all white with wreath and spray
As men's are, dead.   5

Dull porters watched them, and a casual tramp
Stood staring hard,
Sorry to miss them from the upland camp.
Then, unmoved, signals nodded, and a lamp
Winked to the guard.   10

So secretly, like wrongs hushed-up, they went.
They were not ours:
We never heard to which front these were sent.

Nor there if they yet mock what women meant
Who gave them flowers.   15

Shall they return to beatings of great bells
In wild train-loads?
A few, a few, too few for drums and yells,
May creep back, silent, to village wells
Up half-known roads.   20

CHA TILL MACCRUIMEIN

The pipes in the street were playing bravely,
    The marching lads went by,
With merry hearts and voices singing
    My friends marched out to die;
But I was hearing a lonely pibroch   5
    Out of an older war,
"Farewell, farewell, farewell, MacCrimmon,
    MacCrimmon comes no more."

And every lad in his heart was dreaming
    Of honor and wealth to come,   10
And honor and noble pride were calling
    To the tune of the pipes and drum;
But I was hearing a woman singing
    On dark Dunvegan shore,
"In battle or peace, with wealth or honor,   15
    MacCrimmon comes no more."

And there in front of the men were marching,
    With feet that made no mark,
The grey old ghosts of the ancient fighters
    Come back again from the dark;   20

And in front of them all MacCrimmon piping
  A weary tune and sore,
"On the gathering day, for ever and ever,
  MacCrimmon comes no more."

QUESTIONS

1. Vocabulary: *pibroch* (5).
2. The first poem was written by an English poet, the second by a Scottish; both poets were killed in World War I. "Cha Till Maccruimein" is Gaelic and means "MacCrimmon comes no more." The MacCrimmons were a famous race of hereditary pipers from the Isle of Skye. One of them, when his clan was about to leave on a dangerous expedition, composed a lament in which he accurately prophesied his own death in the coming fight. According to Sir Walter Scott, emigrants from the West Highlands and Western Isles usually left their native shore to the accompaniment of this strain. Compare these two poems as to subject and purpose. Taking into account their rhythm, imagery, freshness, and emotional content, decide which is the superior poem.[3]

LITTLE BOY BLUE

The little toy dog is covered with dust,
  But sturdy and staunch he stands;
And the little toy soldier is red with rust,
  And his musket moulds in his hands.
Time was when the little toy dog was new,   5
  And the soldier was passing fair;
And that was the time when our Little Boy Blue
  Kissed them and put them there.

"Now, don't you go till I come," he said,
  "And don't you make any noise!"   10
So, toddling off to his trundle-bed,
  He dreamt of the pretty toys;
And, as he was dreaming, an angel song
  Awakened our Little Boy Blue—
Oh! the years are many, the years are long,   15
  But the little toy friends are true!

Ay, faithful to Little Boy Blue they stand,
  Each in the same old place—
Awaiting the touch of a little hand,
  The smile of a little face;   20

[3] For this pairing I am indebted to Denys Thompson, *Reading and Discrimination*, Revised Edition, London, Chatto & Windus, 1954.

And they wonder, as waiting the long years through
    In the dust of that little chair,
What has become of our Little Boy Blue,
    Since he kissed them and put them there.

THE TOYS

My little Son, who looked from thoughtful eyes
And moved and spoke in quiet grown-up wise,
Having my law the seventh time disobeyed,
I struck him, and dismissed
    With hard words and unkissed,   5
His Mother, who was patient, being dead.
Then, fearing lest his grief should hinder sleep,
    I visited his bed,
But found him slumbering deep,
With darkened eyelids, and their lashes yet   10
From his late sobbing wet.
And I, with moan,
Kissing away his tears, left others of my own;
For, on a table drawn beside his head,
He had put, within his reach,   15
A box of counters and a red-veined stone,
A piece of glass abraded by the beach,
And six or seven shells,
A bottle with bluebells,
And two French copper coins, ranged there with careful art, 20
To comfort his sad heart.
So when that night I prayed
To God, I wept, and said:
Ah, when at last we lie with trancèd breath,
Not vexing Thee in death,   25
And thou rememberest of what toys
We made our joys,
How weakly understood
Thy great commanded good,
Then, fatherly not less   30
Than I whom Thou hast moulded from the clay,
Thou'lt leave Thy wrath, and say,
"I will be sorry for their childishness."

QUESTION

1. One of these poems has an obvious appeal for the beginning reader.
The other is likely to have more meaning for the mature reader. Try to explain
in terms of sentimentality and honesty.

THE LONG VOYAGE

Not that the pines were darker there,
nor mid-May dogwood brighter there,
nor swifts more swift in summer air;
    it was my own country,

having its thunderclap of spring,   5
its long midsummer ripening,
its corn hoar-stiff at harvesting,
    almost like any country,

yet being mine; its face, its speech,
its hills bent low within my reach,   10
its river birch and upland beech
    were mine, of my own country.

Now the dark waters at the bow
fold back, like earth against the plow;
foam brightens like the dogwood now   15
    at home, in my own country.

BREATHES THERE THE MAN

Breathes there the man, with soul so dead,
Who never to himself hath said,
    This is my own, my native land!
Whose heart hath ne'er within him burned,
As home his footsteps he hath turned,   5
    From wandering on a foreign strand?
If such there breathe, go, mark him well;
For him no minstrel raptures swell;
High though his titles, proud his name,
Boundless his wealth as wish can claim—   10
Despite those titles, power, and pelf,
The wretch, concentered all in self,
Living, shall forfeit fair renown,
And, doubly dying, shall go down
To the vile dust from whence he sprung,   15
Unwept, unhonored, and unsung.

QUESTIONS

1. Which poem communicates the more genuine poetic emotion? Which is more rhetorical? Justify your answer.

2. Compare the first poem with "America for Me" (page 230). Which exhibits the greater maturity of attitude?

BOY-MAN

England's lads are miniature men
To start with, grammar in their shiny hats,
And serious: in America who knows when
Manhood begins? Presidents dance and hug
And while the kind King waves and gravely chats   5
America wets on England's old green rug.

The boy-man roars. Worry alone will give
This one the verisimilitude of age.
Those white teeth are his own, for he must live
Longer, grow taller than the Texas race.   10
Fresh are his eyes, his darkening skin the gauge
Of bloods that freely mix beneath his face.

He knows the application of the book
But not who wrote it; shuts it like a shot.
Rather than read he thinks that he will look,   15
Rather than look he thinks that he will talk,
Rather than talk he thinks that he will not
Bother at all; would rather ride than walk.

His means of conversation is the joke,
Humor his language underneath which lies   20
The undecoded dialect of the folk.
Abroad he scorns the foreigner: what's old
Is worn, what's different bad, what's odd unwise.
He gives off heat and is enraged by cold.

Charming, becoming to the suits he wears,   25
The boy-man, younger than his eldest son,
Inherits the state; upon his silver hairs
Time like a panama hat sits at a tilt
And smiles. To him the world has just begun
And every city waiting to be built.   30

Mister, remove your shoulder from the wheel
And say this prayer, "Increase my vitamins,
Make my decisions of the finest steel,
Pour motor oil upon my troubled spawn,
Forgive the Europeans for their sins,   35
Establish them, that values may go on."

1. Vocabulary: *verisimilitude* (8), *spawn* (34).
2. What is the subject of the poem?
3. What is the tone—admiration? mockery? or both?
4. Explain fully the figures of speech in 2, 6, 26, 28–29, and their appropriateness. What kind of irony appears in the last stanza?

AMERICA FOR ME

'Tis fine to see the Old World, and travel up and down
Among the famous palaces and cities of renown,
To admire the crumbly castles and the statues of the kings—
But now I think I've had enough of antiquated things.

> *So it's home again, and home again, America for me!* 5
> *My heart is turning home again, and there I long to be,*
> *In the land of youth and freedom beyond the ocean bars,*
> *Where the air is full of sunlight and the flag is full of stars.*

Oh, London is a man's town, there's power in the air;
And Paris is a woman's town, with flowers in her hair; 10
And it's sweet to dream in Venice, and it's great to study Rome;
But when it comes to living there is no place like home.

I like the German fir-woods, in green battalions drilled;
I like the gardens of Versailles with flashing fountains filled;
But, oh, to take your hand, my dear, and ramble for a day 15
In the friendly western woodlands where Nature has her way!

I know that Europe's wonderful, yet something seems to lack:
The Past is too much with her, and the people looking back.
But the glory of the Present is to make the Future free—
We love our land for what she is and what she is to be. 20

> *Oh, it's home again, and home again, America for me!*
> *I want a ship that's westward bound to plow the rolling sea,*
> *To the blessèd Land of Room Enough beyond the ocean bars,*
> *Where the air is full of sunlight and the flag is full of stars.*

1. In what respects do the attitudes expressed in this poem fit the characterization made in "Boy-Man"?
2. "America for Me" and "Boy-Man" were both written by Americans. Which is more worthy of prolonged consideration? Why?

16

Good Poetry and Great

If a poem has successfully met the test in the question, *How fully has it accomplished its purpose?* we are ready to subject it to our second question, *How important is its purpose?*

Great poetry must, of course, be good poetry. Noble intent alone cannot redeem a work that does not measure high on the scale of accomplishment; otherwise the sentimental and purely didactic verse of much of the last chapter would stand with the world's masterpieces. But once a work has been judged as success-ful on the scale of execution, its final standing will depend on its significance of purpose.

Suppose, for instance, we consider three poems in our text: the limerick "There was a young lady of Niger" (page 200), Elinor Wylie's poem "Velvet Shoes" (page 66), and Shakespeare's sonnet "That Time of Year" (page 202). Each of these would prob-ably be judged by competent critics as highly successful in ac-complishing what it sets out to do. The limerick tells its little story without an unnecessary word, with no "wrong" word, with no dis-tortion of normal sentence order forced by exigencies of meter or rime; the limerick form is ideally suited to the author's humorous purpose; and the manner in which the story is told, with its under-statement, its neat shift in position of the lady and her smile, is economical and delicious. Yet we should hardly call this poetry at all: it does not really communicate experience, nor does it attempt to. It attempts merely to relate a brief anecdote humorously and effectively. Miss Wylie's poem, on the other hand, is poetry, and very good poetry. It appeals richly to our senses and to our imagination: it succeeds excellently in its purpose, to convey the white beauty, peace, and muffled silence of a windless winter day when soft snow is everywhere—in the air, on the trees, and on the sidewalks. Yet when we compare this excellent poem with Shakespeare's, we again see sharp differences. The first engages the senses and the imagination; it does not deeply affect us emotionally or give us much to occupy our minds. It is not as close to the core of human living and suffering and loving as is Shakespeare's sonnet. It is concerned, in fact, primarily with that staple of small talk, the weather. Shakespeare's is concerned with the universal human tragedy of growing old, with approaching death, and with love. Of these three selections, then, Shakespeare's is the greatest. It "says" more than does either Miss Wylie's or the limerick; it communicates a richer experience; it successfully accomplishes a more significant purpose. The discriminating reader will get from it a deeper enjoyment because he has been nourished as well as delighted.

Great poetry engages the whole man in his response—senses, imagination, emotion, intellect; it does not touch him merely on one or two sides of his nature. Great poetry seeks not merely to entertain the reader but to bring him, along with pure pleasure, fresh insights, or renewed insights, and important insights, into the nature of human experience. Great poetry, we might say, gives its reader a broader and deeper understanding of life, of his fellow men, and of himself, always with the qualification, of course, that the kind of insight which literature gives is not necessarily the kind that can be summed up in a simple "lesson" or "moral." It is knowledge—felt knowledge, new knowledge—of the complexities of human nature and of the tragedies and sufferings, the excitements and joys, that characterize human experience.

Is Shakespeare's sonnet a *great* poem? It is, at least, a great *sonnet*. Greatness, like goodness, is relative. If we compare any of Shakespeare's sonnets with his greatest plays—*Macbeth, Othello, Hamlet, King Lear*—another big difference appears. What is undertaken and accomplished in these tragedies is enormously greater, more difficult, and more complex than could ever be undertaken or accomplished in a single sonnet. Greatness in literature, in fact, cannot be entirely dissociated from size. In literature, as in basketball and football, a good big man is better than a good little man. The greatness of a poem is in proportion to the range and depth and intensity of experience that it brings to us: its amount of life.

Shakespeare's plays offer us a multiplicity of life and a depth of living that could never be compressed into the fourteen lines of a sonnet. They organize a greater complexity of life and experience into unity.

Yet, after all, we have provided no easy yardsticks or rule-of-thumb measures for literary judgment. There are no mechanical tests. The final measuring rod can be only the responsiveness, the maturity, the taste and discernment of the cultivated reader. Such taste and discernment are partly a native endowment, partly the product of maturity and experience, partly the achievement of conscious study, training, and intellectual effort. They cannot be achieved suddenly or quickly; they can never be achieved in perfection. The pull is a long pull and a hard pull. But success, even relative success, brings enormous rewards in enrichment and command of life.

* * *

THE DEATH OF THE HIRED MAN [1]

Mary sat musing on the lamp-flame at the table
Waiting for Warren. When she heard his step,
She ran on tip-toe down the darkened passage
To meet him in the doorway with the news
And put him on his guard. "Silas is back." 5
She pushed him outward with her through the door
And shut it after her. "Be kind," she said.
She took the market things from Warren's arms
And set them on the porch, then drew him down
To sit beside her on the wooden steps. 10

"When was I ever anything but kind to him?
But I'll not have the fellow back," he said.
"I told him so last haying, didn't I?
If he left then, I said, that ended it.
What good is he? Who else will harbor him 15
At his age for the little he can do?
What help he is there's no depending on.
Off he goes always when I need him most.
He thinks he ought to earn a little pay,
Enough at least to buy tobacco with, 20
So he won't have to beg and be beholden.

[1] Mr. Frost recorded "The Death of the Hired Man" (LP, Caedman, TC 1060; or LP, National Council of Teachers of English, RL20–1).

'All right,' I say, 'I can't afford to pay
Any fixed wages, though I wish I could.'
'Someone else can.' 'Then someone else will have to.'
I shouldn't mind his bettering himself   25
If that was what it was. You can be certain,
When he begins like that, there's someone at him
Trying to coax him off with pocket-money,—
In haying time, when any help is scarce.
In winter he comes back to us. I'm done."   30

"Sh! not so loud: he'll hear you," Mary said.

"I want him to: he'll have to soon or late."

"He's worn out. He's asleep beside the stove.
When I came up from Rowe's I found him here,
Huddled against the barn-door fast asleep,   35
A miserable sight, and frightening, too—
You needn't smile—I didn't recognize him—
I wasn't looking for him—and he's changed.
Wait till you see."

              "Where did you say he'd been?"

"He didn't say. I dragged him to the house,   40
And gave him tea and tried to make him smoke.
I tried to make him talk about his travels.
Nothing would do: he just kept nodding off."

"What did he say? Did he say anything?"

"But little."

              "Anything? Mary, confess   45
He said he'd come to ditch the meadow for me."

"Warren!"

              "But did he? I just want to know."

"Of course he did. What would you have him say?
Surely you wouldn't grudge the poor old man
Some humble way to save his self-respect.   50
He added, if you really care to know,
He meant to clear the upper pasture, too.
That sounds like something you have heard before?

Warren, I wish you could have heard the way
He jumbled everything. I stopped to look   55
Two or three times—he made me feel so queer—
To see if he was talking in his sleep.
He ran on Harold Wilson—you remember—
The boy you had in haying four years since.
He's finished school, and teaching in his college.   60
Silas declares you'll have to get him back.
He says they two will make a team for work:
Between them they will lay this farm as smooth!
The way he mixed that in with other things.
He thinks young Wilson a likely lad, though daft   65
On education—you know how they fought
All through July under the blazing sun,
Silas up on the cart to build the load,
Harold along beside to pitch it on."

"Yes, I took care to keep well out of earshot."   70

"Well, those days trouble Silas like a dream.
You wouldn't think they would. How some things linger!
Harold's young college boy's assurance piqued him.
After so many years he still keeps finding
Good arguments he sees he might have used.   75
I sympathize. I know just how it feels
To think of the right thing to say too late.
Harold's associated in his mind with Latin.
He asked me what I thought of Harold's saying
He studied Latin like the violin   80
Because he liked it—that an argument!
He said he couldn't make the boy believe
He could find water with a hazel prong—
Which showed how much good school had ever done him.
He wanted to go over that. But most of all   85
He thinks if he could have another chance
To teach him how to build a load of hay—"

"I know, that's Silas' one accomplishment.
He bundles every forkful in its place,
And tags and numbers it for future reference,   90
So he can find and easily dislodge it
In the unloading. Silas does that well.
He takes it out in bunches like big birds' nests.
You never see him standing on the hay
He's trying to lift, straining to lift himself."   95

"He thinks if he could teach him that, he'd be
Some good perhaps to someone in the world.
He hates to see a boy the fool of books.
Poor Silas, so concerned for other folk,
And nothing to look backward to with pride,   100
And nothing to look forward to with hope,
So now and never any different."

Part of a moon was falling down the west,
Dragging the whole sky with it to the hills.
Its light poured softly in her lap. She saw it   105
And spread her apron to it. She put out her hand
Among the harp-like morning-glory strings,
Taut with the dew from garden bed to eaves,
As if she played unheard some tenderness
That wrought on him beside her in the night.   110
"Warren," she said, "he has come home to die:
You needn't be afraid he'll leave you this time."

"Home," he mocked gently.

                        "Yes, what else but home?
It all depends on what you mean by home.
Of course he's nothing to us, any more   115
Than was the hound that came a stranger to us
Out of the woods, worn out upon the trail."

"Home is the place where, when you have to go there,
They have to take you in."

                        "I should have called it
Something you somehow haven't to deserve."   120

Warren leaned out and took a step or two,
Picked up a little stick, and brought it back
And broke it in his hand and tossed it by.
"Silas has better claim on us you think
Than on his brother? Thirteen little miles   125
As the road winds would bring him to his door.
Silas has walked that far no doubt today.
Why doesn't he go there? His brother's rich,
A somebody—director in the bank."

"He never told us that."

                        "We know it though."   130

"I think his brother ought to help, of course.
I'll see to that if there is need. He ought of right
To take him in, and might be willing to—
He may be better than appearances.
But have some pity on Silas. Do you think   135
If he had any pride in claiming kin
Or anything he looked for from his brother,
He'd keep so still about him all this time?"

"I wonder what's between them."

                              "I can tell you.
Silas is what he is—we wouldn't mind him—   140
But just the kind that kinsfolk can't abide.
He never did a thing so very bad.
He don't know why he isn't quite as good
As anybody. Worthless though he is,
He won't be made ashamed to please his brother."   145

"*I* can't think Si ever hurt anyone."

"No, but he hurt my heart the way he lay
And rolled his old head on that sharp-edged chair-back.
He wouldn't let me put him on the lounge.
You must go in and see what you can do.   150
I made the bed up for him there tonight.
You'll be surprised at him—how much he's broken.
His working days are done; I'm sure of it."

"I'd not be in a hurry to say that."

"I haven't been. Go, look, see for yourself.   155
But, Warren, please remember how it is:
He's come to help you ditch the meadow.
He has a plan. You mustn't laugh at him.
He may not speak of it, and then he may.
I'll sit and see if that small sailing cloud   160
Will hit or miss the moon."

                    It hit the moon.
Then there were three there, making a dim row,
The moon, the little silver cloud, and she.

Warren returned—too soon, it seemed to her,

Slipped to her side, caught up her hand and waited.   165

"Warren?" she questioned.

"Dead," was all he answered.

—*Robert Frost [1874–1963]*

QUESTIONS

1. Vocabulary: *beholden* (21), *piqued* (73).
2. What kind of person is Silas? Characterize him as fully as possible, showing, especially, what is revealed about his character by his relationships with Harold Wilson, with his brother, and with Warren and Mary.
3. Characterize Warren and Mary. Are they basically unlike in their natures and attitudes, or not really too far apart? Can you suggest reasons why Warren should at first be less solicitous than Mary?
4. Define as precisely as possible the moral problem faced by Warren and Mary. How would Warren finally have answered it (if an answer had not been made unnecessary)? Give reasons for your answer.
5. Is the poem written in free verse or blank verse? How would you describe its rhythm and language?
6. Using the criteria for literary greatness developed in this chapter, how would you rate this poem as compared with Alfred Noyes's "The Barrel-Organ" (page 176)? Why?

THE LOVE SONG OF J. ALFRED PRUFROCK [2]

S'io credesse che mia risposta fosse
A persona che mai tornasse al mondo,
Questa fiamma staria senza piu scosse.
Ma perciocche giammai di questo fondo
Non torno vivo alcun, s'i'odo il vero,
Senza tema d'infamia ti rispondo.

Let us go then, you and I,
When the evening is spread out against the sky
Like a patient etherized upon a table;
Let us go, through certain half-deserted streets,
The muttering retreats   5
Of restless nights in one-night cheap hotels
And sawdust restaurants with oyster-shells:
Streets that follow like a tedious argument
Of insidious intent
To lead you to an overwhelming question. . . .   10
Oh, do not ask, "What is it?"
Let us go and make our visit.

---

[2] Mr. Eliot has recorded "The Love Song of J. Alfred Prufrock" (LP, Harvard Vocarium, L–6002; or LP, Caedmon, TC 1045).

In the room the women come and go
Talking of Michelangelo.

The yellow fog that rubs its back upon the window-panes,   15
The yellow smoke that rubs its muzzle on the window-panes
Licked its tongue into the corners of the evening,
Lingered upon the pools that stand in drains,
Let fall upon its back the soot that falls from chimneys,
Slipped by the terrace, made a sudden leap,   20
And seeing that it was a soft October night,
Curled once about the house, and fell asleep.

And indeed there will be time
For the yellow smoke that slides along the street,
Rubbing its back upon the window-panes;   25
There will be time, there will be time
To prepare a face to meet the faces that you meet;
There will be time to murder and create,
And time for all the works and days of hands
That lift and drop a question on your plate;   30
Time for you and time for me,
And time yet for a hundred indecisions,
And for a hundred visions and revisions,
Before the taking of a toast and tea.

In the room the women come and go   35
Talking of Michelangelo.

And indeed there will be time
To wonder, "Do I dare?" and, "Do I dare?"
Time to turn back and descend the stair,
With a bald spot in the middle of my hair—   40
[They will say: "How his hair is growing thin!"]
My morning coat, my collar mounting firmly to the chin,
My necktie rich and modest, but asserted by a simple pin—
[They will say: "But how his arms and legs are thin!"]
Do I dare   45
Disturb the universe?
In a minute there is time
For decisions and revisions which a minute will reverse.
For I have known them all already, known them all:—

Have known the evenings, mornings, afternoons,   50
I have measured out my life with coffee spoons;
I know the voices dying with a dying fall
Beneath the music from a farther room.
    So how should I presume?

239

And I have known the eyes already, known them all—   55
The eyes that fix you in a formulated phrase,
And when I am formulated, sprawling on a pin,
When I am pinned and wriggling on the wall,
Then how should I begin
To spit out all the butt-ends of my days and ways?   60
    And how should I presume?

And I have known the arms already, known them all—
Arms that are braceleted and white and bare
[But in the lamplight, downed with light brown hair!]
Is it perfume from a dress   65
That makes me so digress?
Arms that lie along a table, or wrap about a shawl.
    And should I then presume?
    And how should I begin?

                .   .   .   .   .

Shall I say, I have gone at dusk through narrow streets   70
And watched the smoke that rises from the pipes
Of lonely men in shirt-sleeves, leaning out of windows? . . .

I should have been a pair of ragged claws
Scuttling across the floors of silent seas.

                .   .   .   .   .

And the afternoon, the evening, sleeps so peacefully!   75
Smoothed by long fingers,
Asleep . . . tired . . . or it malingers,
Stretched on the floor, here beside you and me.
Should I, after tea and cakes and ices,
Have the strength to force the moment to its crisis?   80
But though I have wept and fasted, wept and prayed,
Though I have seen my head [grown slightly bald] brought in
    upon a platter,
I am no prophet—and here's no great matter;
I have seen the moment of my greatness flicker,
And I have seen the eternal Footman hold my coat, and snicker,   85
And in short, I was afraid.

And would it have been worth it, after all,
After the cups, the marmalade, the tea,
Among the porcelain, among some talk of you and me,
Would it have been worth while,   90
To have bitten off the matter with a smile,
To have squeezed the universe into a ball
To roll it toward some overwhelming question,

To say: "I am Lazarus, come from the dead,
Come back to tell you all, I shall tell you all"—   95
If one, settling a pillow by her head,
    Should say: "That is not what I meant at all.
    That is not it, at all."

And would it have been worth it, after all,
Would it have been worth while,   100
After the sunsets and the dooryards and the sprinkled streets,
After the novels, after the teacups, after the skirts that trail
    along the floor—
And this, and so much more?—
It is impossible to say just what I mean!
But as if a magic lantern threw the nerves in patterns on a screen: 105
Would it have been worth while
If one, settling a pillow or throwing off a shawl,
And turning toward the window, should say:
    "That is not it at all,
    That is not what I meant, at all."   110

        .   .   .   .   .

No! I am not Prince Hamlet, nor was meant to be;
Am an attendant lord, one that will do
To swell a progress, start a scene or two,
Advise the prince; no doubt, an easy tool,
Deferential, glad to be of use,   115
Politic, cautious, and meticulous:
Full of high sentence, but a bit obtuse;
At times, indeed, almost ridiculous—
Almost, at times, the Fool.

I grow old. . . . I grow old. . . .   120
I shall wear the bottoms of my trousers rolled.°   cuffed
Shall I part my hair behind? Do I dare to eat a peach?
I shall wear white flannel trousers, and walk upon the beach.
I have heard the mermaids singing, each to each.

I do not think that they will sing to me.   125

I have seen them riding seaward on the waves
Combing the white hair of the waves blown back
When the wind blows the water white and black.

We have lingered in the chambers of the sea
By sea-girls wreathed with seaweed red and brown   130
Till human voices wake us, and we drown.
                           —*T. S. Eliot* [1888–]

QUESTIONS

1. Vocabulary: *insidious* (9), *Michelangelo* (14), *muzzle* (16), *malingers* (77), *progress* (113), *deferential* (115), *politic* (116), *meticulous* (116), *sentence* (117).

2. This poem may be for you the most difficult in the book, because it uses a "stream of consciousness" technique (that is, presents the apparently random thoughts going through a person's head within a certain time interval), in which the transitional links are psychological rather than logical, and also because it uses allusions with which you may be unfamiliar. Even though you do not at first understand the poem in detail, you should be able to get from it a quite accurate picture of Prufrock's character and personality. What kind of person is he? (Answer this as fully as possible.) From what class of society is he? What one line especially well sums up the nature of his past life? A brief initial orientation may be helpful: Prufrock is apparently on his way, at the beginning of the poem, to a late afternoon tea, at which he wishes (or does he?) to make a declaration of love to some lady who will be present. The "you and I" of the first line are divided parts of Prufrock's own nature, for he is undergoing internal conflict. Does he make the declaration? Why not? Where does the climax of the poem come? If the first half of the poem (up to the climax) is devoted to Prufrock's effort to prepare himself psychologically to make the declaration (or to postponing such effort), what is the latter half (after the climax) devoted to?

3. There are a number of striking or unusual figures of speech in the poem. Most of them in some way reflect Prufrock's own nature or his desires or fears. From this point of view discuss lines 2–3; 15–22 and 75–78; 57–58; 73–74; and 124–31. What figure of speech is lines 73–74? In what respect is the title ironical?

4. The poem makes an extensive use of literary allusion. The Italian epigraph is a passage from Dante's *Inferno* in which a man in Hell tells a visitor that he would never tell his story if there were a chance that it would get back to living ears. In line 29 the phrase "works and days" is the title of a long poem —a description of agricultural life and a call to toil—by the early Greek poet Hesiod. Line 52 echoes the opening speech of Shakespeare's *Twelfth Night*. The prophet of lines 81–83 is John the Baptist, whose head was delivered to Salome by Herod as a reward for her dancing (Matthew 14:1–11, and Oscar Wilde's play *Salome*). Line 92 echoes the closing six lines of Marvell's "To His Coy Mistress" (page 64). Lazarus (94–95) may be either the beggar Lazarus of Luke 16 who was not permitted to return from the dead to warn the brothers of a rich man about Hell, or the Lazarus of John 11 whom Christ raised from death, or both. Lines 111–19 allude to a number of characters from Shakespeare's *Hamlet:* Hamlet himself, the chamberlain Polonius, and various minor characters including probably Rosencrantz, Guildenstern, and Osric. "Full of high sentence" (117) echoes Chaucer's description of the Clerk of Oxford in the Prologue to *The Canterbury Tales*. Relate as many of these allusions as you can to the character of Prufrock. How is Prufrock particularly like Hamlet, and how unlike? Contrast Prufrock with the speaker in "To His Coy Mistress."

5. This poem and "The Death of the Hired Man" are dramatic in structure. One is a drama with several characters who speak in their own voices; the other is a highly allusive soliloquy or interior monologue. In what ways do their dramatic structures facilitate what they have to say?

6. This poem and Charlotte Mew's "The Changeling" (page 159) both might be said to center around a contrast between two worlds—one real, the other unreal. Using the criteria for literary greatness developed in this chapter, how would you rate the two poems as compared to each other? Why?

AMONG SCHOOL CHILDREN

I

I walk through the long schoolroom questioning;
A kind old nun in a white hood replies;
The children learn to cipher and to sing,
To study reading-books and histories,
To cut and sew, be neat in everything   5
In the best modern way—the children's eyes
In momentary wonder stare upon
A sixty-year-old smiling public man.

II

I dream of a Ledaean body, bent
Above a sinking fire, a tale that she   10
Told of a harsh reproof, or trivial event
That changed some childish day to tragedy—
Told, and it seemed that our two natures blent
Into a sphere from youthful sympathy,
Or else, to alter Plato's parable,   15
Into the yolk and white of the one shell.

III

And thinking of that fit of grief or rage
I look upon one child or t'other there
And wonder if she stood so at that age—
For even daughters of the swan can share   20
Something of every paddler's heritage—
And had that color upon cheek or hair,
And thereupon my heart is driven wild:
She stands before me as a living child.

IV

Her present image floats into the mind—   25
Did Quattrocento finger fashion it
Hollow of cheek as though it drank the wind
And took a mess of shadows for its meat?

And I though never of Ledaean kind
Had pretty plumage once—enough of that,   30
Better to smile on all that smile, and show
There is a comfortable kind of old scarecrow.

V

What youthful mother, a shape upon her lap
Honey of generation had betrayed,
And that must sleep, shriek, struggle to escape   35
As recollection or the drug decide,
Would think her son, did she but see that shape
With sixty or more winters on its head,
A compensation for the pang of his birth,
Or the uncertainty of his setting forth?   40

VI

Plato thought nature but a spume that plays
Upon a ghostly paradigm of things;
Solider Aristotle played the taws
Upon the bottom of a king of kings;
World-famous golden-thighed Pythagoras   45
Fingered upon a fiddle-stick or strings
What a star sang and careless Muses heard:
Old clothes upon old sticks to scare a bird.

VII

Both nuns and mothers worship images,
But those the candles light are not as those   50
That animate a mother's reveries,
But keep a marble or a bronze repose.
And yet they too break hearts—O Presences
That passion, piety or affection knows,
And that all heavenly glory symbolize—   55
O self-born mockers of man's enterprise;

VIII

Labor is blossoming or dancing where
The body is not bruised to pleasure soul,
Nor beauty born out of its own despair,
Nor blear-eyed wisdom out of midnight oil.   60
O chestnut-tree, great-rooted blossomer,
Are you the leaf, the blossom or the bole?
O body swayed to music, O brightening glance,
How can we know the dancer from the dance?

—William Butler Yeats [1865–1939]

QUESTIONS

1. Vocabulary: *Quattrocento* (26), *mess* (28), *spume* (41), *paradigm* (42), *bole* (62).

2. William Butler Yeats was a senator of the Irish Free State from 1922 to 1928. This poem, written in 1926, arises out of a visit of inspection to an Irish school, probably Catholic since Ireland is primarily a Catholic country. In stanza II Yeats is thinking of the talented Maud Gonne, to whom he paid court so long and unsuccessfully (see "No Second Troy," Question 1, page 119). Plato (15), discussing love in the *Symposium*, represents male and female as having resulted from the division of an originally single being, round in shape, into two halves which are forever seeking to regain their original unity. What is "a Ledaean body" (9)? See line 10 and "Leda and the Swan" (page 119). What additional fairy-tale allusion is there in lines 20–21? What are the literal and symbolical implications of "bent" (9) and of "a sinking fire" (10)? What is the "present image" of Maud Gonne (25–28)? What figure of speech is "Quattrocento finger" (26), and what historical persons might it refer to?

3. What is the meaning of lines 33–34—especially, why is the child "betrayed"? "Shape" (33) and "winters" (38) are both metonymies; what is their contribution? Why does Yeats use "winters" instead of, say, "springs," as Housman does in "Loveliest of Trees" (page 170)?

4. Plato (41) thought the visible world simply a pale reflection or copy of a divine and more real world of "forms" or "ideas." Aristotle (43), a more realistic philosopher, was tutor to the youthful Alexander the Great, whom he may have occasionally whipped with "taws" (a whip made of leather thongs). Pythagoras (45), a philosopher and mathematician, discovered the laws of vibrating strings upon which harmony is based, thus demonstrating a correspondence between music and mathematics; conceiving of the universe as mathematically ordered and therefore harmonious, he supposed that the planets in their courses must give off varying musical tones—"the music of the spheres." According to ancient legend, he had a golden hip or thigh. What do these philosophers have in common in Yeats's mind, and how does this stanza relate to stanzas IV and V?

5. What "images" are worshipped by nuns (49), and why are nuns mentioned here? What other kinds of "images" have been mentioned in the poem? What are the "Presences" of lines 53–54? Why do they mock "man's enterprise"?

6. What main contrasts have been made in the poem? How does stanza VIII bring together and comment on these contrasts? What two meanings has "Labor" (57)? What is Yeats's conclusion about the relationship of body and mind or body and soul, of the real and the ideal? What is symbolized by the blossoming chestnut tree and the dancing dancer? Why does Yeats use two symbols rather than just one?

7. Using the criteria for literary greatness developed in this chapter, how would you rate "Among School Children" as compared with Swinburne's "When the Hounds of Spring" (page 152)?

EXERCISES

In the following exercises, use both scales of poetic measurement: that of perfection and that of significance of accomplishment.

1. If you have not already done so, go back and decide which is the finer poem, and why, in each of the following pairs:
   a. "The Written Word"—two versions (page 44).
   b. "Richard Cory" (page 39) or "The Rich Man" (page 40).
   c. "Epilogue to *Asolando*" (page 141) or "Epitaph" (page 142).

2. Considering such matters as economy and richness of poetic communication, inevitability of organization, and the complexity and maturity of the attitude or philosophy expressed, decide whether "Barter" or "Stopping by Woods on a Snowy Evening" is the superior poem (page 125).

3. Rank the following ballads according to the power and complexity of their poetic achievement and the human significance of the result: "The Twa Corbies" (page 12), "The Griesly Wife" (page 13), "Edward" (page 209).

4. Rank the following short poems and explain the reasons for your ranking:
   a. "Epitaph on Newton" (page 119), "The Span of Life" (page 186).
   b. "On a Clergyman's Horse Biting Him" (page 67), "Western Wind" page 78), "Of Alphus" (page 95).
   c. "The Turtle" (page 148), "Splinter" (page 182), "On His Seventy-Fifth Birthday" (page 282).
   d. "The Sea-Gull" (page 57), "The Tuft of Kelp" (page 89), "Quatrain" (page 122).
   e. "The Sick Rose" (page 78), "The Horseman" (page 89), "Song: Hark, hark!" (page 181).
   f. "Metrical Feet" (page 179), "The Dark Hills" (page 192), "Jack and His Father" (page 276).

5. "The Eagle" (page 5), "The Twa Corbies" (page 12), and "The Sea-Gull" (page 57) all deal with birds. Rank them on a scale of poetic worth.

6. The following poems are all on seasons of the years. Rank them on a scale of poetic accomplishment: "Winter" (page 6), "To Autumn" (page 51), "Spring" (page 11).

7. "The Man He Killed" (page 20), "Naming of Parts" (page 40), and "Song" (page 158) all treat the subject of war. Rank them according to their poetic worth.

8. "A Valediction: Forbidding Mourning" (page 62), "To Lucasta, Going to the Wars" (page 99), and "The 'Je Ne Sais Quoi'" (page 172) all in one way or another treat the subject of love. Evaluate and rank them.

9. You have read a number of poems in this book by Robert Browning. Rank the following in order of their excellence, and defend your ranking: "Meeting at Night" and "Parting at Morning" (considered as one poem) (pages 46 and 47), "My Star" (page 70), "My Last Duchess" (page 109), "Song" (page 127), "Epilogue to *Asolando*" (page 141).

10. Answer the same question with the following poems by Alfred, Lord Tennyson: "The Eagle" (page 5), "Ulysses" (page 79), "The Deserted House" (page 88), and "The Oak" (page 171).

11. "The House on the Hill" (page 88), and "Mr. Flood's Party" (page 292) both evoke a sense of loneliness. Which more surely guarantees the poetic reputation of Edwin Arlington Robinson?

12. Herrick's "To the Virgins, to Make Much of Time" (page 76) and Marvell's "To His Coy Mistress" (page 64) are both *carpe diem* poems of acknowledged excellence. Which achieves the more complex unity?

13. Explore the similarities and differences of the following two poems; then evaluate them in relation to each other: "The Groundswell" (page 48), "Dover Beach" (page 256).

14. Each of the following pairs is written by a single author. Pick the poem that you think represents the higher poetic accomplishment, and explain why:
   a. "Hillside Thaw" (page 54) or " 'Out, Out—' " (page 114).
   b. "The Sonnet" (page 208) or "Silent Noon" (page 295).
   c. "Edward" (page 209) or "Lord Randal" (page 211).
   d. "Ozymandias" (page 97) or "England in 1819" (page 191).
   e. "The World Is Too Much with Us" (page 34) or "London, 1802" (page 65).
   f. "You, Andrew Marvell" (page 72) or "Ars Poetica" (page 134).
   g. "There, is no frigate like a book" (page 33) or "Apparently with no surprise" (page 137).
   h. "I like to see it lap the miles" (page 190) or "Because I could not stop for Death" (page 267).
   i. "A Valediction: Forbidding Mourning" (page 62) or "Song" (page 269).
   j. "Winter" (page 6) or "Spring" (page 11).
   k. "John Gorham" (page 30) or "Another Dark Lady" (page 31).

Part Two

Poems for Further Reading

MORNING SONG FROM "SENLIN"

It is morning, Senlin says, and in the morning
When the light drips through the shutters like the dew,
I arise, I face the sunrise,
And do the things my fathers learned to do.
Stars in the purple dusk above the rooftops
Pale in a saffron mist and seem to die,
And I myself on a swiftly tilting planet
Stand before a glass and tie my tie.

Vine leaves tap my window,
Dew-drops sing to the garden stones,
The robin chirps in the chinaberry tree
Repeating three clear tones.

It is morning. I stand by the mirror
And tie my tie once more.
While waves far off in a pale rose twilight
Crash on a coral shore.
I stand by a mirror and comb my hair:
How small and white my face!—
The green earth tilts through a sphere of air
And bathes in a flame of space.

There are houses hanging above the stars
And stars hung under a sea.
And a sun far off in a shell of silence
Dapples my walls for me.

It is morning, Senlin says, and in the morning
Should I not pause in the light to remember god?
Upright and firm I stand on a star unstable,
He is immense and lonely as a cloud.
I will dedicate this moment before my mirror
To him alone, for him I will comb my hair.
Accept these humble offerings, cloud of silence!
I will think of you as I descend the stair.

Vine leaves tap my window,
The snail-track shines on the stones,
Dew-drops flash from the chinaberry tree
Repeating two clear tones.

It is morning, I awake from a bed of silence,
Shining I rise from the starless waters of sleep.
The walls are about me still as in the evening,
I am the same, and the same name still I keep.   40
The earth revolves with me, yet makes no motion,
The stars pale silently in a coral sky.
In a whistling void I stand before my mirror,
Unconcerned, and tie my tie.

There are horses neighing on far-off hills   45
Tossing their long white manes,
And mountains flash in the rose-white dusk,
Their shoulders black with rains.
It is morning. I stand by the mirror
And surprise my soul once more;   50
The blue air rushes above my ceiling,
There are suns beneath my floor.

. . . It is morning, Senlin says, I ascend from darkness
And depart on the winds of space for I know not where,
My watch is wound, a key is in my pocket,   55
And the sky is darkened as I descend the stair.
There are shadows across the windows, clouds in heaven,
And a god among the stars; and I will go
Thinking of him as I might think of daybreak
And humming a tune I know.   60

Vine leaves tap at the window,
Dew-drops sing to the garden stones,
The robin chirps in the chinaberry tree
Repeating three clear tones.

—*Conrad Aiken [1889–   ]*

A BOOKSHOP IDYLL

Between the *gardening* and the *cookery*
    Comes the brief *Poetry* shelf;
By the Nonesuch Donne, a thin anthology
    Offers itself.

Critical, and with nothing else to do,   5
    I scan the Contents page,
Relieved to find the names are mostly new;
    No one my age.

Like all strangers, they divide by sex:
    Landscape near Parma   10
Interests a man, so does *The Double Vortex,*
    So does *Rilke and Buddha.*

"I travel, you see," "I think" and "I can read"
    These titles seem to say;
But *I Remember You, Love is my Creed,*   15
    Poem for J.,

The ladies' choice, discountenance my patter
    For several seconds;
From somewhere in this (as in any) matter
    A moral beckons.   20

Should poets bicycle-pump the human heart
    Or squash it flat?
Man's love is of man's life a thing apart;
    Girls aren't like that.

We men have got love well weighed up; our stuff   25
    Can get by without it.
Women don't seem to think that's good enough;
    They write about it.

And the awful way their poems lay them open
    Just doesn't strike them.   30
Women are really much nicer than men:
    No wonder we like them.

Deciding this, we can forget those times
    We sat up half the night
Chock-full of love, crammed with bright thoughts, names, rhymes, 35
    And couldn't write.

                        —*Kingsley Amis [1922–]*

THE SILVER SWAN

        The silver swan, who living had no note,
        When death approached, unlocked her silent throat;
        Leaning her breast against the reedy shore,
        Thus sung her first and last, and sung no more:
        Farewell, all joys; O death, come close mine eyes;
        More geese than swans now live, more fools than wise.

                        —*Anonymous [c. 1612]*

WHEN IN MY PILGRIMAGE

When in my pilgrimage I reach
The river that we all must cross
And land upon that farther beach
Where earthly gains are counted loss,

May I not earthly loss repair?   5
Well, if those fish should rise again,
There shall be no more parting there—
Celestial gut will stand the strain.

And, issuing from the portal, one
Who was himself a fisherman   10
Will drop his keys and, shouting, run
To help me land leviathan.

—*Anonymous*

SIR PATRICK SPENCE

The king sits in Dumferling toune,
    Drinking the blude-reid wine;
"O whar will I get guid sailor,
    To sail this schip of mine?"

Up and spak an eldern knicht,   5
    Sat at the kings richt kne:
"Sir Patrick Spence is the best sailor,
    That sails upon the se."

The king has written a braid letter,
    And signd it wi his hand,   10
And sent it to Sir Patrick Spence,
    Was walking on the sand.

The first line that Sir Patrick red,
    A loud lauch lauched he;
The next line that Sir Patrick red,   15
    The teir blinded his ee.

"O wha is this has don this deid,
    This ill deid don to me,
To send me out this time o' the yeir,
    To sail upon the se!   20

"Mak haste, mak haste, my mirry men all,
    Our guid schip sails the morne."
"O say no sae, my master deir,
    For I feir a deadlie storme.

"Late, late yestreen I saw the new moone,   25
    Wi the auld moone in hir arme,
And I feir, I feir, my deir master,
    That we will cum to harme."

O our Scots nobles wer richt laith
    To weet thair cork-heild schoone;°   cork-heeled shoes
Bot lang owre a' the play wer playd,   31
    Thair hats they swam aboone.

O lang, lang may thair ladies sit,
    Wi thair fans into their hand,
Or eir they se Sir Patrick Spence   35
    Cum sailing to the land.

O lang, lang may the ladies stand,
    Wi thair gold kems in thair hair,
Waiting for thair ain deir lords,
    For they'll se thame na mair.   40

Haf owre, haf owre, to Aberdour,
    It's fiftie fadom deip,
And thair lies guid Sir Patrick Spence,
    Wi the Scots lords at his feit.

                                          —*Anonymous*

TO MARGUERITE

Yes! in the sea of life enisled,
With echoing straits between us thrown,
Dotting the shoreless watery wild,
We mortal millions live *alone*.
The islands feel the enclasping flow   5
And then their endless bounds they know.

But when the moon their hollows lights,
And they are swept by balms of spring,
And in their glens, on starry nights,
The nightingales divinely sing;   10
And lovely notes, from shore to shore,
Across the sounds and channels pour—

Oh! then a longing like despair
Is to their farthest caverns sent;
For surely once, they feel, we were   15
Parts of a single continent!
Now round us spreads the watery plain—
Oh might our marges meet again!

Who ordered that their longing's fire
Should be, as soon as kindled, cooled?   20
Who renders vain their deep desire?—
A God, a God their severance ruled!
And bade betwixt their shores to be
The unplumbed, salt, estranging sea.

—*Matthew Arnold [1822–1888]*

DOVER BEACH

The sea is calm tonight,
The tide is full, the moon lies fair
Upon the straits;—on the French coast the light
Gleams and is gone; the cliffs of England stand,
Glimmering and vast, out in the tranquil bay.   5
Come to the window, sweet is the night-air!
Only, from the long line of spray
Where the sea meets the moon-blanched land,
Listen! you hear the grating roar
Of pebbles which the waves draw back, and fling,   10
At their return, up the high strand,
Begin, and cease, and then again begin,
With tremulous cadence slow, and bring
The eternal note of sadness in.

Sophocles long ago   15
Heard it on the Aegean, and it brought
Into his mind the turbid ebb and flow
Of human misery; we
Find also in the sound a thought,
Hearing it by this distant northern sea.   20

The Sea of Faith
Was once, too, at the full, and round earth's shore
Lay like the folds of a bright girdle furled
But now I only hear
Its melancholy, long, withdrawing roar,   25
Retreating, to the breath
Of the night-wind, down the vast edges drear
And naked shingles° of the world.   pebbled beaches

Ah, love, let us be true
To one another! for the world, which seems   30
To lie before us like a land of dreams,
So various, so beautiful, so new,
Hath really neither joy, nor love, nor light,
Nor certitude, nor peace, nor help for pain;
And we are here as on a darkling plain   35
Swept with confused alarms of struggle and flight,
Where ignorant armies clash by night.

—*Matthew Arnold [1822–1888]*

THE SHIELD OF ACHILLES

        She looked over his shoulder
            For vines and olive trees,
        Marble well-governed cities,
            And ships upon untamed seas,
        But there on the shining metal   5
            His hands had put instead
        An artificial wilderness
            And a sky like lead.

A plain without a feature, bare and brown,
    No blade of grass, no sign of neighborhood,   10
Nothing to eat and nowhere to sit down,
    Yet, congregated on its blankness, stood
    An unintelligible multitude.
A million eyes, a million boots in line,
Without expression, waiting for a sign.   15

Out of the air a voice without a face
    Proved by statistics that some cause was just
In tones as dry and level as the place:
    No one was cheered and nothing was discussed;
    Column by column in a cloud of dust   20
They marched away enduring a belief
Whose logic brought them, somewhere else, to grief.

        She looked over his shoulder
            For ritual pieties,
        White flower-garlanded heifers,   25
            Libation and sacrifice,
        But there on the shining metal
            Where the altar should have been,
        She saw by his flickering forge-light
            Quite another scene.   30

Barbed wire enclosed an arbitrary spot
   Where bored officials lounged (one cracked a joke)
And sentries sweated, for the day was hot:
   A crowd of ordinary decent folk
   Watched from without and neither moved nor spoke   35
As three pale figures were led forth and bound
To three posts driven upright in the ground.

The mass and majesty of this world, all
   That carries weight and always weighs the same,
Lay in the hands of others; they were small   40
   And could not hope for help and no help came:
   What their foes like to do was done, their shame
Was all the worst could wish; they lost their pride
And died as men before their bodies died.

     She looked over his shoulder   45
       For athletes at their games,
     Men and women in a dance
       Moving their sweet limbs
     Quick, quick, to music,
       But there on the shining shield   50
     His hands had set no dancing-floor
     But a weed-choked field.

A ragged urchin, aimless and alone,
   Loitered about that vacancy; a bird
Flew up to safety from his well-aimed stone: 55
   That girls are raped, that two boys knife a third,
   Were axioms to him, who'd never heard
Of any world where promises were kept
Or one could weep because another wept.

     The thin-lipped armorer,   60
       Hephaestos, hobbled away;
     Thetis of the shining breasts
       Cried out in dismay
     At what the god had wrought
       To please her son, the strong
     Iron-hearted man-slaying Achilles
     Who would not live long.

          —*W. H. Auden* [1907–]

    THE SHIELD OF ACHILLES. The poem has for its background the famous account in the
Iliad (Book XVIII) of the making of Achilles' shield by the god of the forge, Hephaestos,
at the request of Achilles' mother, Thetis.

SONG

Old Adam, the carrion crow,
  The old crow of Cairo;
He sat in the shower, and let it flow
  Under his tail and over his crest;
    And through every feather   5
    Leaked the wet weather;
And the bough swung under his nest;
For his beak it was heavy with marrow.
  Is that the wind dying? O no;
  It's only two devils, that blow   10
  Through a murderer's bones, to and fro,
  In the ghosts' moonshine.

Ho! Eve, my grey carrion wife,
  When we have supped on kings' marrow,
Where shall we drink and make merry our life?   15
  Our nest it is Queen Cleopatra's skull,
    'Tis cloven and cracked,
    And battered and hacked,
But with tears of blue eyes it is full;
Let us drink then, my raven of Cairo!   20
  Is that the wind dying? O no;
  It's only two devils, that blow
  Through a murderer's bones, to and fro,
  In the ghosts' moonshine.

—Thomas Lovell Beddoes [1803–1849]

THE TIGER

Tiger! Tiger! burning bright
In the forests of the night,
What immortal hand or eye
Could frame thy fearful symmetry?

In what distant deeps or skies   5
Burnt the fire of thine eyes?
On what wings dare he aspire?
What the hand dare seize the fire?

And what shoulder, and what art,
Could twist the sinews of thy heart?   10
And when thy heart began to beat,
What dread hand forged thy dread feet?

What the hammer? what the chain?
In what furnace was thy brain?
What the anvil? what dread grasp   15
Dare its deadly terrors clasp?

When the stars threw down their spears,
And watered heaven with their tears,
Did he smile his work to see?
Did he who made the Lamb make thee?   20

Tiger! Tiger! burning bright
In the forests of the night,
What immortal hand or eye,
Dare frame thy fearful symmetry?

—*William Blake [1757–1827]*

THE DIVINE IMAGE

To Mercy, Pity, Peace, and Love
All pray in their distress;
And to these virtues of delight
Return their thankfulness.

For Mercy, Pity, Peace, and Love   5
Is God, our father dear;
And Mercy, Pity, Peace, and Love
Is Man, his child and care.

For Mercy has a human heart,
Pity, a human face,   10
And Love, the human form divine,
And Peace, the human dress.

Then every man, of every clime,
That prays in his distress,
Prays to the human form divine,   15
Love, Mercy, Pity, Peace.

And all must love the human form,
In heathen, turk, or jew;
Where Mercy, Love, and Pity dwell,
There God is dwelling too.   20

—*William Blake [1757–1827]*

SO WE'LL GO NO MORE A-ROVING

So we'll go no more a-roving
So late into the night,
Though the heart be still as loving,
And the moon be still as bright.

For the sword outwears its sheath,   5
And the soul wears out the breast,
And the heart must pause to breathe,
And Love itself have rest.

Though the night was made for loving,
And the day returns too soon,   10
Yet we'll go no more a-roving
By the light of the moon.

—*George Gordon, Lord Byron [1788–1824]*

WHEN THOU MUST HOME

When thou must home to shades of underground,
And there arrived, a new admirèd guest,
The beauteous spirits do engirt thee round,
White Iope, blithe Helen and the rest,
To hear the stories of thy finished love   5
From that smooth tongue, whose music hell can move:

Then wilt thou speak of banqueting delights,
Of masques and revels which sweet youth did make,
Of tourneys and great challenges of knights,
And all these triumphs for thy beauty's sake.   10
When thou hast told these honors done to thee,
Then tell, O! tell, how thou didst murder me.

—*Thomas Campion [1567–1620]*

NO PLATONIC LOVE

Tell me no more of minds embracing minds,
And hearts exchanged for hearts;
That spirits spirits meet, as winds do winds,
And mix their subt'lest parts;
That two unbodied essences may kiss,   5
And then like angels, twist and feel one bliss.

I was that silly thing that once was wrought
    To practise this thin love:
I climbed from sex to soul, from soul to thought;
    But thinking there to move,   10
Headlong I rolled from thought to soul, and then
From soul I lighted at the sex again.

As some strict down-looked men pretend to fast,
    Who yet in closets eat;
So lovers who profess they spirits taste,   15
    Feed yet on grosser meat;
I know they boast they souls to souls convey,
Howe'er they meet, the body is the way.

Come, I will undeceive thee, they that tread
    Those vain aerial ways,   20
Are like young heirs and alchemists misled
    To waste their wealth and days,
For searching thus to be forever rich,
They only find a medicine for the itch.

—*William Cartwright [1611–1643]*

THE LATEST DECALOGUE

Thou shalt have one God only; who
Would be at the expense of two?
No graven images may be
Worshipped, except the currency.
Swear not at all; for, for thy curse   5
Thine enemy is none the worse.
At church on Sunday to attend
Will serve to keep the world thy friend.
Honor thy parents; that is, all
From whom advancement may befall.   10
Thou shalt not kill; but need'st not strive
Officiously to keep alive.
Do not adultery commit;
Advantage rarely comes of it.
Thou shalt not steal: an empty feat,   15
When it's so lucrative to cheat.
Bear not false witness; let the lie
Have time on its own wings to fly.
Thou shalt not covet, but tradition
Approves all forms of competition.   20

—*Arthur Hugh Clough [1819–1861]*

KUBLA KHAN

In Xanadu did Kubla Khan
A stately pleasure-dome decree:
Where Alph, the sacred river, ran
Through caverns measureless to man
    Down to a sunless sea.
So twice five miles of fertile ground
With walls and towers were girdled round:
And here were gardens bright with sinuous rills,
Where blossomed many an incense-bearing tree;
And here were forests ancient as the hills,   10
Enfolding sunny spots of greenery.

But oh! that deep romantic chasm which slanted
Down the green hill athwart a cedarn cover!
A savage place! as holy and enchanted
As e'er beneath a waning moon was haunted   15
By woman wailing for her demon-lover!
And from this chasm, with ceaseless turmoil seething,
As if this earth in fast thick pants were breathing,
A mighty fountain momently was forced:
Amid whose swift half-intermitted burst   20
Huge fragments vaulted like rebounding hail,
Or chaffy grain beneath the thresher's flail:
And 'mid these dancing rocks at once and ever
It flung up momently the sacred river.
Five miles meandering with a mazy motion   25
Through wood and dale the sacred river ran,
Then reached the caverns measureless to man,
And sank in tumult to a lifeless ocean:
And 'mid this tumult Kubla heard from far
Ancestral voices prophesying war!   30
    The shadow of the dome of pleasure
    Floated midway on the waves;
    Where was heard the mingled measure
    From the fountain and the caves.
It was a miracle of rare device,   35
A sunny pleasure-dome with caves of ice!

    A damsel with a dulcimer
    In a vision once I saw:
    It was an Abyssinian maid,
    And on her dulcimer she played,   40
    Singing of Mount Abora.
    Could I revive within me
    Her symphony and song,
    To such a deep delight, 'twould win me,

That with music loud and long,   45
I would build that dome in air,
That sunny dome! those caves of ice!
And all who heard should see them there,
And all should cry, Beware! Beware!
His flashing eyes, his floating hair!   50
Weave a circle round him thrice,
And close your eyes with holy dread,
For he on honey-dew hath fed,
And drunk the milk of Paradise.

—Samuel Taylor Coleridge [1772–1834]

SONG

Pious Selinda goes to prayers
    If I but ask the favor,
And yet the tender fool's in tears
    When she believes I'll leave her.

Would I were free from this restraint,
    Or else had hopes to win her;
Would she could make of me a saint,
    Or I of her a sinner.

—William Congreve [1670–1729]

THE TREES IN THE GARDEN

The trees in the garden rained flowers.
Children ran there joyously.
They gathered the flowers
Each to himself.
Now there were some   5
Who gathered great heaps—
Having opportunity and skill—
Until, behold, only chance blossoms
Remained for the feeble.
Then a little spindling tutor   10
Ran importantly to the father, crying:
"Pray, come hither!
See this unjust thing in your garden!"
But when the father had surveyed,
He admonished the tutor: 15
"Not so, small sage!
This thing is just.

For, look you,
Are not they who possess the flowers
Stronger, bolder, shrewder   20
Than they who have none?
Why should the strong—
The beautiful strong—
Why should they not have the flowers?"
Upon reflection, the tutor bowed to the ground,   25
"My lord," he said,
"The stars are displaced
By this towering wisdom."
                                    —*Stephen Crane [1871–1900]*

INCIDENT

Once riding in old Baltimore
    Heart-filled, head-filled with glee,
I saw a Baltimorean
    Keep looking straight at me.

Now I was eight and very small,   5
    And he was no whit bigger,
And so I smiled, but he poked out
    His tongue, and called me, "Nigger."

I saw the whole of Baltimore
    From May until December;   10
Of all the things that happened there
    That's all that I remember.
                                    —*Countée Cullen [1903–1946]*

THE LISTENERS

"Is there anybody there?" said the Traveller,
    Knocking on the moonlit door;
And his horse in the silence champed the grasses
    Of the forest's ferny floor:
And a bird flew up out of the turret,   5
    Above the Traveller's head:
And he smote upon the door again a second time;
    "Is there anybody there?" he said.
But no one descended to the Traveller;
    No head from the leaf-fringed sill   10
Leaned over and looked into his grey eyes,
    Where he stood perplexed and still.

But only a host of phantom listeners
    That dwelt in the lone house then
Stood listening in the quiet of the moonlight   15
    To that voice from the world of men:
Stood thronging the faint moonbeams on the dark stair,
    That goes down to the empty hall,
Hearkening in an air stirred and shaken
    By the lonely Traveller's call.   20
And he felt in his heart their strangeness,
    Their stillness answering his cry,
While his horse moved, cropping the dark turf,
    'Neath the starred and leafy sky;
For he suddenly smote on the door, even   25
    Louder, and lifted his head:—
"Tell them I came, and no one answered,
    That I kept my word," he said.
Never the least stir made the listeners,
    Though every word he spake   30
Fell echoing through the shadowiness of the still house
    From the one man left awake:
Ay, they heard his foot upon the stirrup,
    And the sound of iron on stone,
And how the silence surged softly backward,   35
    When the plunging hoofs were gone.

                         —Walter de la Mare [1873–1956]

MY LIFE HAD STOOD, A LOADED GUN

My life had stood, a loaded gun,
In corners, till a day
The owner passed, identified,
And carried me away.

And now we roam in sovereign woods,   5
And now we hunt the doe,
And every time I speak for him,
The mountains straight reply.

And do I smile, such cordial light
Upon the valley glow,   10
It is as a Vesuvian face
Had let its pleasure through.

And when at night, our good day done,
I guard my master's head,
'Tis better than the eider-duck's   15
Deep pillow, to have shared.

To foe of his I'm deadly foe:
None stir the second time
On whom I lay a yellow eye
Or an emphatic thumb.   20

Though I than he may longer live,
He longer must than I,
For I have but the power to kill,
Without the power to die.

                              —*Emily Dickinson [1830–1886]*

BECAUSE I COULD NOT STOP FOR DEATH

Because I could not stop for Death,
He kindly stopped for me;
The carriage held but just ourselves
And Immortality.

We slowly drove; he knew no haste,   5
And I had put away
My labor and my leisure too,
For his civility.

We passed the school, where children strove,
At recess, in the ring,   10
We passed the fields of gazing grain,
We passed the setting sun.

Or rather, he passed us;
The dews drew quivering and chill;
For only gossamer, my gown;   15
My tippet, only tulle.

We paused before a house that seemed
A swelling of the ground;
The roof was scarcely visible,
The cornice, in the ground.   20

Since then, 'tis centuries, and yet
Feels shorter than the day
I first surmised the horses' heads
Were toward eternity.

—*Emily Dickinson [1830–1886]*

THE GOOD-MORROW

I wonder, by my troth, what thou and I
Did, till we loved? were we not weaned till then?
But sucked on country pleasures, childishly?
Or snorted we in the Seven Sleepers' den?
'Twas so; but this, all pleasures fancies be.   5
If ever any beauty I did see,
Which I desired, and got, 'twas but a dream of thee.

And now good morrow to our waking souls,
Which watch not one another out of fear;
For love all love of other sights controls,   10
And makes one little room an everywhere.
Let sea-discoverers to new worlds have gone;
Let maps to other,° worlds on worlds have shown;   *others*
Let us possess one world; each hath one, and is one.

My face in thine eye, thine in mine appears,   15
And true plain hearts do in the faces rest;
Where can we find two better hemispheres
Without sharp north, without declining west?
Whatever dies, was not mixed equally;
If our two loves be one, or thou and I
Love so alike that none can slacken, none can die.

—*John Donne [1572–1631]*

THE GOOD-MORROW. 4. *Seven Sleepers' den:* a cave where, according to Christian legend,
seven youths escaped persecution and slept for two centuries.

THE SUN RISING

Busy old fool, unruly Sun,
Why dost thou thus,
Through windows, and through curtains, call on us?
Must to thy motions lovers' seasons run?
Saucy pedantic wretch, go chide   5
Late school boys and sour prentices,
Go tell court-huntsmen that the king will ride,
Call country ants to harvest offices;

Love, all alike, no season knows nor clime,
Nor hours, days, months, which are the rags of time.   10

     Thy beams so reverend and strong
      Why shouldst thou think?
I could eclipse and cloud them with a wink,
But that I would not lose her sight so long.
     If her eyes have not blinded thine,   15
      Look, and tomorrow late tell me,
     Whether both th' Indias of spice and mine
     Be where thou left'st them, or lie here with me.
Ask for those kings whom thou saw'st yesterday,
And thou shalt hear, "All here in one bed lay."   20

     She's all states, and all princes I;
      Nothing else is.
Princes do but play us; compared to this,
All honor's mimic, all wealth alchemy.
     Thou, Sun, art half as happy as we,   25
      In that the world's contracted thus;
     Thine age asks ease, and since thy duties be
     To warm the world, that's done in warming us.
Shine here to us, and thou art everywhere;
This bed thy center is, these walls thy sphere.   30

—John Donne [1572–1631]

SONG

     Go and catch a falling star,
      Get with child a mandrake root,
     Tell me where all past years are,
      Or who cleft the devil's foot,
Teach me to hear mermaids singing,   5
Or to keep off envy's stinging,
       And find
       What wind
Serves to advance an honest mind.

If thou be'st born to strange sights,   10
     Things invisible to see,
Ride ten thousand days and nights,
     Till age snow white hairs on thee.
Thou, when thou return'st, wilt tell me,
All strange wonders that befell thee,   15
       And swear
       No where
Lives a woman true and fair.

If thou find'st one, let me know;
    Such a pilgrimage were sweet.   20
Yet do not; I would not go,
    Though at next door we might meet.
Though she were true when you met her,
And last till you write your letter,
                Yet she   25
                Will be
False, ere I come, to two or three.

—John Donne [1572–1631]

SONG. 2. *mandrake:* supposed to resemble a human being because of its forked root.

BATTER MY HEART, THREE-PERSONED GOD

Batter my heart, three-personed God, for you
As yet but knock, breathe, shine, and seek to mend;
That I may rise and stand, o'erthrow me, and bend
Your force to break, blow, burn, and make me new.
I, like an usurped town, to another due,   5
Labor to admit you, but Oh, to no end.
Reason, your viceroy in me, me should defend,
But is captived, and proves weak or untrue.
Yet dearly I love you, and would be lovèd fain,
But am betrothed unto your enemy;   10
Divorce me, untie, or break that knot again,
Take me to you, imprison me, for I,
Except you enthrall me, never shall be free,
Nor ever chaste, except you ravish me.

—John Donne [1572–1631]

VERGISSMEINICHT

Three weeks gone and the combatants gone,
returning over the nightmare ground
we found the place again, and found
the soldier sprawling in the sun.

The frowning barrel of his gun   5
overshadowing. As we came on
that day, he hit my tank with one
like the entry of a demon.

Look. Here in the gunpit spoil
the dishonored picture of his girl   10
who has put: *Steffi.° Vergissmeinicht*   a girl's name
in a copybook gothic script.

We see him almost with content
abased, and seeming to have paid
and mocked at by his own equipment   15
that's hard and good when he's decayed.

But she would weep to see to-day
how on his skin the swart flies move;
the dust upon the paper eye
and the burst stomach like a cave.   20

For here the lover and killer are mingled
who had one body and one heart.
And death who had the soldier singled
has done the lover mortal hurt.

—*Keith Douglas [1920–1944]*

VERGISSMEINICHT. The German title means "Forget Me Not." The author, an English
poet, fought with a tank battalion in World War II and was killed in the invasion of
Normandy.

DAYS

Daughters of Time, the hypocritic Days,
Muffled and dumb like barefoot dervishes,°   Moslem monks
And marching single in an endless file,
Bring diadems and fagots in their hands.
To each they offer gifts after his will,   5
Bread, kingdoms, stars, and sky that holds them all.
I, in my pleachèd° garden, watched the pomp,   covered with in-
Forgot my morning wishes, hastily   tertwined
Took a few herbs and apples, and the Day   boughs
Turned and departed silent. I, too late,   10
Under her solemn fillet saw the scorn.

—*Ralph Waldo Emerson [1803–1882]*

THE SILKEN TENT

She is as in a field a silken tent
At midday when a sunny summer breeze
Has dried the dew and all its ropes relent,
So that in guys it gently sways at ease,
And its supporting central cedar pole,   5
That is its pinnacle to heavenward
And signifies the sureness of the soul,
Seems to owe naught to any single cord,

271

But strictly held by none, is loosely bound
By countless silken ties of love and thought   10
To everything on earth the compass round,
And only by one's going slightly taut
In the capriciousness of summer air
Is of the slightest bondage made aware.

—*Robert Frost [1874–1963]*

THE SILKEN TENT. This poem was recorded by Mr. Frost (LP, Yale Series of Recorded Poets, YP 320).

SIX POETS IN SEARCH OF A LAWYER

Finesse be first, whose elegance deplores
All things save beauty, and the swinging doors;
Whose cleverness in writing verse is just
Exceeded by his lack of taste and lust;
Who lives off lady lovers of his verse   5
And thanks them by departing with their purse;
Who writes his verse in order to amaze,
To win the Pulitzer, or *Time*'s sweet praise;
Who will endure a moment, and then pass,
As hopeless as an olive in his glass.   10

Dullard be second, as he always will,
From lack of brains as well as lack of skill.
Expert in some, and dillettante in all
The ways of making poems gasp and fall,
He teaches at a junior college where   15
He's recognized as Homer's son and heir.
Respectable, brown-suited, it is he
Who represents on forums poetry,
And argues to protect the libeled Muse,
Who'd tear his flimsy tongue out, could she choose.   20

His opposite is anarchistic *Bomb*,
Who writes a manifesto with aplomb.
Revolt! Revolt! No matter why or when,
It's novelty, old novelty again.
Yet *Bomb* if read intently may reveal   25
A talent not to murder but to steal;
First from old *Gone*, whose fragmentary style
Disguised his sawdust Keats a little while;
And now from one who writes at very best
What ne'er was thought and much the less expressed.   30

Lucre be next, who takes to poetry
The businessman he swore he would not be.
Anthologies and lecture tours and grants
Create a solvency which disenchants.
He writes his poems now to suit his purse,   35
Short-lined and windy, and reserves his curse
For all the little magazines so fine
That offer only fifty cents a line.
He makes his money, certainly, to write,
But writes for money. Such is appetite.   40

Of *Mucker* will I tell, who tries to show
He is a kind of poet men don't know.
To shadow box at literary teas
And every girl at Bennington to seize,
To talk of baseball rather than of Yeats,   45
To drink straight whisky while the bard creates—
This is his pose, and so his poems seem
Incongruous in proving life a dream.
Some say, with Freud, that *Mucker* has a reason
For acting virile in and out of season.   50

Scoundrel be last. Be deaf, be dumb, be blind,
Who writes satiric verses on his kind.

—*Donald Hall* [1928–   ]

SIX POETS IN SEARCH OF A LAWYER. 30. Cf. Alexander Pope, *Essay on Criticism*, II,
97–98: "True wit is Nature to advantage dressed,/ What oft was thought, but ne're so
well expressed."

AFTERWARDS

When the Present has latched its postern behind my tremulous stay,
   And the May month flaps its glad green leaves like wings,
Delicate-filmed as new-spun silk, will the neighbors say,
   "He was a man who used to notice such things"?

If it be in the dusk when, like an eyelid's soundless blink,   5
   The dewfall-hawk comes crossing the shades to alight
Upon the wind-warped upland thorn, a gazer may think,
   "To him this must have been a familiar sight."

If I pass during some nocturnal blackness, mothy and warm,
   When the hedgehog travels furtively over the lawn,   10
One may say, "He strove that such innocent creatures should
      come to no harm,
   But he could do little for them; and now he is gone."

273

If, when hearing that I have been stilled at last, they stand at
    the door,
  Watching the full-starred heavens that winter sees,
Will this thought rise on those who will meet my face no more,   15
  "He was one who had an eye for such mysteries"?

And will any say when my bell of quittance is heard in the gloom,
  And a crossing breeze cuts a pause in its outrollings,
Till they rise again, as they were a new bell's boom,
  "He hears it not now, but used to notice such things"?   20

—*Thomas Hardy [1840–1928]*

REDEMPTION

    Having been tenant long to a rich Lord,
      Not thriving, I resolvèd to be bold,
      And make a suit unto him to afford
    A new small-rented lease and cancel the old.
    In heaven at his manor I him sought.   5
      They told me there that he was lately gone
      About some land which he had dearly bought
    Long since on earth, to take possessïon.
    I straight returned, and knowing his great birth,
      Sought him accordingly in great resorts,   10
      In cities, theaters, gardens, parks, and courts.
    At length I heard a ragged noise and mirth
      Of thieves and murderers; there I him espied,
      Who straight, *Your suit is granted,* said, and died.

—*George Herbert [1593–1633]*

CORINNA'S GOING A-MAYING

    Get up, get up for shame, the blooming morn
    Upon her wings presents the god unshorn.
      See how Aurora throws her fair
      Fresh-quilted colors through the air:
      Get up, sweet slug-a-bed, and see   5
      The dew bespangling herb and tree.
    Each flower has wept and bowed toward the east
    Above an hour since: yet you not dressed;
      Nay; not so much as out of bed?
      When all the birds have matins said   10
      And sung their thankful hymns, 'tis sin,
      Nay, profanation, to keep in,

Whenas a thousand virgins on this day
Spring, sooner than the lark, to fetch in May.

Rise, and put on your foliage, and be seen   15
To come forth, like the spring-time, fresh and green,
   And sweet as Flora. Take no care
   For jewels for your gown or hair:
Fear not; the leaves will strew
Gems in abundance upon you: 20
Besides, the childhood of the day has kept,
Against you come, some orient pearls unwept;
   Come and receive them while the light
   Hangs on the dew-locks of the night:
   And Titan on the eastern hill   25
   Retires himself, or else stands still
Till you come forth. Wash, dress, be brief in praying:
Few beads are best when once we go a-Maying.

Come, my Corinna, come; and, coming, mark
How each field turns a street, each street a park   30
   Made green and trimmed with trees; see how
   Devotion gives each house a bough
Or branch; each porch, each door ere this
An ark, a tabernacle is,
Made up of white-thorn, neatly interwove;   35
As if here were those cooler shades of love.
   Can such delights be in the street
   And open fields and we not see't?
   Come, we'll abroad; and let's obey
   The proclamation made for May: 40
And sin no more, as we have done, by staying;
But, my Corinna, come, let's go a-Maying.

There's not a budding boy or girl this day
But is got up, and gone to bring in May.
   A deal of youth, ere this, is come   45
   Back, and with white-thorn laden home.
   Some have despatched their cakes and cream
   Before that we have left to dream:
And some have wept, and wooed, and plighted troth,
And chose their priest, ere we can cast off sloth: 50
   Many a green-gown has been given;
   Many a kiss, both odd and even:
   Many a glance too has been sent
   From out the eye, love's firmament;
Many a jest told of the keys betraying   55
This night, and locks picked, yet we're not a-Maying.

Come, let us go while we are in our prime;
And take the harmless folly of the time.
  We shall grow old apace, and die
  Before we know our liberty.   60
  Our life is short, and our days run
  As fast away as does the sun;
And, as a vapor or a drop of rain,
Once lost, can ne'er be found again,   64
  So when or° you or I are made   either
  A fable, song, or fleeting shade,
  All love, all liking, all delight
  Lies drowned with us in endless night.
Then while time serves, and we are but decaying,
Come, my Corinna, come, let's go a-Maying.   70

                —*Robert Herrick* [*1591–1674*]

JACK AND HIS FATHER

"Jack," quoth his father, "how shall I ease take?
If I stand, my legs ache; and if I kneel
My knees ache; if I go, then my feet ache;
If I lie, my back aches; if I sit, I feel
My hips ache; and lean I never so weel,
My elbows ache." "Sir," quoth Jack, "pain to exile,
Since all these ease not, best ye hang awhile."

              —*John Heywood* [*c. 1497–c. 1580*]

EVE

Eve, with her basket, was
Deep in the bells and grass,
Wading in bells and grass
Up to her knees,
Picking a dish of sweet   5
Berries and plums to eat,
Down in the bells and grass
Under the trees.

Mute as a mouse in a
Corner the cobra lay,   10
Curled round a bough of the
Cinnamon tall. . . .
Now to get even and
Humble proud heaven and
Now was the moment or   15
Never at all.

"Eva!" Each syllable
Light as a flower fell,
"Eva!" he whispered the
Wondering maid,   20
Soft as a bubble sung
Out of a linnet's lung,
Soft and most silverly
"Eva!" he said.

Picture that orchard sprite,   25
Eve, with her body white,
Supple and smooth to her
Slim finger tips,
Wondering, listening,
Listening, wondering,   30
Eve with a berry
Half-way to her lips.

Oh had our simple Eve
Seen through the make-believe!
Had she but known the   35
Pretender he was!
Out of the boughs he came,
Whispering still her name,
Tumbling in twenty rings
Into the grass.   40

Here was the strangest pair
In the world anywhere,
Eve in the bells and grass
Kneeling, and he
Telling his story low. . . .   45
Singing birds saw them go
Down the dark path to
The Blasphemous Tree.

Oh, what a clatter when
Titmouse and Jenny Wren   50
Saw him successful and
Taking his leave!
How the birds rated him,
How they all hated him!
How they all pitied   55
Poor motherless Eve!

Picture her crying
Outside in the lane,
Eve, with no dish of sweet
Berries and plums to eat,   60
Haunting the gate of the
Orchard in vain. . . .
Picture the lewd delight
Under the hill tonight—
"Eva!" the toast goes round,   65
"Eva!" again.

—Ralph Hodgson [1872–1962]

BREDON HILL

In summertime on Bredon
  The bells they sound so clear;
Round both the shires they ring them
  In steeples far and near,
  A happy noise to hear.   5

Here of a Sunday morning
  My love and I would lie,
And see the coloured counties,
  And hear the larks so high
  About us in the sky.   10

The bells would ring to call her
  In valleys miles away:
"Come all to church, good people;
  Good people, come and pray."
  But here my love would stay.   15

And I would turn and answer
  Among the springing thyme,
"Oh, peal upon our wedding,
  And we will hear the chime,
  And come to church in time."   20

But when the snows at Christmas
  On Bredon top were strown,
My love rose up so early
  And stole out unbeknown
  And went to church alone.   25

They tolled the one bell only,
    Groom there was none to see,
The mourners followed after,
    And so to church went she,
    And would not wait for me.   30

The bells they sound on Bredon,
    And still the steeples hum.
"Come all to church, good people,"—
    Oh, noisy bells, be dumb;
    I hear you, I will come.   35

                    —A. E. Housman [1859–1936]

ECHO'S LAMENT OF NARCISSUS

Slow, slow, fresh fount, keep time with my salt tears;
    Yet slower yet, oh faintly, gentle springs;
List to the heavy part the music bears,
    Woe weeps out her division when she sings.
        Droop herbs and flowers,   5
        Fall grief in showers;
        Our beauties are not ours;
            Oh, I could still,
Like melting snow upon some craggy hill,
    Drop, drop, drop, drop,   10
Since nature's pride is now a withered daffodil.

                    —Ben Jonson [1573?–1637]

ODE ON A GRECIAN URN

Thou still unravished bride of quietness,
    Thou foster-child of silence and slow time,
Sylvan historian, who canst thus express
    A flowery tale more sweetly than our rhyme:
What leaf-fringed legend haunts about thy shape   5
    Of deities or mortals, or of both,
        In Tempe or the dales of Arcady?
    What men or gods are these? What maidens loth?
What mad pursuit? What struggle to escape?
    What pipes and timbrels? What wild ecstasy?   10

Heard melodies are sweet, but those unheard
Are sweeter; therefore, ye soft pipes, play on;
Not to the sensual ear, but, more endeared,
Pipe to the spirit ditties of no tone:
Fair youth, beneath the trees, thou canst not leave   15
Thy song, nor ever can those trees be bare;
Bold Lover, never, never canst thou kiss,
Though winning near the goal—yet, do not grieve;
She cannot fade, though thou hast not thy bliss,
For ever wilt thou love, and she be fair!   20

Ah, happy, happy boughs! that cannot shed
Your leaves, nor ever bid the Spring adieu;
And, happy melodist, unwearièd,
For ever piping songs for ever new;
More happy love! more happy, happy love!   25
For ever warm and still to be enjoyed,
For ever panting and for ever young;
All breathing human passion far above,
That leaves a heart high-sorrowful and cloyed,
A burning forehead, and a parching tongue.   30

Who are these coming to the sacrifice?
To what green altar, O mysterious priest,
Lead'st thou that heifer lowing at the skies,
And all her silken flanks with garlands drest?
What little town by river or sea shore,   35
Or mountain-built with peaceful citadel,
Is emptied of its folk, this pious morn?
And, little town, thy streets for evermore
Will silent be; and not a soul to tell
Why thou art desolate, can e'er return.   40

O Attic shape! Fair attitude! with brede
Of marble men and maidens overwrought,
With forest branches and the trodden weed;
Thou, silent form, dost tease us out of thought
As doth eternity: Cold Pastoral!   45
When old age shall this generation waste,
Thou shalt remain, in midst of other woe
Than ours, a friend to man, to whom thou say'st,
Beauty is truth, truth beauty,—that is all
Ye know on earth, and all ye need to know.   50

—*John Keats [1795–1821]*

ODE ON A GRECIAN URN. 49-50. In the 1820 edition of Keats's poems the words "Beauty
is truth, truth beauty" were enclosed in quotation marks. Critics have disagreed as to

whether only this statement is uttered by the Urn, with the remainder of the poem
spoken *to* the Urn (or the figures on the Urn) by the speaker of the poem; or whether
the entire last two lines are spoken by the Urn.

ODE ON MELANCHOLY

No, no, go not to Lethe, neither twist
  Wolf's-bane,° tight-rooted, for its poisonous wine;   poisonous plant
Nor suffer thy pale forehead to be kissed
  By nightshade,° ruby grape of Proserpine;   poisonous plant
Make not your rosary of yew°-berries,   tree of mourning
  Nor let the beetle, nor the death-moth be   6
    Your mournful Psyche, nor the downy owl
A partner in your sorrow's mysteries;°   religious rites
  For shade to shade will come too drowsily,
    And drown the wakeful anguish of the soul.   10

But when the melancholy fit shall fall
  Sudden from heaven like a weeping cloud,
That fosters the droop-headed flowers all,
  And hides the green hill in an April shroud;
Then glut thy sorrow on a morning rose,   15
  Or on the rainbow of the salt sand wave,
    Or on the wealth of globèd peonies;
Or if thy mistress some rich anger shows,
  Emprison her soft hand, and let her rave,
    And feed deep, deep upon her peerless eyes.   20

She dwells with Beauty—Beauty that must die;
  And Joy, whose hand is ever at his lips
Bidding adieu; and aching Pleasure nigh,
  Turning to Poison while the bee-mouth sips:
Aye, in the very temple of Delight   25
  Veiled Melancholy has her sovran shrine,
    Though seen of none save him whose strenuous tongue
Can burst Joy's grape against his palate fine;
  His soul shall taste the sadness of her might,
    And be among her cloudy trophies hung.   30

               —*John Keats [1795–1821]*

ODE ON MELANCHOLY. 1. *Lethe:* river in the Greek Hades which caused forgetfulness.
4. *Proserpine:* queen of Hades. 6. *death-moth:* moth with skull-like markings. 7. *Psyche:*
the soul, symbolized sometimes by a butterfly, sometimes by a beautiful maiden loved by
Cupid (desire).

ON HIS SEVENTY-FIFTH BIRTHDAY

I strove with none, for none was worth my strife;
Nature I loved, and next to Nature, Art;
I warmed both hands before the fire of Life;
It sinks; and I am ready to depart.

—*Walter Savage Landor [1775–1864]*

CHURCH GOING

Once I am sure there's nothing going on
I step inside, letting the door thud shut.
Another church: matting, seats, and stone,
And little books; sprawlings of flowers, cut
For Sunday, brownish now; some brass and stuff   5
Up at the holy end; the small neat organ;
And a tense, musty, unignorable silence,
Brewed God knows how long. Hatless, I take off
My cycle-clips in awkward reverence,

Move forward, run my hand around the font.   10
From where I stand, the roof looks almost new—
Cleaned, or restored? Someone would know: I don't.
Mounting the lectern, I peruse a few
Hectoring large-scale verses, and pronounce
"Here endeth" much more loudly than I'd meant.   15
The echoes snigger briefly. Back at the door
I sign the book, donate an Irish sixpence,
Reflect the place was not worth stopping for.

Yet stop I did: in fact I often do,
And always end much at a loss like this,   20
Wondering what to look for; wondering, too,
When churches fall completely out of use
What we shall turn them into, if we shall keep
A few cathedrals chronically on show,
Their parchment, plate and pyx in locked cases,   25
And let the rest rent-free to rain and sheep.
Shall we avoid them as unlucky places?

Or, after dark, will dubious women come
To make their children touch a particular stone;
Pick simples for a cancer; or on some   30
Advised night see walking a dead one?
Power of some sort or other will go on
In games, in riddles, seemingly at random;

But superstition, like belief, must die,
And what remains when disbelief has gone?   35
Grass, weedy pavement, brambles, buttress, sky,

A shape less recognizable each week,
A purpose more obscure. I wonder who
Will be the last, the very last, to seek
This place for what it was; one of the crew   40
That tap and jot and know what rood-lofts were?
Some ruin-bibber, randy° for antique,   wild, lustful
Or Christmas-addict, counting on a whiff
Of gown-and-bands and organ-pipes and myrrh?
Or will he be my representative,   45

Bored, uninformed, knowing the ghostly silt
Dispersed, yet tending to this cross of ground
Through suburb scrub because it held unspilt
So long and equably what since is found
Only in separation—marriage, and birth,   50
And death, and thoughts of these—for whom was built
This special shell? For though I've no idea
What this accoutred frowsty barn is worth,
It pleases me to stand in silence here;

A serious house on serious earth it is,   55
In whose blent air all our compulsions meet,
Are recognized, and robed as destinies.
And that much never can be obsolete,
Since someone will forever be surprising
A hunger in himself to be more serious,
And gravitating with it to this ground,   60
Which, he once heard, was proper to grow wise in,
If only that so many dead lie round.

—*Philip Larkin* [1922–   ]

CITY LIFE

When I am in a great city, I know that I despair.
I know there is no hope for us, death waits, it is useless to care.

For oh the poor people, that are flesh of my flesh,
I, that am flesh of their flesh,
when I see the iron hooked into their faces   5
their poor, their fearful faces
I scream in my soul, for I know I cannot
take the iron hooks out of their faces, that make them so drawn,

nor cut the invisible wires of steel that pull them
back and forth, to work,   10
back and forth to work,
like fearful and corpse-like fishes hooked and being played
by some malignant fisherman on an unseen shore
where he does not choose to land them yet, hooked fishes of
   the factory world.

—*D. H. Lawrence [1885–1930]*

SEA-SHELL MURMURS

The hollow sea-shell which for years hath stood
   On dusty shelves, when held against the ear
   Proclaims its stormy parent; and we hear
The faint far murmur of the breaking flood.

We hear the sea. The sea? It is the blood   5
   In our own veins, impetuous and near,
   And pulses keeping pace with hope and fear
And with our feelings' every shifting mood.

Lo, in my heart I hear, as in a shell,
   The murmur of a world beyond the grave,   10
Distinct, distinct, though faint and far it be.

Thou fool; this echo is a cheat as well,—
   The hum of earthly instincts; and we crave
A world unreal as the shell-heard sea.

—*Eugene Lee-Hamilton [1845–1907]*

THE GARDEN

How vainly men themselves amaze,°   perplex
To win the palm,° the oak,° or bays,°   tokens of victory
And their incessant labors see
Crowned from some single herb or tree
Whose short and narrow-vergèd shade   5
Does prudently their toils upbraid,
While all the flowers and trees do close
To weave the garlands of repose!

Fair Quiet, have I found thee here,
And Innocence, thy sister dear!   10
Mistaken long, I sought you then
In busy companies of men.
Your sacred plants, if here below,
Only among the plants will grow.
Society is all but rude   15
To° this delicious solitude.   compared to

No white nor red° was ever seen   colors of female beauty
So amorous° as this lovely green.   lovable
Fond lovers, cruel as their flame,
Cut in these trees their mistress' name.   20
Little, alas! they know or heed
How far these beauties hers exceed!
Fair trees! wheres'e'r your barks I wound,
No name shall but your own be found.

When we have run our passion's heat,   25
Love hither makes his best retreat.
The gods, that mortal beauty chase,
Still in a tree did end their race.
Apollo hunted Daphne so,
Only that she might laurel grow.   30
And Pan did after Syrinx speed,
Not as a nymph, but for a reed.

What wondrous life is this I lead!
Ripe apples drop about my head;
The luscious clusters of the vine   35
Upon my mouth do crush their wine;
The nectarine, and curious peach,
Into my hands themselves do reach;
Stumbling on melons, as I pass,
Insnared with flowers, I fall on grass.   40

Meanwhile the mind, from pleasure less,
Withdraws into its happiness:
The mind, that ocean where each kind°   species, class of things
Does straight its own resemblance find;
Yet it creates, transcending these,   45
Far other worlds, and other seas,
Annihilating all that's made
To a green thought in a green shade.

Here at the fountain's sliding foot,
Or at some fruit-tree's mossy root, 50
Casting the body's vest° aside, vesture
My soul into the boughs does glide:
There, like a bird, it sits and sings,
Then whets° and combs its silver wings, preens
And, till prepared for longer flight, 55
Waves in its plumes the various light.

Such was that happy garden-state,° Eden
While man there walked without a mate;
After a place so pure and sweet,
What other help could yet be meet! ° suitable
But 'twas beyond a mortal's share 61
To wander solitary there:
Two paradises 'twere in one,
To live in paradise alone.

How well the skilful gardener drew 65
Of flowers and herbs this dial new;
Where, from above, the milder sun
Does through a fragrant zodiac run,
And, as it works, the industrious bee
Computes its time as well as we! 70
How could such sweet and wholesome hours
Be reckoned but with herbs and flowers?

—*Andrew Marvell [1621–1678]*

THE GARDEN. 27–32. *The gods,* etc.: Daphne, to escape Apollo, was turned into a laurel; Syrinx, pursued by Pan, was changed into a reed, from which Pan made his pipes (Ovid's *Metamorphosis*). 41. *pleasure less:* lesser pleasures, e.g., of society and of the senses. 60. *help,* a pun with *meet:* Eve was created to be Adam's *helpmeet* or helpmate. 66. *dial:* a floral sundial with planted signs of the zodiac.

LUCIFER IN STARLIGHT

On a starred night Prince Lucifer uprose
Tired of his dark dominion swung the fiend
Above the rolling ball in cloud part screened,
Where sinners hugged their specter of repose.
Poor prey to his hot fit of pride were those. 5
And now upon his western wing he leaned,
Now his huge bulk o'er Afric's sands careened,
Now the black planet shadowed Arctic snows.

Soaring through wider zones that pricked his scars   9
With memory of the old revolt from Awe,°   Satan's rebellion
He reached a middle height, and at the stars,   against God
Which are the brain of heaven, he looked, and sank.
Around the ancient track marched, rank on rank,
The army of unalterable law.

—*George Meredith [1828–1909]*

A CARRIAGE FROM SWEDEN

They say there is a sweeter air
    where it was made, than we have here;
    a Hamlet's castle atmosphere.
At all events there is in Brooklyn
something that makes me feel at home.   5

No one may see this put-away
    museum-piece, this country cart
    that inner happiness made art;
and yet, in this city of freckled
integrity it is a vein   10

of resined straightness from north-wind
    hardened Sweden's once-opposed-to-
    compromise archipelago
of rocks. Washington and Gustavus
Adolphus, forgive our decay.   15

Seats, dashboard and sides of smooth gourd-
    rind texture, a flowered step, swan-
    dart brake, and swirling crustacean-
tailed equine amphibious creatures
that garnish the axle-tree! What   20

a fine thing! What unannoying
    romance! And how beautiful, she
    with the natural stoop of the
snowy egret, grey-eyed and straight-haired,
for whom it should come to the door,—   25

of whom it reminds me. The split
    pine fair hair, steady gannet-clear
    eyes and the pine-needled-path deer-
swift step; that is Sweden, land of the
free and the soil for a spruce-tree—   30

vertical though a seedling—all
    needles: from a green trunk, green shelf
    on shelf fanning out by itself.
The deft white-stockinged dance in thick-soled
shoes! Denmark's sanctuaried Jews!   35

The puzzle-jugs and hand-spun rugs,
    the root-legged kracken° shaped like dogs,   wooden
    the hanging buttons and the frogs   stools
that edge the Sunday jackets! Sweden,
you have a runner called the Deer, who   40

when he's won a race, likes to run
    more; you have the sun-right gable-
    ends due east and west, the table
spread as for a banquet; and the put-
in twin vest-pleats with a fish-fin   45

effect when you need none. Sweden,
    what makes the people dress that way
    and those who see you wish to stay?
The runner, not too tired to run more
at the end of the race? And that   50

cart, dolphin-graceful? A Dalgrén
    light-house, self-lit?—responsive and
    responsible. I understand;
it's not pine-needle-paths that give spring
when they're run on, it's a Sweden   55

of moated white castles,—the bed
    of white flowers densely grown in an S
    meaning Sweden and stalwartness,
skill, and a surface that says
Made in Sweden: carts are my trade.   60

                                          —*Marianne Moore* [1887–   ]

    A CARRIAGE FROM SWEDEN. 14. *Gustavus Adolphus:* Swedish king and military hero
(1594–1632). 35. *Denmark's sanctuaried Jews:* Many Jewish refugees fled to Sweden after
the German invasion of Denmark in World War II. 52. *Dalgrén light-house:* Gustaf Dalén,
Swedish scientist, won a Nobel Prize in 1912 chiefly for his invention of an automatic regu-
lator, responsive to the sun's rays, for turning on and off the gas lights used in marine
buoys and beacons and in railway signals.

SPRING

Spring, the sweet Spring, is the year's pleasant king;
Then blooms each thing, then maids dance in a ring,
Cold doth not sting, the pretty birds do sing,
    Cuckoo, jug-jug, pu-we, to-witta-woo!

The palm and may make country houses gay,   5
Lambs frisk and play, the shepherds pipe all day,
And we hear aye birds tune this merry lay,
    Cuckoo, jug-jug, pu-we, to-witta-woo!

The fields breathe sweet, the daisies kiss our feet,
Young lovers meet, old wives a-sunning sit,   10
In every street these tunes our ears do greet,
    Cuckoo, jug-jug, pu-we, to-witta-woo!
        Spring! the sweet Spring!

                —Thomas Nashe [1567–1601]

LOVE POEM

My clumsiest dear, whose hands shipwreck vases,
At whose quick touch all glasses chip and ring,
Whose palms are bulls in china, burs in linen,
And have no cunning with any soft thing

Except all ill-at-ease fidgeting people: 5
The refugee uncertain at the door
You make at home; deftly you steady
The drunk clambering on his undulant floor.

Unpredictable dear, the taxi drivers' terror,
Shrinking from far headlights pale as a dime   10
Yet leaping before red apoplectic streetcars—
Misfit in any space. And never on time.

A wrench in clocks and the solar system. Only
With words and people and love you move at ease.
In traffic of wit expertly manoeuvre   15
And keep us, all devotion, at your knees.

Forgetting your coffee spreading on our flannel,
Your lipstick grinning on our coat,
So gayly in love's unbreakable heaven
Our souls on glory of spilt bourbon float.   20

Be with me, darling, early and late. Smash glasses—
I will study wry music for your sake.
For should your hands drop white and empty
All the toys of the world would break.

                —John Frederick Nims [1914–]

EPISTLE TO A YOUNG LADY,
ON HER LEAVING THE TOWN
AFTER THE CORONATION

As some fond virgin, whom her mother's care
Drags from the town to wholesome country air,
Just when she learns to roll a melting eye,
And hear a spark,° yet think no danger nigh—   beau
From the dear man unwilling she must sever,   5
Yet takes one kiss before she parts forever—
Thus from the world fair Zephalinda flew,
Saw others happy, and with sighs withdrew;
Not that their pleasures caused her discontent:
She sighed not that they stayed, but that she went.   10
    She went—to plain-work and to purling brooks,
Old-fashioned halls, dull aunts, and croaking rooks;
She went from opera, park, assembly, play,
To morning walks, and prayers three hours a day;   14
To part her time 'twixt reading and bohea,°   black tea
To muse, and spill her solitary tea;
Or o'er cold coffee trifle with the spoon,
Count the slow clock, and dine exact at noon;
Divert her eyes with pictures in the fire,
Hum half a tune, tell stories to the squire;   20
Up to her godly garret after seven,
There starve and pray, for that's the way to heaven.
    Some squire, perhaps, you take delight to rack,
Whose game is "whisk,"° whose treat a toast in sack;   whist
Who visits with a gun, presents you birds,   25
Then gives a smacking buss, and cries, "No words!"
Or with his hound comes hollowing from the stable,
Makes love with nods, and knees beneath a table;
Whose laughs are hearty, though his jests are coarse,
And loves you best of all things—but his horse.   30
    In some fair evening, on your elbow laid,
You dream of triumphs in the rural shade;
In pensive thought recall the fancied scene,
See coronations rise on every green:
Before you pass the imaginary sights   35
Of Lords, and Earls, and Dukes, and gartered Knights,
While the spread fan o'ershades your closing eyes,
Then gives one flirt, and all the vision flies.
Thus vanish sceptres, coronets, and balls,
And leave you in lone woods, or empty walls!   40
    So when your slave, at some dear idle time
(Not plagued with headaches, or the want of rhyme)

Stands in the streets, abstracted from the crew,
And while he seems to study, thinks of you;
Just when his fancy paints your sprightly eyes,   45
Or sees the blush of soft Parthenia rise,
Gay pats my shoulder, and you vanish quite,
Streets, chairs,° and coxcombs rush upon my sight.   sedan chairs
Vexed to be still in town, I knit my brow,
Look sour, and hum a tune—as you may now.   50

—Alexander Pope [1688–1744]

EPISTLE TO A YOUNG LADY. The young lady, whom Pope here calls *Zephalinda* (7), was
in actuality his good friend Teresa Blount, and *Parthenia* (46) was his even better
friend, her younger sister, Martha. *Your slave* (41) is Pope himself, and *Gay* (47) is the
poet John Gay, also a good friend of Pope's. The coronation was that of George I in 1714.

SUNBURNED ULYSSES

Sunburned Ulysses, when he leaned over the water
And heard through the lapping of the waves
That calculating music, heard more than the noise of wind
    or the noise of water:
As he strained his ears, he heard the monotonous profound
Music of lost mariners moving landward through the water,   5
He heard, rising from graves of sand, sea-pitted
    and sea-pillared graves,
The sobbing and interminable voices of the drowned.

Scarcely to be grasped as anything other than music,
Being almost wholly woven into the sound of waves,
    he heard
Emerging from the crested, sun-dipped lethargy   10
    of the afternoon,
Distinct and terrifying words. Yet not a word
Could he recall—or at least, he never told, being in love
With no one; hard and isolated, in love with change alone,
With a bird's yearning to move seasonally and the sharp,
    mean eyes of a bird.

O blacker and deeper than the depths off Portugal,   15
Some of us have glimpsed that rock, that goddess
    rising from the sea,
And as we labor to find for what we were intended,
Slowly, as the spirit is sharpened, the senses are vilified.
Even the sly faces and the weatherbeaten faces all, all
Are caught and brought to punishment. Though they have   20
    not died,
Their eyes are those of a dead man, or a dead animal.

Black-eyed Ulysses, being an astute and eagle-hearted man,
A heavily loined, lumbering man with a bird's eye
  and a bird's unrest,
As he listened and heard through the lapping of the waves
That loud, heart-breaking music, understood. Sweat poured   25
  from his brown chest.
Loving the unattainable and forbidden, in love with change
  alone,
He recognized the frightful necessity in the song of the sirens:
  for he likewise possessed
Flesh fanned easily into fire, and a heart as hard as a stone.

                                    —*Frederic Prokosch* [1908–   ]

SUNBURNED ULYSSES. See discussion in Question 8 of "Ulysses," Alfred, Lord Tennyson,
p. 81 of Part One.

PIAZZA PIECE

—I am a gentleman in a dustcoat trying
To make you hear. Your ears are soft and small
And listen to an old man not at all,
They want the young men's whispering and sighing.
But see the roses on your trellis dying   5
And hear the spectral singing of the moon;
For I must have my lovely lady soon,
I am a gentleman in a dustcoat trying.

—I am a lady young in beauty waiting
Until my truelove comes, and then we kiss.   10
But what grey man among the vines is this
Whose words are dry and faint as in a dream?
Back from my trellis, Sir, before I scream!
I am a lady young in beauty waiting.

                                    —*John Crowe Ransom* [1888–   ]

MR. FLOOD'S PARTY

Old Eben Flood, climbing alone one night
Over the hill between the town below
And the forsaken upland hermitage
That held as much as he should ever know
On earth again of home, paused warily.   5
The road was his with not a native near;
And Eben, having leisure, said aloud,
For no man else in Tilbury Town to hear:

"Well, Mr. Flood, we have the harvest moon
Again, and we may not have many more;   10
The bird is on the wing, the poet says,
And you and I have said it here before.
Drink to the bird." He raised up to the light
The jug that he had gone so far to fill,
And answered huskily: "Well, Mr. Flood,   15
Since you propose it, I believe I will."

Alone, as if enduring to the end
A valiant armor of scarred hopes outworn,
He stood there in the middle of the road
Like Roland's ghost winding a silent horn.   20
Below him, in the town among the trees,
Where friends of other days had honored him,
A phantom salutation of the dead
Rang thinly till old Eben's eyes were dim.

Then, as a mother lays her sleeping child   25
Down tenderly, fearing it may awake,
He set the jug down slowly at his feet
With trembling care, knowing that most things break;
And only when assured that on firm earth
It stood, as the uncertain lives of men   30
Assuredly did not, he paced away,
And with his hand extended paused again:

"Well, Mr. Flood, we have not met like this
In a long time; and many a change has come
To both of us, I fear, since last it was   35
We had a drop together. Welcome home!"
Convivially returning with himself,
Again he raised the jug up to the light;
And with an acquiescent quaver said:
"Well, Mr. Flood, if you insist, I might.   40

"Only a very little, Mr. Flood—
For auld lang syne. No more, sir; that will do."
So, for the time, apparently it did,
And Eben evidently thought so too;
For soon amid the silver loneliness   45
Of night he lifted up his voice and sang,
Secure, with only two moons listening,
Until the whole harmonious landscape rang—

"For auld lang syne." The weary throat gave out,
The last word wavered, and the song was done.   50
He raised again the jug regretfully
And shook his head, and was again alone.
There was not much that was ahead of him,
And there was nothing in the town below—
Where strangers would have shut the many doors   55
That many friends had opened long ago.

—Edwin Arlington Robinson [1869–1935]

MR. FLOOD'S PARTY. 11. *bird:* Mr. Flood is quoting from *The Rubáiyát of Omar Khayyám*, "The bird of Time . . . is on the wing." 20. *Roland:* hero of the French epic poem *The Song of Roland*. He died fighting a rear-guard action for Charlemagne against the Moors in Spain; before his death he sounded a call for help on his famous horn, but the king's army arrived too late.

I KNEW A WOMAN

I knew a woman, lovely in her bones,
When small birds sighed, she would sigh back at them;
Ah, when she moved, she moved more ways than one:
The shapes a bright container can contain!
Of her choice virtues only gods should speak,   5
Or English poets who grew up on Greek
(I'd have them sing in chorus, cheek to cheek).

How well her wishes went! She stroked my chin,
She taught me Turn, and Counter-turn, and Stand;
She taught me Touch, that undulant white skin;   10
I nibbled meekly from her proffered hand;
She was the sickle; I, poor I, the rake,
Coming behind her for her pretty sake
(But what prodigious mowing we did make).

Love likes a gander, and adores a goose: 15
Her full lips pursed, the arrant note to seize;
She played it quick, she played it light and loose;
My eyes, they dazzled at her flowing knees;
Her several parts could keep a pure repose,
Or one hip quiver with a mobile nose   20
(She moved in circles, and those circles moved).

Let seed be grass, and grass turn into hay:
I'm martyr to a motion not my own;
What's freedom for? To know eternity.
I swear she cast a shadow white as stone.   25
But who would count eternity in days?
These old bones live to learn her wanton ways:
(I measure time by how a body sways).

—*Theodore Roethke* [1908–1963]

SILENT NOON

Your hands lie open in the long fresh grass,—
The finger-points look through like rosy blooms:
Your eyes smile peace. The pasture gleams and glooms
'Neath billowing skies that scatter and amass.
All round our nest, far as the eye can pass,   5
Are golden kingcup-fields with silver edge
Where the cow-parsley skirts the hawthorn-hedge.
'Tis visible silence, still as the hour-glass.

Deep in the sun-searched growths the dragon-fly
Hangs like a blue thread loosened from the sky:—   10
So this winged hour is dropped to us from above.
Oh! clasp we to our hearts, for deathless dower,
This close-companioned inarticulate hour
When twofold silence was the song of love.

—*Dante Gabriel Rossetti* [1828–1882]

FEAR NO MORE

Fear no more the heat o' the sun,
    Nor the furious winter's rages;
Thou thy worldly task hast done,
    Home art gone, and ta'en thy wages.
Golden lads and girls all must,   5
As chimney-sweepers, come to dust.

Fear no more the frown o' the great;
    Thou art past the tyrant's stroke;
Care no more to clothe and eat;
    To thee the reed is as the oak.   10
The sceptre, learning, physic,° must   art of healing
All follow this, and come to dust.

295

Fear no more the lightning-flash,
    Nor the all-dreaded thunder-stone;°   thunderbolt
Fear not slander, censure rash;   15
    Thou hast finished joy and moan.
All lovers young, all lovers must
Consign to thee,° and come to dust.   yield to your condition

—*William Shakespeare [1564–1616]*

LET ME NOT TO THE MARRIAGE OF TRUE MINDS

Let me not to the marriage of true minds
Admit impediments. Love is not love
Which alters when it alteration finds,
Or bends with the remover to remove.
O no! it is an ever-fixèd mark   5
That looks on tempests and is never shaken;
It is the star to every wandering bark,
Whose worth's unknown, although his height be taken.
Love's not Time's fool, though rosy lips and cheeks
Within his bending sickle's compass come;   10
Love alters not with his brief hours and weeks,
But bears it out even to the edge of doom.
    If this be error and upon me proved,
    I never writ, nor no man ever loved.

—*William Shakespeare [1564–1616]*

SINCE BRASS, NOR STONE, NOR EARTH

Since brass, nor stone, nor earth, nor boundless sea,
But sad mortality o'er-sways their power,
How with this rage shall beauty hold a plea,
Whose action is no stronger than a flower?
O, how shall summer's honey breath hold out   5
Against the wrackful siege of battering days,
When rocks impregnable are not so stout,
Nor gates of steel so strong, but Time decays?
O fearful meditation! where, alack,
Shall Time's best jewel from Time's chest lie hid?   10
Or what strong hand can hold his swift foot back?
Or who his spoil of beauty can forbid?
    O, none, unless this miracle have might,
    That in black ink my love may still shine bright.

—*William Shakespeare [1564–1616]*

MY MISTRESS' EYES ARE NOTHING LIKE THE SUN

My mistress' eyes are nothing like the sun;
Coral is far more red than her lips' red:
If snow be white, why then her breasts are dun;
If hairs be wires, black wires grow on her head.
I have seen roses damasked,° red and white,   of different colors
But no such roses see I in her cheeks;   6
And in some perfumes is there more delight
Than in the breath that from my mistress reeks.
I love to hear her speak, yet well I know
That music hath a far more pleasing sound: 10
I grant I never saw a goddess go,—
My mistress, when she walks, treads on the ground.
   And yet, by heaven, I think my love as rare
   As any she belied with false compare.

—*William Shakespeare [1564–1616]*

DOCTOR, DOCTOR, A LITTLE OF YOUR LOVE

"Doctor, doctor, a little of your love
   And a little of your skill,
I can no longer sight my gun,
   No longer can I kill."

"Soldier, soldier, I cannot find the cause   5
   And I will not set you free,
But take this pill and go your way
   To your own company."

"Chaplain, chaplain, a little of your love
   And a little of your grace,   10
I can no longer think my thoughts
   Nor bear the demon's face."

"My son, my son, I cannot find the cause
   And I will not set you free,
But take this book and go your way   15
   To your own company."

"Captain, captain, a little of your love
   And likewise of your loyalty,
I can no longer land at dawn
   Nor ride the troopship sea."   20

"Soldier, soldier, I cannot find the cause
    And I will not set you free
But take this leave and go your way
    To your own company."

With doctor's pill and chaplain's book   25
    And captain's furlough free,
The soldier went and hanged himself
    On a Signal Corps cross-tree.

O soldier, soldier, where now are your eyes
    That once so much did see?   30
The vultures have plucked them from his face
    Just over our company.

Karl Shapiro [1913–   ]

THE GLORIES OF OUR BLOOD AND STATE

The glories of our blood and state
    Are shadows, not substantial things;
There is no armor against fate;
    Death lays his icy hand on kings.
        Scepter and crown   5
        Must tumble down,
And in the dust be equal made
With the poor crooked scythe and spade.

Some men with swords may reap the field,
    And plant fresh laurels where they kill;   10
But their strong nerves at last must yield,
    They tame but one another still.
        Early or late,
        They stoop to fate,
And must give up their murmuring breath   15
When they, pale captives, creep to death.

The garlands wither on your brow,
    Then boast no more your mighty deeds;
Upon death's purple altar now
    See where the victor-victim bleeds.   20
        Your heads must come
        To the cold tomb;
Only the actions of the just
Smell sweet and blossom in their dust.

—James Shirley [1596–1666]

LEAVE ME, O LOVE

Leave me, O Love, which reachest but to dust;
And thou, my mind, aspire to higher things;
Grow rich in that which never taketh rust.
Whatever fades, but fading pleasure brings.
Draw in thy beams, and humble all thy might   5
To that sweet yoke where lasting freedoms be,
Which breaks the clouds, and opens forth the light,
That doth both shine and give us sight to see.
O, take fast hold! let that light be thy guide
In this small course which birth draws out to death—   10
And think how evil becometh him to slide,
Who seeketh heaven, and comes of heavenly breath.
    Then farewell, world; thy uttermost I see:
    Eternal Love, maintain thy life in me.

—Sir Philip Sidney [1554–1586]

WITH HOW SAD STEPS, O MOON

With how sad steps, O moon, thou climb'st the skies!
    How silently, and with how wan a face!
    What! may it be that even in heavenly place
    That busy archer° his sharp arrows tries?   cupid
Sure, if that long-with-love-acquainted eyes   5
    Can judge of love, thou feel'st a lover's case:
    I read it in thy looks,—thy languished grace
    To me, that feel the like, thy state descries.
Then, even of fellowship, O moon, tell me,
    Is constant love deemed there but want of wit?   10
    Are beauties there as proud as here they be?
Do they above love to be loved, and yet
    Those lovers scorn whom that love doth possess?
    Do they call virtue there ungratefulness?

—Sir Philip Sidney [1554–1586]

THE CIRCUS; OR ONE VIEW OF IT

Said the circus man, Oh what do you like
Best of all about my show—
The circular rings, three rings in a row,
With animals going around, around,
Tamed to go running round, around,   5
And around, round, around they go;

Or perhaps you like the merry-go-round,
Horses plunging sedately up,
Horses sedately plunging down,
Going around the merry-go-round;   10
Or perhaps you like the clown with a hoop,
Shouting, rolling the hoop around;
Or the elephants walking around in a ring
Each trunk looped to a tail's loop,
Loosely ambling around the ring;   15
How do you like this part of the show?
Everything's busy and on the go;
The peanut men cry out and sing,
The round fat clown rolls on the ground,
The trapeze ladies sway and swing,   20
The circus horses plunge around
The circular rings, three rings in a row;
Here they come, and here they go.
And here you sit, said the circus man,
Around in a circle to watch my show;   25
Which is show and which is you,
Now that we're here in this circus show,
Do I know? Do you know?
But hooray for the clowns and the merry-go-round,
The painted horses plunging round,   30
The live, proud horses stamping the ground,
And the clowns and the elephants swinging around;
Come to my show; hooray for the show,
Hooray for the circus all the way round!
Said the round exuberant circus man.   35
Hooray for the show! said the circus man.

—Theodore Spencer [1902–1949]

THE CIRCUS. This poem has been recorded by Mr. Spencer (78 rpm, Harvard Vocarium, P–1032).

TRUST NOT THE TREASON

Trust not the treason of those smiling looks
Until ye have their guileful trains° well tried,   lures
For they are like but unto golden hooks
That from the foolish fish their baits do hide:
So she with flattering smiles weak hearts doth guide   5
Unto her love, and tempt to their decay,
Whom, being caught, she kills with cruel pride,
And feeds at pleasure on the wretched prey.
Yet even whilst her bloody hands them slay,
Her eyes look lovely, and upon them smile,   10
That they take pleasure in her cruel play,
And, dying, do themselves of pain beguile.

O mighty charm! which makes men love their bane,
And think they die with pleasure, live with pain.

—*Edmund Spenser* [1552?–1599]

A GLASS OF BEER

The lanky hank of a she in the inn over there
Nearly killed me for asking the loan of a glass of beer;
May the devil grip the whey-faced slut by the hair,
And beat bad manners out of her skin for a year.

That parboiled ape, with the toughest jaw you will see   5
On virtue's path, and a voice that would rasp the dead,
Came roaring and raging the minute she looked at me,
And threw me out of the house on the back of my head!

If I asked her master he'd give me a cask a day;
But she, with the beer at hand, not a gill would arrange!   10
May she marry a ghost and bear him a kitten, and may
The High King of Glory permit her to get the mange.

—*James Stephens* [1882–1950]

A HIGH-TONED OLD CHRISTIAN WOMAN

Poetry is the supreme fiction, madame.
Take the moral law and make a nave of it
And from the nave build haunted heaven. Thus,
The conscience is converted into palms,
Like windy citherns hankering for hymns.   5
We agree in principle. That's clear. But take
The opposing law and make a peristyle,
And from the peristyle project a masque
Beyond the planets. Thus, our bawdiness,
Unpurged by epitaph, indulged at last,   10
Is equally converted into palms,
Squiggling like saxophones. And palm for palm,
Madame, we are where we began. Allow,
Therefore, that in the planetary scene
Your disaffected flagellants, well-stuffed,   15
Smacking their muzzy bellies in parade,
Proud of such novelties of the sublime,
Such tink and tank and tunk-a-tunk-tunk,
May, merely may, madame, whip from themselves
A jovial hullabaloo among the spheres.   20
This will make widows wince. But fictive things
Wink as they will. Wink most when widows wince.

—*Wallace Stevens* [1879–1955]

DESCRIPTION OF SPRING,
WHEREIN EACH THING RENEWS
SAVE ONLY THE LOVER

The soote° season that bud and bloom forth brings   sweet
With green hath clad the hill and eke° the vale,   also
The nightingale with feathers new she sings,
The turtle° to her make° hath told her tale.   turtle-dove; mate
Summer is come, for every spray now springs,   5
The hart hath hung his old head on the pale,°   paling fence
The buck in brake his winter coat he flings,
The fishes float with new repaired scale,
The adder all her slough away she slings,   9
The swift swallow pursueth the flies smale,°   small
The busy bee her honey now she mings,°   mixes
Winter is worn, that was the flowers' bale:
And thus I see, among these pleasant things
Each care decays—and yet my sorrow springs.

—*Henry Howard, Earl of Surrey [1517?–1547]*

DESCRIPTION OF SPRING. 6. The hart has shed his antlers by rubbing them against the fence.

A SATIRICAL ELEGY
ON THE DEATH OF A LATE FAMOUS GENERAL

His Grace! impossible! what dead!
Of old age too, and in his bed!
And could that Mighty Warrior fall?
And so inglorious, after all!
Well, since he's gone, no matter how,   5
The last loud trump must wake him now:
And, trust me, as the noise grows stronger,
He'd wish to sleep a little longer.
And could he be indeed so old
As by the newspapers we're told?   10
Threescore, I think, is pretty high;
'Twas time in conscience he should die.
This world he cumbered long enough;
He burnt his candle to the snuff;
And that's the reason, some folks think,   15
He left behind so great a s---k.
Behold his funeral appears,
Nor widow's sighs, nor orphan's tears,
Wont at such times each heart to pierce,
Attend the progress of his hearse.   20

But what of that, his friends may say,
He had those honors in his day.
True to his profit and his pride,
He made them weep before he died.

Come hither, all ye empty things—   25
Ye bubbles raised by breath of Kings—
Who float upon the tide of state,
Come hither, and behold your fate.
Let pride be taught by this rebuke
How very mean a thing's a Duke: 30
From all his ill-got honors flung,
Turned to that dirt from whence he sprung.

—Jonathan Swift [1667–1745]

HOUSEWIFERY

Make me, O Lord, thy spinning wheel complete.
  Thy Holy Word my distaff make for me.
Make mine affections thy swift fliers° neate,   revolving arms in a
  And make my soul thy holy spool to be.   spinning wheel
  My conversation make to be thy reel   5
  And reel the yarn thereon spun of thy wheel.

Make me thy loom then, knit therein this twine;
  And make thy Holy Spirit, Lord, wind quills;° spindles
Then weave the web thyself. The yarn is fine.
  Thine ordinances make my fulling° mills.   cloth processing
  Then dye the same in heavenly colors choice,
  All pinked° with varnished flowers of Paradise. ornamentally
                                        punched with holes

Then clothe therewith mine understanding, will,
  Affections, judgment, conscience, memory,
My words and actions, that their shine may fill   15
  My ways with glory and thee glorify.
  Then mine apparel shall display before ye
  That I am clothed in holy robes for glory.

—Edward Taylor [1645–1729]

DO NOT GO GENTLE INTO THAT GOOD NIGHT

Do not go gentle into that good night,
Old age should burn and rave at close of day;
Rage, rage against the dying of the light.·

Though wise men at their end know dark is right,
Because their words had forked no lightning they   5
Do not go gentle into that good night.

Good men, the last wave by, crying how bright
Their frail deeds might have danced in a green bay,
Rage, rage against the dying of the light.

Wild men who caught and sang the sun in flight,   10
And learn, too late, they grieved it on its way,
Do not go gentle into that good night.

Grave men, near death, who see with blinding sight
Blind eyes could blaze like meteors and be gay,
Rage, rage against the dying of the light.   15

And you, my father, there on the sad height,
Curse, bless, me now with your fierce tears, I pray.
Do not go gentle into that good night.
Rage, rage against the dying of the light.

—*Dylan Thomas [1914–1953]*

THE GALLOWS

There was a weasel lived in the sun
With all his family,
Till a keeper shot him with his gun
And hung him up on a tree,
Where he swings in the wind and the rain   5
In the sun and in the snow,
Without pleasure, without pain,
On the dead oak tree bough.

There was a crow who was no sleeper,
But a thief and a murderer   10
Till a very late hour; and this keeper
Made him one of the things that were,
To hang and flap in the rain and wind,
In the sun and in the snow.
There are no more sins to be sinned   15
On the dead oak tree bough.

There was a magpie, too,
Had a long tongue and a long tail;
He could both talk and do—
But what did that avail?   20

He, too, flaps in the wind and rain
Alongside weasel and crow.
Without pleasure, without pain,
On the dead oak tree bough.

And many other beasts,   25
And birds, skin, bone and feather,
Have been taken from their feasts
And hung up there together,
To swing and have endless leisure
In the sun and in the snow,   30
Without pain, without pleasure,
On the dead oak tree bough.

—*Edward Thomas [1878–1917]*

PEACE

My soul, there is a country
  Far beyond the stars,
Where stands a wingèd sentry
  All skillful in the wars.
There, above noise and danger,   5
  Sweet Peace sits crowned with smiles,
And One born in a manger
  Commands the beauteous files.
He is thy gracious friend,
  And—O my soul, awake!—   10
Did in pure love descend
  To die here for thy sake.
If thou canst get but thither,
  There grows the flower of peace,
The rose that cannot wither,   15
  Thy fortress and thy ease.
Leave then thy foolish ranges,
  For none can thee secure
But One who never changes,
  Thy God, thy life, thy cure.   20

—*Henry Vaughan [1622–1695]*

ON A GIRDLE

That which her slender waist confined
Shall now my joyful temples bind;
No monarch but would give his crown
His arms might do what this has done.

It was my heaven's extremest sphere,   5
The pale which held that lovely deer.
My joy, my grief, my hope, my love,
Did all within this circle move!

A narrow compass, and yet there
Dwelt all that's good and all that's fair;   10
Give me but what this riband bound,
Take all the rest the sun goes round.

—Edmund Waller [1606–1687]

TO NIGHT

Mysterious Night! when our first parent knew
Thee from report divine, and heard thy name,
Did he not tremble for this lovely frame,
This glorious canopy of light and blue?
Yet 'neath the curtain of translucent dew,   5
Bathed in the rays of the great setting flame,
Hesperus with the host of heaven came,
And lo! creation widened on man's view.
Who could have thought such darkness lay concealed
Within thy beams, O Sun! or who could find,   10
While fly, and leaf, and insect stood revealed,
That to such countless orbs thou mad'st us blind!
    Why do we, then, shun Death with anxious strife?—
    If Light can thus deceive, wherefore not Life?

—Joseph Blanco White [1775–1841]

A NOISELESS PATIENT SPIDER

A noiseless patient spider,
I marked where on a little promontory it stood isolated,
Marked how to explore the vacant vast surrounding,
It launched forth filament, filament, filament, out of itself,
Ever unreeling them, ever tirelessly speeding them.   5

And you O my soul where you stand,
Surrounded, detached, in measureless oceans of space,
Ceaselessly musing, venturing, throwing, seeking the spheres to
    connect them,
Till the bridge you will need be formed, till the ductile anchor hold,
Till the gossamer thread you fling catch somewhere, O my soul.   10

—Walt Whitman [1819–1892]

THERE WAS A CHILD WENT FORTH

There was a child went forth every day,
And the first object he looked upon, that object he became,
And that object became part of him for the day or a certain part of the
day,
Or for many years or stretching cycles of years.

The early lilacs became part of this child,   5
And grass and white and red morning-glories, and white and red clover,
and the song of the phoebe-bird,
And the Third-month lambs and the sow's pink-faint litter, and the mare's
foal and the cow's calf,
And the noisy brood of the barnyard or by the mire of the pond-side,
And the fish suspending themselves so curiously below there, and the
beautiful curious liquid,
And the water-plants with their graceful flat heads, all became part of
him.   10

The field-sprouts of Fourth-month and Fifth-month became part of him,
Winter-grain sprouts and those of the light-yellow corn, and the esculent
roots of the garden,
And the apple-trees covered with blossoms and the fruit afterward, and
wood-berries, and the commonest weeds by the road,
And the old drunkard staggering home from the outhouse of the tavern
whence he had lately risen,
And the schoolmistress that passed on her way to the school,   15
And the friendly boys that passed, and the quarrelsome boys,
And the tidy and fresh-cheeked girls, and the barefoot negro boy and
girl,
And all the changes of city and country wherever he went.

His own parents, he that had fathered him and she that had conceived
him in her womb and birthed him,
They gave this child more of themselves than that,   20
They gave him afterward every day, they became part of him.

The mother at home quietly placing the dishes on the supper-table,
The mother with mild words, clean her cap and gown, a wholesome
odor falling off her person and clothes as she walks by,
The father, strong, self-sufficient, manly, mean, angered, unjust,
The blow, the quick loud word, the tight bargain, the crafty lure,   25
The family usages, the language, the company, the furniture, the yearn-
ing and swelling heart,
Affection that will not be gainsayed, the sense of what is real, the thought
if after all it should prove unreal,

The doubts of day-time and the doubts of night-time, the curious
    whether and how,
Whether that which appears so is so, or is it all flashes and specks?
Men and women crowding fast in the streets, if they are not flashes and
    specks what are they?   30
The streets themselves and the façades of houses, and goods in the win-
    dows,
Vehicles, teams, the heavy-planked wharves, the huge crossing at the
    ferries,
The village on the highland seen from afar at sunset, the river between,
Shadows, aureola and mist, the light falling on roofs and gables of white
    or brown two miles off,
The schooner near by sleepily dropping down the tide, the little boat
    slack-towed astern,   35
The hurrying tumbling waves, quick-broken crests, slapping,
The strata of colored clouds, the long bar of maroon-tint away solitary
    by itself, the spread of purity it lies motionless in,
The horizon's edge, the flying sea-crow, the fragrance of salt marsh and
    shore mud,
These became part of that child who went forth every day, and who now
    goes, and will always go forth every day.

                                            —*Walt Whitman [1819–1892]*

OUT OF THE CRADLE ENDLESSLY ROCKING

Out of the cradle endlessly rocking,
Out of the mocking-bird's throat, the musical shuttle,
Out of the Ninth-month midnight,
Over the sterile sands and the fields beyond where the child leaving his
    bed wandered alone, bareheaded, barefoot,
Down from the showered halo,   5
Up from the mystic play of shadows twining and twisting as if they were
    alive,
Out from the patches of briers and blackberries,
From the memories of the bird that chanted to me,
From your memories sad brother, from the fitful risings and fallings I
    heard,
From under that yellow half-moon late-risen and swollen as if with
    tears,   10
From those beginning notes of yearning and love there in the mist,
From the thousand responses of my heart never to cease,
From the myriad thence aroused words,
From the word stronger and more delicious than any,
From such as now they start the scene revisiting,   15
As a flock, twittering, rising, or overhead passing,

Borne hither, ere all eludes me, hurriedly,
A man, yet by these tears a little boy again,
Throwing myself on the sand, confronting the waves,
I, chanter of pains and joys, uniter of here and hereafter,   20
Taking all hints to use them, but swiftly leaping beyond them,
A reminiscence sing.

Once Paumanok,
When the lilac-scent was in the air and Fifth-month grass was growing,
Up this seashore in some briers,   25
Two feathered guests from Alabama, two together,
And their nest, and four light-green eggs spotted with brown,
And every day the he-bird to and fro near at hand,
And every day the she-bird crouched on her nest, silent, with bright
    eyes,
And every day I, a curious boy, never too close, never disturbing
    them,   30
Cautiously peering, absorbing, translating.

Shine! shine! shine!
Pour down your warmth, great sun!
While we bask, we two together,

Two together!   35
Winds blow south, or winds blow north,
Day come white, or night come black,
Home, or rivers and mountains from home,
Singing all time, minding no time,
While we two keep together.   40

Till of a sudden,
May-be killed, unknown to her mate,
One forenoon the she-bird crouched not on the nest,
Nor returned that afternoon, nor the next,
Nor ever appeared again.   45

And thenceforward all summer in the sound of the sea,
And at night under the full of the moon in calmer weather,
Over the hoarse surging of the sea,
Or flitting from brier to brier by day,
I saw, I heard at intervals the remaining one, the he-bird,   50
The solitary guest from Alabama.

Blow! blow! blow!
Blow up sea-winds along Paumanok's shore;
I wait and I wait till you blow my mate to me.

Yes, when the stars glistened,   55
All night long on the prong of a moss-scalloped stake,
Down almost amid the slapping waves,
Sat the lone singer wonderful causing tears.

He called on his mate,
He poured forth the meanings which I of all men know.   60

Yes my brother I know,
The rest might not, but I have treasured every note,
For more than once dimly down to the beach gliding,
Silent, avoiding the moonbeams, blending myself with the shadows,
Recalling now the obscure shapes, the echoes, the sounds and sights after
    their sorts,   65
The white arms out in the breakers tirelessly tossing,
I, with bare feet, a child, the wind wafting my hair,
Listened long and long.

Listened to keep, to sing, now translating the notes,
Following you my brother.   70

Soothe! soothe! soothe!
Close on its wave soothes the wave behind,
And again another behind embracing and lapping, every one close,
But my love soothes not me, not me.

Low hangs the moon, it rose late,   75
It is lagging—O I think it is heavy with love, with love.

O madly the sea pushes upon the land,
With love, with love.

O night! do I not see my love fluttering out among the breakers?
What is that little black thing I see there in the white?   80

Loud! loud! loud!
Loud I call to you, my love!
High and clear I shoot my voice over the waves,
Surely you must know who is here, is here,
You must know who I am, my love.   85

Low-hanging moon!
What is that dusky spot in your brown yellow?
O it is the shape, the shape of my mate!
O moon do not keep her from me any longer.

Land! land! O land!   90
Whichever way I turn, O I think you could give me my mate back again
    if you only would,
For I am almost sure I see her dimly whichever way I look.

O rising stars!
Perhaps the one I want so much will rise, will rise with some of you.

O throat! O trembling throat!   95
Sound clearer through the atmosphere!
Pierce the woods, the earth,
Somewhere listening to catch you must be the one I want.

Shake out carols!
Solitary here, the night's carols!   100
Carols of lonesome love! death's carols!
Carols under that lagging, yellow, waning moon!
O under that moon where she droops almost down into the sea!
O reckless despairing carols.

But soft! sink low!   105
Soft, let me just murmur,
And do you wait a moment you husky-noised sea,
For somewhere I believe I heard my mate responding to me,
So faint, I must be still, be still to listen,
But not altogether still, for then she might not come immediately to
    me.   110

Hither my love!
Here I am! Here!
With this just-sustained note I announce myself to you,
This gentle call is for you my love, for you.

Do not be decoyed elsewhere,   115
That is the whistle of the wind, it is not my voice,
That is the fluttering, the fluttering of the spray,
Those are the shadows of leaves.

O darkness! O in vain!
O I am very sick and sorrowful.   120

O brown halo in the sky near the moon, drooping upon the sea!
O troubled reflection in the sea!
O throat! O throbbing heart!
And I singing uselessly, uselessly all the night.

O past! O happy life! O songs of joy!
In the air, in the woods, over fields,
Loved! loved! loved! loved! loved!
But my mate no more, no more with me!
We two together no more.

The aria sinking,   130
All else continuing, the stars shining,
The winds blowing, the notes of the bird continuous echoing,
With angry moans the fierce old mother incessantly moaning,
On the sands of Paumanok's shore gray and rustling,
The yellow half-moon enlarged, sagging down, drooping, the face of the
    sea almost touching,   135
The boy ecstatic, with his bare feet the waves, with his hair the atmos-
    phere dallying,
The love in the heart long pent, now loose, now at last tumultuously
    bursting,
The aria's meaning, the ears, the soul, swiftly depositing,
The strange tears down the cheeks coursing,
The colloquy there, the trio, each uttering,   140
The undertone, the savage old mother incessantly crying,
To the boy's soul's questions sullenly timing, some drowned secret hiss-
    ing,
To the outsetting bard.

Demon or bird! (said the boy's soul,)
Is it indeed toward your mate you sing? or is it really to me?   145
For I, that was a child, my tongue's use sleeping, now I have heard
    you,
Now in a moment I know what I am for, I awake,
And already a thousand singers, a thousand songs, clearer, louder and
    more sorrowful than yours,
A thousand warbling echoes have started to life within me, never to
    die.

O you singer solitary, singing by yourself, projecting me,   150
O solitary me listening, never more shall I cease perpetuating you,
Never more shall I escape, never more the reverberations,
Never more the cries of unsatisfied love be absent from me,
Never again leave me to be the peaceful child I was before what there
    in the night,
By the sea under the yellow and sagging moon,   155
The messenger there aroused, the fire, the sweet hell within,
The unknown want, the destiny of me.

O give me the clue! (it lurks in the night here somewhere,)
O if I am to have so much, let me have more!

A word then, (for I will conquer it,)   160
The word final, superior to all,
Subtle, sent up—what is it?—I listen;
Are you whispering it, and have been all the time, you sea-waves?
Is that it from your liquid rims and wet sands?

Whereto answering, the sea,
Delaying not, hurrying not,
Whispered me through the night, and very plainly before daybreak,
Lisped to me the low and delicious word death,
And again death, death, death, death,
Hissing melodious, neither like the bird nor like my aroused child's
    heart,   170
But edging near as privately for me rustling at my feet,
Creeping thence steadily up to my ears and laving me softly all over
Death, death, death, death, death.

Which I do not forget,
But fuse the song of my dusky demon and brother,   175
That he sang to me in the moonlight on Paumanok's gray beach,
With the thousand responsive songs at random,
My own songs awaked from that hour,
And with them the key, the word up from the waves,
The word of the sweetest song and all songs,   180
That strong and delicious word which, creeping to my feet,
(Or like some old crone rocking the cradle, swathed in sweet garments,
    bending aside,)
The sea whispered me.

                            —*Walt Whitman* [*1819–1892*]

OUT OF THE CRADLE ENDLESSLY ROCKING. 23. *Paumanok:* Indian name for Long Island,
where Whitman grew up.

A BAROQUE WALL-FOUNTAIN IN THE VILLA SCIARRA

        Under the bronze crown
Too big for the head of the stone cherub whose feet
        A serpent has begun to eat,
Sweet water brims a cockle and braids down

        Past spattered mosses, breaks   5
On the tipped edge of a second shell, and fills
        The massive third below. It spills
In threads then from the scalloped rim, and makes

313

A scrim or summery tent
For a faun-ménage and their familiar goose.   10
    Happy in all that ragged, loose
Collapse of water, its effortless descent

    And flatteries of spray,
The stocky god upholds the shell with ease,
    Watching, about his shaggy knees,   15
The goatish innocence of his babes at play;

    His fauness all the while
Leans forward, slightly, into a clambering mesh
    Of water-lights, her sparkling flesh
In a saecular ecstasy, her blinded smile   20

    Bent on the sand floor
Of the trefoil pool, where ripple-shadows come
    And go in swift reticulum,
More addling to the eye than wine, and more

    Interminable to thought   25
Than pleasure's calculus. Yet since this all
    Is pleasure, flash, and waterfall,
Must it not be too simple? Are we not

    More intricately expressed
In the plain fountains that Maderna set   30
    Before St. Peter's—the main jet
Struggling aloft until it seems at rest

    In the act of rising, until
The very wish of water is reversed,
    That heaviness borne up to burst   35
In a clear, high, cavorting head, to fill

    With blaze, and then in gauze
Delays, in a gnatlike shimmering, in a fine
    Illumined version of itself, decline,
And patter on the stones its own applause?   40

    If that is what men are
Or should be, if those water-saints display
    The pattern of our areté,
What of these showered fauns in their bizarre,

    Spangled, and plunging house?   45
They are at rest in fulness of desire
    For what is given, they do not tire
Of the smart of the sun, the pleasant water-douse

And riddled pool below,
Reproving our disgust and our ennui   50
With humble insatiety.
Francis, perhaps, who lay in sister snow

Before the wealthy gate
Freezing and praising, might have seen in this
    No trifle, but a shade of bliss—   55
That land of tolerable flowers, that state

As near and far as grass
Where eyes become the sunlight, and the hand
    Is worthy of water: the dreamt land
Toward which all hungers leap, all pleasures pass.   60

—*Richard Wilbur [1921–   ]*

A BAROQUE WALL-FOUNTAIN IN THE VILLA SCIARRA. The Villa Sciarra is in Rome, as is
also St. Peter's Cathedral (31). 20. *saecular:* a variant spelling of *secular* which here
gathers in the sense of *saeculum,* a period of long duration, an age. 30. *Maderna:* Italian
architect (1556–1629). 43. *areté:* a Greek word meaning roughly "virtue" (Wilbur's note).
52. *Francis:* St. Francis of Assisi.

STRANGE FITS OF PASSION

Strange fits° of passion have I known: whims
And I will dare to tell,
But in the Lover's ear alone,
What once to me befell.

When she I loved looked every day   5
Fresh as a rose in June,
I to her cottage bent my way,
Beneath an evening-moon.

Upon the moon I fixed my eye,
All over the wide lea;   10
With quickening pace my horse drew nigh
Those paths so dear to me.

And now we reached the orchard-plot;
And, as we climbed the hill,
The sinking moon to Lucy's cot°   cottage
Came near, and nearer still.   16

In one of those sweet dreams I slept,
Kind Nature's gentlest boon!
And all the while my eyes I kept
On the descending moon.   20

My horse moved on; hoof after hoof
He raised, and never stopped:
When down behind the cottage roof,
At once, the bright moon dropped.

What fond° and wayward thoughts will slide   foolish
Into a Lover's head!   26
"O mercy!" to myself I cried,
"If Lucy should be dead!"

—*William Wordsworth [1770–1850]*

RESOLUTION AND INDEPENDENCE

There was a roaring in the wind all night;
The rain came heavily and fell in floods;
But now the sun is rising calm and bright;
The birds are singing in the distant woods;
Over his own sweet voice the Stock-dove broods;   5
The Jay makes answer as the Magpie chatters;
And all the air is filled with pleasant noise of waters.

All things that love the sun are out of doors;
The sky rejoices in the morning's birth;
The grass is bright with rain-drops;—on the moors   10
The hare is running races in her mirth;
And with her feet she from the plashy earth
Raises a mist; that, glittering in the sun,
Runs with her all the way, wherever she doth run.

I was a Traveller then upon the moor;   15
I saw the hare that raced about with joy;
I heard the woods and distant waters roar;
Or heard them not, as happy as a boy:
The pleasant season did my heart employ:
My old remembrances went from me wholly: 20
And all the ways of men, so vain and melancholy.

But, as it sometimes chanceth, from the might
Of joy in minds that can no further go,
As high as we have mounted in delight
In our dejection do we sink as low;   25
To me that morning did it happen so;
And fears and fancies thick upon me came;
Dim sadness—and blind thoughts, I knew not, nor could name.

I heard the skylark warbling in the sky;
And I bethought me of the playful hare: 30
Even such a happy child of earth am I;
Even as these blissful creatures do I fare;
Far from the world I walk, and from all care;
But there may come another day to me—
Solitude, pain of heart, distress, and poverty. 35

My whole life I have lived in pleasant thought,
As if life's business were a summer mood;
As if all needful things would come unsought
To genial faith, still rich in genial good;
But how can He expect that others should 40
Build for him, sow for him, and at his call
Love him, who for himself will take no heed at all?

I thought of Chatterton, the marvellous Boy,
The sleepless Soul that perished in his pride;
Of Him who walked in glory and in joy 45
Following his plough, along the mountainside:
By our own spirits are we deified:
We Poets in our youth begin in gladness;
But thereof come in the end despondency and madness.

Now, whether it were by peculiar grace, 50
A leading from above, a something given,
Yet it befell that, in this lonely place,
When I with these untoward thoughts had striven,
Beside a pool bare to the eye of heaven
I saw a Man before me unawares: 55
The oldest man he seemed that ever wore grey hairs.

As a huge stone is sometimes seen to lie
Couched on the bald top of an eminence;
Wonder to all who do the same espy,
By what means it could thither come, and whence; 60
So that it seems a thing endued with sense:
Like a sea-beast crawled forth, that on a shelf
Of rock or sand reposeth, there to sun itself;

Such seemed this Man, not all alive nor dead,
Nor all asleep—in his extreme old age: 65
His body was bent double, feet and head
Coming together in life's pilgrimage;
As if some dire constraint of pain, or rage
Of sickness felt by him in times long past,
A more than human weight upon his frame had cast. 70

Himself he propped, limbs, body, and pale face,
Upon a long grey staff of shaven wood:
And, still as I drew near with gentle pace,
Upon the margin of that moorish flood
Motionless as a cloud the old Man stood,   75
That heareth not the loud winds when they call;
And moveth all together, if it move at all.

At length, himself unsettling, he the pond
Stirred with his staff, and fixedly did look
Upon the muddy water, which he conned,   80
As if he had been reading in a book:
And now a stranger's privilege I took;
And, drawing to his side, to him did say,
"This morning gives us promise of a glorious day."

A gentle answer did the old Man make,   85
In courteous speech which forth he slowly drew:
And him with further words I thus bespake,
"What occupation do you there pursue?
This is a lonesome place for one like you."
Ere he replied, a flash of mild surprise   90
Broke from the sable orbs of his yet-vivid eyes.

His words came feebly, from a feeble chest,
But each in solemn order followed each,
With something of a lofty utterance drest—
Choice word and measured phrase, above the reach   95
Of ordinary men; a stately speech;
Such as grave Livers do in Scotland use,
Religious men, who give to God and man their dues.

He told, that to these waters he had come
To gather leeches, being old and poor: 100
Employment hazardous and wearisome!
And he had many hardships to endure:
From pond to pond he roamed, from moor to moor;
Housing, with God's help, by choice or chance;
And in this way he gained an honest maintenance.   105

The old Man still stood talking by my side;
But now *his* voice to me was like a stream
Scarce heard; nor word from word could I divide;
And the whole body of the Man did seem
Like one whom I had met with in a dream;   110
Or like a man from some far region sent,
To give me human strength, by apt admonishment.

My former thoughts returned: the fear that kills;
And hope that is unwilling to be fed;
Cold, pain, and labour, and all fleshly ills;   115
And mighty Poets in their misery dead.
—Perplexed, and longing to be comforted
My question eagerly did I renew,
"How is it that you live, and what is it you do?"

He with a smile did then his words repeat;   120
And said that, gathering leeches, far and wide
He travelled; stirring thus about his feet
The waters of the pools where they abide.
"Once I could meet with them on every side;
But they have dwindled long by slow decay;   125
Yet still I persevere, and find them where I may."

While he was talking thus, the lonely place,
The old Man's shape, and speech—all troubled me:
In my mind's eye I seemed to see him pace
About the weary moors continually,   130
Wandering about alone and silently.
While I these thoughts within myself pursued,
He, having made a pause, the same discourse renewed.

And soon with this he other matter blended,
Cheerfully uttered, with demeanour kind,   135
But stately in the main; and, when he ended,
I could have laughed myself to scorn to find
In that decrepit Man so firm a mind.
"God," said I, "be my help and stay secure;
I'll think of the Leech-gatherer on the lonely moor!"   140

—William Wordsworth [1770–1850]

RESOLUTION AND INDEPENDENCE. 43. *Chatterton:* A promising young English poet
(1752–1770) who, reduced to despair by poverty, poisoned himself at the age of 17. 45.
Him who walked . . . : Robert Burns, the peasant poet (1759–1796), died in want at
the age of 37.

THE SOLITARY REAPER

Behold her, single in the field,
Yon solitary Highland lass!
Reaping and singing by herself;
Stop here, or gently pass!
Alone she cuts and binds the grain,   5
And sings a melancholy strain;
O listen! for the vale profound
Is overflowing with the sound.

No nightingale did ever chaunt
More welcome notes to weary bands   10
Of travellers in some shady haunt
Among Arabian sands.
A voice so thrilling ne'er was heard
In springtime from the cuckoo-bird,
Breaking the silence of the seas   15
Among the farthest Hebrides.

Will no one tell me what she sings?—
Perhaps the plaintive numbers° flow   measures
For old, unhappy, far-off things,
And battles long ago.   20
Or is it some more humble lay,°   song
Familiar matter of today?
Some natural sorrow, loss, or pain,
That has been, and may be again?

Whate'er the theme, the maiden sang   25
As if her song could have no ending;
I saw her singing at her work,
And o'er the sickle bending—
I listened, motionless and still;
And, as I mounted up the hill,   30
The music in my heart I bore
Long after it was heard no more.

—*William Wordsworth* [1770–1850]

THE SOLITARY REAPER. 2. *Highland:* Scottish upland. The girl is singing in the Highland language, a form of Gaelic, quite different from English. 16. *Hebrides:* islands off the northwest tip of Scotland.

THEY FLEE FROM ME

They flee from me that sometime did me seek,
  With naked foot stalking in my chamber.
I have seen them gentle, tame, and meek,
  That now are wild, and do not remember
    That sometime they put themselves in danger   5
To take bread at my hand; and now they range,
Busily seeking with a continual change.

Thanked be fortune, it hath been otherwise
  Twenty times better; but once, in special,
In thin array, after a pleasant guise,   10
  When her loose gown from her shoulders did fall,
  And she me caught in her arms long and small.

Therewith all sweetly did me kiss,
And softly said, "Dear heart, how like you this?"

It was no dream: I lay broad waking.   15
    But all is turned, thorough° my gentleness,   through
Into a strange fashion of forsaking;
    And I have leave to go of° her goodness,   because of
And she also to use newfangleness.
But since that I so kindëly am served,   20
I would fain know what she hath deserved.

                        —*Sir Thomas Wyatt [1503?–1542]*

THEY FLEE FROM ME. 20. *kindëly:* kindly. In addition to its modern meaning, it means
typically, i.e., according to her type or kind.

A PRAYER FOR MY DAUGHTER

Once more the storm is howling, and half hid
Under this cradle-hood and coverlid
My child sleeps on. There is no obstacle
But Gregory's wood and one bare hill
Whereby the haystack- and roof-levelling wind,   5
Bred on the Atlantic, can be stayed;
And for an hour I have walked and prayed
Because of the great gloom that is in my mind.

I have walked and prayed for this young child an hour
And heard the sea-wind scream upon the tower,   10
And under the arches of the bridge, and scream
In the elms above the flooded stream;
Imagining in excited reverie
That the future years had come,
Dancing to a frenzied drum,   15
Out of the murderous innocence of the sea.

May she be granted beauty and yet not
Beauty to make a stranger's eye distraught,
Or hers before a looking-glass, for such,
Being made beautiful overmuch,   20
Consider beauty a sufficient end,
Lose natural kindness and maybe
The heart-revealing intimacy
That chooses right, and never find a friend.

Helen being chosen found life flat and dull   25
And later had much trouble from a fool,
While that great Queen, that rose out of the spray,
Being fatherless could have her way
Yet chose a bandy-leggèd smith for man.
It's certain that fine women eat   30
A crazy salad with their meat
Whereby the Horn of Plenty is undone.

In courtesy I'd have her chiefly learned;
Hearts are not had as a gift but hearts are earned
By those that are not entirely beautiful;   35
Yet many, that have played the fool
For beauty's very self, has charm made wise,
And many a poor man that has roved,
Loved and thought himself beloved,
From a glad kindness cannot take his eyes.   40

May she become a flourishing hidden tree
That all her thoughts may like the linnet be,
And have no business but dispensing round
Their magnanimities of sound,
Nor but in merriment begin a chase,   45
Nor but in merriment a quarrel.
O may she live like some green laurel
Rooted in one dear perpetual place.

My mind, because the minds that I have loved,
The sort of beauty that I have approved,   50
Prosper but little, has dried up of late,
Yet knows that to be choked with hate
May well be of all evil chances chief.
If there's no hatred in a mind
Assault and battery of the wind   55
Can never tear the linnet from the leaf.

An intellectual hatred is the worst,
So let her think opinions are accursed.
Have I not seen the loveliest woman born
Out of the mouth of Plenty's horn,   60
Because of her opinionated mind
Barter that horn and every good
By quiet natures understood
For an old bellows full of angry wind?

Considering that, all hatred driven hence,   65
The soul recovers radical innocence

And learns at last that it is self-delighting,
Self-appeasing, self-affrighting,
And that its own sweet will is Heaven's will;
She can, though every face should scowl   70
And every windy quarter howl
Or every bellows burst, be happy still.

And may her bridegroom bring her to a house
Where all's accustomed, ceremonious;
For arrogance and hatred are the wares   75
Peddled in the thoroughfares.
How but in custom and in ceremony
Are innocence and beauty born?
Ceremony's a name for the rich horn,
And custom for the spreading laurel tree.   80

—William Butler Yeats [1865–1939]

A PRAYER FOR MY DAUGHTER. 10, 14. *tower, future years:* When Yeats wrote this poem
he lived in an old tower near the west coast of Ireland. It was a time of civil strife, and
Yeats foresaw worse times coming. 25–26. Helen of Troy found life dull as the wife
of Menelaus, was later given trouble by Paris, who abducted her to Troy, precipitating
the Trojan War. 27. *great Queen:* Aphrodite, goddess of beauty, born full grown out of
the ocean, chose for her husband the lame and ill-favored Hephaestos, god of the forge.
32. *Horn of Plenty:* the cornucopia, which poured out to its recipient anything he desired.
59–64: *loveliest woman born:* Maud Gonne, whom Yeats wooed unsuccessfully (see "No
Second Troy," Question 1, page 119, and "Among School Children," Question 2, page
245), became a speaker for political and nationalistic causes.

SAILING TO BYZANTIUM

That is no country for old men. The young
In one another's arms, birds in the trees
—Those dying generations—at their song,
The salmon-falls, the mackerel-crowded seas,
Fish, flesh, or fowl, commend all summer long   5
Whatever is begotten, born, and dies.
Caught in that sensual music all neglect
Monuments of unageing intellect.

An aged man is but a paltry thing,
A tattered coat upon a stick, unless   10
Soul clap its hands and sing, and louder sing
For every tatter in its mortal dress,
Nor is there singing school but studying
Monuments of its own magnificence;
And therefore I have sailed the seas and come   15
To the holy city of Byzantium.

O sages standing in God's holy fire
As in the gold mosaic of a wall,
Come from the holy fire, perne in a gyre,°   spin in spiralling or
And be the singing-masters of my soul.   cone-shaped flight
Consume my heart away; sick with desire   21
And fastened to a dying animal
It knows not what it is; and gather me
Into the artifice of eternity.

Once out of nature I shall never take   25
My bodily form from any natural thing,
But such a form as Grecian goldsmiths make
Of hammered gold and gold enamelling
To keep a drowsy Emperor awake;
Or set upon a golden bough to sing   30
To lords and ladies of Byzantium
Of what is past, or passing, or to come.

—*William Butler Yeats [1865–1939]*

SAILING TO BYZANTIUM. *Byzantium:* Ancient eastern capital of the Holy Roman Empire; here symbolically a holy city of the imagination. 1. *That:* Ireland; or the ordinary sensual world. 27–31. *such a form . . . :* The Byzantine Emperor Theophilus had made for himself mechanical golden birds which sang upon the branches of a golden tree.

TWO PASSAGES FROM *SATIRE ON WOMEN*

Lavinia is polite, but not profane;°   irreligious
To church as constant as to Drury Lane.
She decently, in form, pays Heaven its due,
And makes a civil visit to her pew.
Her lifted fan, to give a solemn air,   5
Conceals her face, which passes for a prayer;
Curtsies to curtsies, then, with grace succeed,
Not one the fair omits, but at the creed.
Or if she joins the service, 'tis to speak;
Through dreadful silence the pent heart might break;   10
Untaught to bear it, women talk away
To God himself, and fondly think they pray.
But sweet their accent, and their air refined;
For they're before their Maker,—and mankind.
When ladies once are proud of praying well,   15
Satan himself will toll the parish bell.

Atheists are few; most nymphs° a godhead own,°   maidens;
And nothing but his attributes dethrone.   acknowledge
From atheists far, they steadfastly believe
God is, and is almighty—to forgive.   20
His other excellence they'll not dispute;
But mercy, sure, is his chief attribute.
Shall pleasures of a short duration chain
A lady's soul in everlasting pain?
Will the great author us poor worms destroy   25
For now and then a sip of transient joy?
No, he's forever in a smiling mood,
He's like themselves; or how could he be good?
And they blaspheme who blacker schemes suppose.
Devoutly, thus, Jehovah they depose,   30
The pure! the just! and set up in his stead
A Deity, that's perfectly well bred.

—*Edward Young [1683–1765]*

SATIRE ON WOMEN. 1. *Drury Lane:* A fashionable London theater.

Index of Authors, Titles, and First Lines

Authors' names appear in capitals, titles of poems in italics, and first lines of poems in roman type. Numbers in roman type indicate the page of the selection, and italic numbers indicate discussion of the poem.

A decrepit old gas man named Peter 204
A line in long array where they wind 67, 124
A noiseless patient spider 306
A planet doesn't explode of itself 112
A poem should be palpable and mute 134
A Sonnet is a moment's monument 208
A stranger came to the door at eve 14, 59
A sudden blow: the great wings beating still 119
A tutor who tooted the flute 204
Acre of Grass, An 130
ADAMS, FRANKLIN P.
    The Rich Man 40
Afterwards 273
AIKEN, CONRAD
    Morning Song from "Senlin" 251
All day I hear the noise of waters 194
All dripping in tangles green 89
All that I know 70, 71–72, 75
America for Me 175, 230
AMIS, KINGSLEY
    A Bookshop Idyll 252
Among School Children 243
An ant on the tablecloth 107
An old, mad, blind, despised, and dying king 191
And here face down beneath the sun 72, 74–75

ANONYMOUS
    Edward 209
    Fine Flowers in the Valley 104
    God's Will for You and Me 222
    I sing of a maiden 205
    In the garden there strayed 122
    A Handful of Limericks 200, 203
    Little Jack Horner 123
    Lord Randal 150, 211
    Love 146, 217
    Of Alphus 95
    On a Clergyman's Horse Biting Him 67
    Pease porridge hot 180
    Sir Patrick Spence 254
    The Silver Swan 253
    The Twa Corbies 12, 56
    The Written Word 44
    Two Rivers 13
    Western Wind 78, 124
    When in My Pilgrimage 254
Another Dark Lady 31, 56, 59
Apparently with no surprise 137, 138–39
ARNOLD, MATTHEW
    Dover Beach 256
    To Marguerite 255
Ars Poetica 134
As a dare-gale skylark scanted in a dull cage 132
As I was walking all alane 12, 56

326

As some fond virgin, whom her mother's care 290
As virtuous men pass mildly away 62
At midnight in the silence of the sleep-time 141
AUDEN, W. H.
  O Where Are You Going? 199
  That night when joy began 151
  The Shield of Achilles 257
  The Unknown Citizen 106
Autumnus 161
Avenge, O Lord, thy slaughtered saints 193

Barely a twelvemonth after 111
Baroque Wall-Fountain in the Villa Sciarra, A 313
BARR, MATTHIAS
  Only a baby small 224
Barrel-Organ, The 176
Barter 125, 126

Base Details 43
Batter my heart, three-personed God 270
Because I could not stop for Death 267
BEDDOES, THOMAS LOVELL
  Song 259
Behold her, single in the field 315
BELLOC, HILAIRE
  Lines for a Christmas Card 101
Bench of Boors, The 195
Bent double, like old beggars under sacks 8, 59
BEST, CHARLES
  A Sonnet of the Moon 143
Between the *gardening* and the *cookery* 252
BLAKE, WILLIAM
  The Chimney Sweeper 96
  The Divine Image 260
  The Sick Rose 78
  The Tiger 56, 259
Bookshop Idyll, A 252
Boy-Man 229
Breathes there the man with soul so dead 228
Bredon Hill 278
BROWNING, ROBERT
  Epilogue to Asolando 141
  Meeting at Night 46, 46–48, 56, 59
  My Last Duchess 109, 124
  My Star 70, 71–72, 75
  Parting at Morning 47
  Song 127
BRYANT, WILLIAM CULLEN
  To a Waterfowl 128
BURFORD, WILLIAM
  A Christmas Tree 213
BURNS, ROBERT
  A Red, Red Rose 92
Busy old fool, unruly Sun 268
BYRON, GEORGE GORDON, LORD
  So we'll go no more a-roving 261

Caged Skylark, The 131
CAMPION, THOMAS
  When thou must home 261
Carpenter's Son, The 120
Carriage from Sweden, A 287
CARTWRIGHT, WILLIAM
  No Platonic Love 261

Cavalry Crossing a Ford 67, 124
Cha Till Maccruimein 225
Changeling, The 159
Chimney Sweeper, The 96
Christmas Tree, A 213
Church Going 282
Circus, The 299
City Life 283
CLOUGH, ARTHUR HUGH
  Say not the struggle nought availeth 220
  The Latest Decalogue 262
COLERIDGE, SAMUEL TAYLOR
  Kubla Khan 263
  Metrical Feet 179
Coming of Good Luck, The 89
Coming of Wisdom with Time, The 140
CONGREVE, WILLIAM
  Song 264
Constant Lover, The 108
Corinna's Going a-Maying 274
Counting-Out Rhyme 158
COWLEY, MALCOLM
  The Long Voyage 228
CRANE, STEPHEN
  The Trees in the Garden 264
CRAPSEY, ADELAIDE
  On Seeing Weather-Beaten Trees 89
CULLEN, COUNTÉE
  Incident 265
CUMMINGS, E. E.
  if everything happens that can't be done 173
  in Just- 117
Curiosity 81

Dance, The 196
Dark Hills, The 192
Daughters of Time, the hypocritic Days 271
DAVIES, WILLIAM H.
  The Villain 137, 138–39
Days 271
DE LA MARE, WALTER
  The Horseman 89
  The Listeners 265
Death Is a Dialogue 223
Death of the Hired Man, The 233
Death stands above me, whispering low 56, 59
Departmental 107
Description of Spring, Wherein Each Thing Renews Save Only the Lover 302
Description of the Morning, A 51
Deserted House, The 88
Design 129
Devil, Maggot and Son 27
DICKINSON, EMILY
  Apparently with no surprise 137, 138–39
  Because I could not stop for Death 267
  Death Is a Dialogue 223
  I like to see it lap the miles 190
  If I can stop one heart from breaking 223
  My Life Closed Twice 91
  My life had stood, a loaded gun 266
  There is no frigate like a book 33
Dirge 127
Divine Image, The 260
Do not go gentle into that good night 203, 303
Doctor, doctor, a little of your love 297

DONNE, JOHN
  A Valediction: Forbidding Mourning 62
  Batter my heart, three-personed God 270
  Song 269
  The Good-Morrow 268
  The Sun Rising 268
DOUGLAS, KEITH
  Vergissmeinicht 150, 270
Dover Beach 256
Down the close, darkening lanes they sang
  their way 224
DRAYTON, MICHAEL
  Since There's No Help 140
DRYDEN, JOHN
  Lines on a Paid Militia 58
Dulce et Decorum Est 8, 59

Eagle, The 5, 47, 54, 92
Earth 112
Echo's Lament of Narcissus 279
Edward 209
Eight O'Clock 194
ELIOT, T. S.
  The Love Song of J. Alfred Prufrock 238
EMERSON, RALPH WALDO
  Days 271
England in 1819 191
England's lads are miniature men 229
Epilogue to Asolando 141
Epistle to a Young Lady, on Her Leaving
  the Town After the Coronation 290
Epitaph 142, 150
Epitaph on Newton 119
Escapist's Song 213
Eve 276
Exspecto Resurrectionem 77

Fear no more the heat o' the sun 295
Fine Flowers in the Valley 104
Finesse be first, whose elegance deplores 273
Fair daffodils, we weep to see 204
FALLON, PADRAIC
  Mary Hynes 101, 150
FIELD, EUGENE
  Little Boy Blue 226
FLETCHER, JOHN GOULD
  The Groundswell 48
For me, the naked and the nude 35, 57
FRANKLIN, BENJAMIN
  Quatrain 122
FROST, ROBERT
  A Hillside Thaw 54
  A Prayer in Spring 221
  Departmental 107
  Design 129
  Love and a Question 14, 59
  "Out, Out—" 114, 115–16
  Stopping by Woods 125, 126, 136–37
  The Death of the Hired Man 233
  The Road Not Taken 68, 69–70, 71, 75,
    92
  The Rose Family 93
  The Silken Tent 271
  The Span of Life 186, 187

Gallows, The 304
Garden, The 284
Gather ye rosebuds while ye may 76
Get up, get up for shame 275

Glass of Beer, A 301
Glory be to God for dappled things 222
Go and catch a falling star 269
God's Grandeur 155
God's Will for You and Me 222
Good-Morrow, The 268
GRAVES, ROBERT
  The Naked and the Nude 35, 57
Greatly shining 52
Grey Squirrel, The 105
Griesly Wife, The 13, 123–24
Groundswell, The 48

Had he and I but met 20, 21–22
Had we but world enough, and time 64
HALL, DONALD
  My son, my executioner 223
  Six Poets in Search of a Lawyer 272
Hap 28
Harbor, The 156
HARDY, THOMAS
  Afterwards 273
  Hap 28
  The Man He Killed 20, 21–22
  The Subalterns 29, 57
Hark, hark! 181
Hark to the whimper of the sea-gull 57
Having been tenant long to a rich Lord 274
He clasps the crag with crooked hands 5,
  47, 54, 92
He stood, and heard the steeple 194
He was found by the Bureau of Statistics 106
HEATH-STUBBS, JOHN
  Epitaph 142, 150
Heaven-Haven 193
HERBERT, GEORGE
  Love 61
  Peace 85
  Redemption 274
Here the hangman stops his cart 120
HERRICK, ROBERT
  Corinna's Going a-Maying 274
  The Coming of Good Luck 89
  To Daffodils 204
  To the Virgins, to Make Much of Time 76
  Upon Julia's Voice 183, 184
HEYWOOD, JOHN
  Jack and His Father 276
High-Toned Old Christian Woman, A 301
Hillside Thaw, A 54
His Grace! impossible! what dead! 302
HODGSON, RALPH
  Eve 276
HOFFENSTEIN, SAMUEL
  Love Song 44
HOPKINS. GERARD MANLEY
  God's Grandeur 155
  Heaven-Haven 193
  Pied Beauty 222
  Spring 50
  The Caged Skylark 131
Horseman, The 89
Horses, The 111
House on the Hill, The 88, 203
Housewifery 303
HOUSMAN, A. E.
  Bredon Hill 278
  Eight O'Clock 194
  Is my team ploughing 22, 23–24, 57

Loveliest of Trees 170
O Who Is That Young Sinner 174
On moonlit heath and lonesome bank 49
Terence, this is stupid stuff 15
The Carpenter's Son 120
The Immortal Part 132
How vainly men themselves amaze 285

I am a gentleman in a dustcoat trying 292
I can't forget 62
I found a dimpled spider 129
I have desired to go 193
I heard a horseman 89
I knew a woman, lovely in her bones 294
I like to see it lap the miles 190
I met a traveler from an antique land 97
I sat next the Duchess at tea 203
I sing of a maiden 205
I strove with none 282
I walk down the garden paths 82
I walk through the long schoolroom questioning 243
I wonder, by my troth, what thou and I 268
If but some vengeful god would call to me 28
if everything happens that can't be done 173
If I can stop one heart from breaking 223
If I profane with my unworthiest hand 209
If I were fierce, and bald, and short of breath 43
If you think you are beaten, you are 220
Immortal Part, The 132
In bed I muse on Tenier's boors 195
In Breughel's great picture, The Kermess 196
in Just- 117
In summertime on Bredon 278
In the garden there strayed 122
In Xanadu did Kubla Khan 263
Incident 265
Is it as plainly in our living shown 89
Is my team ploughing 22, 23–24, 57
"Is there anybody there?" said the Traveller 265
It is morning, Senlin says 251
It is most true that eyes are formed to serve 26
It is not growing like a tree 25
It little profits that an idle king 79, 184–85, 186
It was my thirtieth year to heaven 150, 206

Jack and His Father 276
Jack, eating rotten cheese 122
"Je Ne Sais Quois," The 172
John Gorham 30, 175
JONSON, BEN
  Echo's Lament of Narcissus 279
  It is not growing like a tree 25
JOYCE, JAMES
  All Day I Hear 194
Judging Distances 41
Just to be tender, just to be true 222

KEATS, JOHN
  Ode on a Grecian Urn 279
  Ode on Melancholy 281

On First Looking into Chapman's Homer 201
To Autumn 51, 56
Kubla Khan 263

LANDOR, WALTER SAVAGE
  Death Stands Above Me 56, 59
  On His Seventy-Fifth Birthday 282
  To Age 145
  Yes; I Write Verses 144
LARKIN, PHILIP
  Church Going 282
Latest Decalogue, The 262
Lavinia is polite, but not profane 324
LAWRENCE, D. H.
  City Life 283
Leave me, O Love, which reachest but to dust 299
Leda and the Swan 119
LEE-HAMILTON, EUGENE
  Sea-Shell Murmurs 284
Let me not to the marriage of true minds 296
Let us walk in the white snow 66, 231–32
Let us go then, you and I 238
Lie still, my newly married wife 13, 123–24
Life and Thought have gone away 88
Life has loveliness to sell 125, 126
Like a small grey 105
Limericks, A Handful of 203
Lines for a Christmas Card 101
Lines on a Paid Militia 58
Listeners, The 265
LISTER, R. P.
  Target 143
Little Boy Blue 226
Little Jack Horner 123
Live thy Life 171, 218
London, 1802 65
Long Voyage, The 228
Look how the pale Queen of the silent night 143
Lord Randal 211, 150
Love (Anonymous) 146, 217
Love (George Herbert) 61
Love and a Question 14, 59
Love bade me welcome 61
Love Poem 289
Love Song 44
Love Song of J. Alfred Prufrock, The 238
LOVELACE, RICHARD
  To Althea, from Prison 99
  To Lucasta, Going to the Wars 98, 164–68
Loveliest of trees, the cherry now 170
LOWELL, AMY
  Patterns 82
  Wind and Silver 52
Lucifer in Starlight 286

Macbeth, from 59–60, 116
McGINLEY, PHYLLIS
  This Side of Calvin 140
MacLEISH, ARCHIBALD
  Ars Poetica 134
  You, Andrew Marvell 72, 74–75
MACKINTOSH, E. A.
  Cha Till Maccruimein 225
Make me, O Lord, thy spinning wheel 303

Man He Killed, The 20, 21–22
Man Who Thinks He Can, The 220
MANIFOLD, JOHN
  The Griesly Wife 13, 123–24
MARVELL, ANDREW
  The Garden 284
  To His Coy Mistress 64
Mary sat musing on the lamp-flame at the table 233
Mary Hynes 101, 150
May all my enemies go to hell 101
Meeting at Night 46, 46–48, 56, 59
MELVILLE, HERMAN
  The Bench of Boors 195
  The Night-March 67
  The Tuft of Kelp 89
MEREDITH, GEORGE
  Lucifer in Starlight 286
METCALFE, JAMES J.
  Pray in May 221
Metrical Feet 179
MEW, CHARLOTTE
  Exspecto Resurrectionem 77
  The Changeling 159
MILLAY, EDNA ST. VINCENT
  Counting-Out Rhyme 158
MILTON, JOHN
  On His Blindness 118
  On the Late Massacre in Piemont 193
MOORE, MARIANNE
  A Carriage from Sweden 287
Morning Song from "Senlin" 251
Mr. Flood's Party 292
Mr. Heath-Stubbs as you must understand 142, 150
Much have I travelled in the realms of gold 201
MUIR, EDWIN
  The Horses 111
My clumsiest dear, whose hands shipwreck vases 289
My Last Duchess 109, 124
My life closed twice before its close 91
My life had stood, a loaded gun 266
My little Son, who looked from thoughtful eyes 227
My mistress' eyes are nothing like the sun 297
My son, my executioner 223
My soul, there is a country 305
My Star 70, 71–72, 75
Mysterious Night! when our first parent knew 306

Naked and the Nude, The 35, 57
Naming of Parts 40
NASH, OGDEN
  The Sea-Gull 57
  The Turtle 148, 148–49
NASHE, THOMAS
  Spring 288
Nature and Nature's laws lay hid in night 119
Night-March, The 67
NIMS, JOHN FREDERICK
  Love Poem 289
No egg on Friday Alph will eat 95
No longer mourn for me when I am dead 105

No, no, go not to Lethe 281
No Platonic Love 261
No Second Troy 118
Noiseless Patient Spider, A 306
Not only how far away, but the way that you say it 41
Not that the pines were darker there 228
Nothing is so beautiful as spring 50
Now hardly here and there a hackney-coach 51
NOYES, ALFRED
  The Barrel-Organ 176

O, my luve is like a red, red rose 92
O Rose, thou art sick 78
O Western wind, when wilt thou blow 78, 124
"O where are you going?" said reader to rider 199
O where ha' you been, Lord Randal, my son 150, 211
O who is that young sinner 174
Oak, The 171, 218
O'CONNOR, FRANK
  Devil, Maggot and Son 27
Ode on a Grecian Urn 279
Ode on Melancholy 281
Of a Contented Mind 130
Of Alphus 95
Oh, give us pleasure in the flowers today 221
Oh! King Who hast the key 77
Old Adam, the carrion crow 259
On a Clergyman's Horse Biting Him 67
On a Girdle 305
On a starred night Prince Lucifer uprose 286
On First Looking into Chapman's Homer 201
On His Blindness 118
On His Seventy-Fifth Birthday 282
On moonlit heath and lonesome bank 49
On Seeing Weather-Beaten Trees 89
On the Late Massacre in Piemont 193
Once I am sure there's nothing going on 282
Once more the storm is howling 321
Once riding in old Baltimore 265
Only a baby small 224
O'REILLY, JOHN BOYLE
  A White Rose 70, 71–72
Out of the cradle endlessly rocking 308
"Out, Out—" 114, 115–16
Out upon it! I have loved 107
OWEN, WILFRED
  Dulce et Decorum Est 8, 59
  The Parable of the Old Men and the Young 121
  The Send-Off 224
Ozymandias 97

Parable of the Old Men and the Young, The 121
Parting at Morning 47
Parting, Without a Sequel 157
Passing through huddled and ugly walls 156
PATMORE, COVENTRY
  The Toys 227
Patterns 82

Peace (George Herbert) 85
Peace (Henry Vaughan) 305
Pease porridge hot 180
Piazza di Spagna, Early Morning 62
Piazza Piece 292
Picture and book remain 130
Pied Beauty 222
Pious Selinda goes to prayers 264
Poem in October 150, 206
Poetry is the supreme fiction 301
"Poor wanderer," said the leaden sky 29, 57
POPE, ALEXANDER
   Epistle to a Young Lady 290
   Epitaph on Newton 119
   Sound and Sense 190
PRAED, WINTHROP MACKWORTH
   Song 158
Pray in May 221
Prayer for My Daughter, A 321
Prayer in Spring, A 221
PROKOSCH, FREDERICK
   Sunburned Ulysses 291

Quatrain 122

RANSOM, JOHN CROWE
   Parting, Without a Sequel 157
   Piazza Piece 292
Redemption 274
REED, HENRY
   Judging Distances 41
   Naming of Parts 40
REID, ALASTAIR
   Curiosity 81
Red, Red Rose, A 92
Resolution and Independence 316
Rich Man, The 40
Richard Cory 39, 47, 97
Road Not Taken, The 68, 69–70, 71, 75, 92
ROBINSON, EDWIN ARLINGTON
   Another Dark Lady 31, 56, 59
   John Gorham 30, 175
   Mr. Flood's Party 292
   Richard Cory 39, 47, 97
   The Dark Hills 192
   The House on the Hill 88, 203
ROETHKE, THEODORE
   I Knew a Woman 294
Romeo and Juliet, from 209
Rose Family, The 93
ROSSETTI, DANTE GABRIEL
   Silent Noon 295
   The Sonnet 208
Rough wind, that moanest loud 127
Round the cape of a sudden came the sea 47

Said the circus man, Oh what do you like 299
Sailing to Byzantium 323
SANDBURG, CARL
   Splinter 182
   The Harbor 147
SASSOON, SIEGFRIED
   Base Details 43
Satire on Women, Two Passages from 324
Satirical Elegy on the Death of a Late Famous General, A 302

Say not the struggle naught availeth 220
Says Tweed to Till 13
SCOTT, SIR WALTER
   Breathes There the Man 228
Sea-Gull, The 57
Sea-Shell Murmurs 284
Season of mists and mellow fruitfulness 51, 56
Second Coming, The 87
Send-Off, The 224
SHAKESPEARE, WILLIAM
   Fear No More 295
   from *Macbeth* 59–60, 116
   from *Romeo and Juliet,* 209
   Let me not to the marriage of true minds 296
   My mistress' eyes are nothing like the sun 297
   No Longer Mourn for Me 105
   Since Brass, nor Stone, nor Earth 296
   Song 181
   Spring 11, 45, 54, 57, 185–86
   That Time of Year 202, 231–32
   Winter 6, 7–8
SHAPIRO, KARL
   Boy-Man 229
Doctor, doctor, a little of your love 297
She has finished and sealed the letter 157
She is as in a field a silken tent 271
She looked over his shoulder 257
She sat down below a thorn 104
She should have died hereafter 59–60, 116
SHELLEY, PERCY BYSSHE
   Dirge 127
   England in 1819 191
   Ozymandias 97
   Shield of Achilles, The 257
SHIRLEY, JAMES
   The glories of our blood and state 298
Sick Rose, The 78
SIDNEY, SIR PHILIP
   It is most true that eyes are formed to serve 26
   Leave Me, O Love 299
   With How Sad Steps, O Moon 299
Silken Tent, The 271
Silent Noon 295
Silver bark of beech, and sallow 158
Silver Swan, The 253
Since brass, nor stone, nor earth 296
Since there's no help 140
Sir Patrick Spence 254
Six Poets in Search of a Lawyer 272
Slow, slow, fresh fount 279
So Abram rose, and clave the wood, and went 121
So Good Luck came, and on my roof did light 89
So smooth, so sweet, so silv'ry is thy voice 183, 184
So we'll go no more a-roving 261
Solitary Reaper, The 319
Song: Go and catch a falling star 269
Song: Hark, hark! 181
Song: Old Adam, the carrion crow 259
Song: Pious Selinda goes to prayers 264
Song: The pints and the pistols 158
Song: The year's at the spring 127

Sonnet, The 208
Sonnet of the Moon, A 143
Sound and Sense 190
Span of Life, The 186, 187
SPENCER, THEODORE
    Escapist's Song 213
    The Circus 299
SPENSER, EDMUND
    Trust Not the Treason 300
Splinter 182
Spring (Gerard Manley Hopkins) 50
Spring (Thomas Nashe) 288
Spring (Shakespeare) 11, 45, 54, 57, 185–86, 200
Spring, the sweet Spring 288
Star 213
STEPHENS, JAMES
    A Glass of Beer 301
STEVENS, WALLACE
    A High-Toned Old Christian Woman 301
Stopping by Woods on a Snowy Evening 125, 126, 136–37
Strange fits of passion have I known 315
Subalterns, The 29, 57
SUCKLING, SIR JOHN
    The Constant Lover 108
Sun Rising, The 268
Sunburned Ulysses 291
SURREY, HENRY HOWARD, EARL OF
    Description of Spring 302
Sweet Peace, where dost thou dwell? 85
SWIFT, JONATHAN
    A Description of the Morning 51
    A Satirical Elegy 302
SWINBURNE, ALGERNON CHARLES
    When the Hounds of Spring 152
SYLVESTER, JOSHUA
    Autumnus 161

Target 143
TAYLOR, EDWARD
    Housewifery 303
TEASDALE, SARA
    Barter 125, 126
Tell me no more of minds embracing minds 261
Tell me not, Sweet, I am unkind 99, 164–68
Tell me what you're doing over here, John Gorham 30, 175
TENNYSON, ALFRED, LORD
    The Deserted House 88
    The Eagle 5, 47, 54, 92
    The Oak 171, 218
    Ulysses 79, 184–86
Terence, this is stupid stuff 15
That is no country for old men 323
That night when joy began 151
That Sunday, on my oath, the rain was a heavy overcoat 101, 150
That time of year thou mayst in me behold 202, 231–32
That which her slender waist confined 305
That's my last Duchess painted on the wall 109, 124
The buzz-saw snarled and rattled in the yard 114, 115–16
The country rings around with loud alarms 58

The first woman I loved, he said 213
The glories of our blood and state 298
The gray sea and the long black land 46, 46–48, 56, 59
The hollow sea-shell which for years hath stood 284
The king sits in Dumferling toune 254
The lanky hank of a she in the inn over there 301
The little toy dog is covered with dust 226
The moon holds nothing in her arms 143
The old dog barks backward 186, 187
The pints and the pistols 158
The pipes in the street were playing bravely 225
The red rose whispers of passion 70, 71–72
The Reverend Dr. Harcourt, folk agree 140
The rich man has his motor-car 40
The rose is a rose 93
The sea is calm tonight 256
The soote season that bud and bloom forth brings 302
The steed bit his master 67
The trees in the garden rained flowers 264
The turtle lives 'twixt plated decks 148, 148–49
The voice of the last cricket 182
The world is charged with the grandeur of God 155
The world is too much with us 34, 56
The written word 44
The year's at the spring 127
There is no frigate like a book 33
There was a child went forth 307
There was a roaring in the wind all night 316
There was a weasel lived in the sun 304
There was a young lady of Lynn 204
There was a young lady of Niger 200, 231–32
There was a young maid who said, "Why 204
There was a young woman named Bright 204
There was an old man of Peru 204
There's a barrel-organ carolling 176
There's the wonderful love of a beautiful maid 146, 217
They are all gone away 88, 203
They flee from me that sometime did me seek 320
They say there is a sweeter air 287
Think not, because I wonder where you fled 31, 56, 59
Thirty days hath September 219
This Side of Calvin 140
THOMAS, DYLAN
    Do not go gentle into that good night 203, 303
    Poem in October 150, 206
THOMAS, EDWARD
    The Gallows 304
Thou shalt have one God only 262
Thou still unravished bride of quietness 279
Though leaves are many, the root is one 140
Three things seek my death 27
Three weeks gone and the combatants gone 150, 270
Tiger! Tiger! burning bright 56, 259

'Tis fine to see the Old World *175*, *230*
To a Waterfowl 128
To Age 145
To Althea, from Prison 99
To Autumn 51, *56*
To Daffodils 204
To His Coy Mistress 64
To Lucasta, Going to the Wars 98, *164–68*
To Marguerite 255
To Mercy, Pity, Peace, and Love 260
To Night 306
To the Virgins, to Make Much of Time 76
To think to know the country 54
Today the birds are singing and 221
To-day we have naming of parts 40
Toll no bell for me, dear Father 159
Toys, The 227
Trochee trips from long to short 179
True ease in writing comes from art 190
Trust not the treason of those smiling looks 300
Tuft of Kelp, The 89
Turning and turning in the widening gyre 87
Turtle, The 148, *148–49*
Twa Corbies, The 12, *56*
Two Rivers 13
Two roads diverged in a yellow wood 68, *69–70*, *71*, *75*, *92*

Ulysses 79, *184–86*
Under the bronze crown 313
Unknown Citizen, The 106
Upon Julia's Voice 183, *184*

Valediction: Forbidding Mourning, A 62
VAN DYKE, HENRY
  America for Me 175, *230*
VAUGHAN, HENRY
  Peace 305
VAUX, THOMAS
  Of a Contented Mind 130
Velvet Shoes 66, *231–32*
Vergissmeinicht 150, *270*
Villain, The 137, *138–39*

WALLER, EDMUND
  On a Girdle 305
Welcome, old friend! These many years 145
Well, Mr. Flood, we have the harvest moon 293
Western Wind 78, *124*
WHEELOCK, JOHN HALL
  Earth 112
When all is done and said 130
When daisies pied and violets blue 11, *45*, *54*, *57*, *185–86*
When I am in a great city 283
When I consider how my light is spent 118
When I meet the morning beam 132
When icicles hang by the -wall 6, *7–8*
When in my pilgrimage I reach 254
When love with unconfinèd wings 99
When my mother died I was very young 96
When the hounds of spring are on winter's traces 152
When the Present has latched its postern 273

When thou must home to shades of under-ground 261
Whenever Richard Cory went down town 39, *47*, *97*
While joy gave clouds the light of stars 137, *138–39*
WHITE, JOSEPH BLANCO
  To Night 306
White Rose, A 70, *71–72*
WHITEHEAD, WILLIAM
  The "Je Ne Sais Quoi" 172
Whither, midst falling dew 128
WHITMAN, WALT
  A noiseless patient spider 306
  Cavalry Crossing a Ford 67, *124*
  Out of the cradle endlessly rocking 308
  There Was a Child Went Forth 307
Whose woods these are I think I know 125, *126*, *136–37*
Why dois your brand sae drap wi bluid 209
Why should I blame her that she filled my days 118
WILBUR, RICHARD
  A Baroque Wall-Fountain 313
  Piazza di Spagna, Early Morning 62
WILLIAMS, WILLIAM CARLOS
  The Dance 196
Wind and Silver 52
Winter 6, *7–8*
WINTLE, WALTER
  The Man Who Thinks He Can 220
With banners furled, and clarions mute 67
With heavy doleful clamor 48
With how sad steps, O moon, thou climb'st the skies 299
WOLFE, HUMBERT
  The Grey Squirrel 105
WORDSWORTH, WILLIAM
  London, 1802 65
  Resolution and Independence 316
  Strange Fits of Passion 315
  The Solitary Reaper 319
  The World Is Too Much with Us 34, *56*
Written Word, The 44
WYATT, SIR THOMAS
  They Flee from Me 320
WYLIE, ELINOR
  Velvet Shoes 66, *231–32*

YEATS, WILLIAM BUTLER
  A Prayer for My Daughter 321
  Among School Children 243
  An Acre of Grass 130
  Leda and the Swan 219
  No Second Troy 118
  Sailing to Byzantium 323
  The Coming of Wisdom with Time 140
  The Second Coming 87
Yes; I write verses now and then 144
Yes, I'm in love, I feel it now 172
Yes! in the sea of life enisled 255
You, Andrew Marvell 72, *74–75*
YOUNG, EDWARD
  Two Passages from Satire of Women 324
Your hands lie open in the long fresh grass 295
Your little hands 44

Allegory 76–77
Alliteration 149–50
Allusion 113–17
Anapestic foot 164
Apostrophe 156–57
Approximate rime 150
Assonance 149–50

Ballad 15
Blank verse 169

Cacophony 183
Connotation 32–37
Consonance 149–50
Continuous form 198

Dactylic foot 164
Denotation 32–37
Didactic poetry 218
Dimeter 164
Dipodic verse 175
Double rime 157
Dramatic framework 21–24
Dramatic irony 95–96
Duple meter 164

End rime 150
End-stopped line 170
English sonnet 202
Euphony 183

Feminine rime 150
Figure of speech 53–54, 58–60
Fixed form 200–03
Foot 163–64
Free verse 169–70

Grammatical pause 170, 184–85

Heptameter 164
Hexameter 164
Hyperbole 91–92

Iambic foot 164
Idea 123–27
Imagery 45–48
Internal rime 150
Irony 93–97
Irony of situation 97
Italian sonnet 200–01

Limerick 200
Line 164

Masculine rime 150
Meaning 123–24
Metaphor 54–55
Meter 162–69
Metonymy 57–58
Metrical pause 179
Monometer 164
Monosyllabic foot 164
Musical devices 147–55

Octameter 164
Octave 200
Onomatopoeia 181–82
Overstatement 91–92
Oxymoron 112

Paradox 90–91
Paraphrase 26–27
Pentameter 164
Personification 55–56
Phonetic intensive 182

Prose 163
Prose meaning 123–24

Refrain 151
Rhetorical pause 170, 184–85
Rhetorical poetry 217–18
Rhythm 162, 168–69
Rime 150
Rime scheme 199–200
Run-on line 170

Sarcasm 93–94
Satire 93–94
Scansion 164–68
Sentimentality 217
Sestet 200
Simile 54
Single rime 158
Sonnet 200–03
Spondee 164
Stanza 164, 198–200
Stanzaic form 198–200
Symbol 68–75
Synecdoche 57

Tetrameter 164
Theme 25
Tone 135–39
Total meaning 123–24
Trimeter 164
Triple meter 164
Triple rime 157–58
Trochaic foot 164

Understatement 92

Verbal irony 93–95
Verse 163
Villanelle 203